)10

SOUL SEARCHERS

For those who have carried this anthology in their prayers
And in thanksgiving to Thérèse Martin

Soul Searchers

An Anthology
of Spiritual Journeys

Compiled by
TERESA DE BERTODANO

A LION BOOK

Copyright in the collection © 2001 Teresa de Bertodano
This edition copyright © 2001 Lion Publishing

Teresa de Bertodano asserts the moral right
to be identified as the compiler of this work

Published by
Lion Publishing plc
Sandy Lane West, Oxford, England
www.lion-publishing.co.uk
ISBN 0 7459 5041 8

First edition 2001
10 9 8 7 6 5 4 3 2 1 0

A catalogue record for this book is available
from the British Library

Typeset in 12/14 Venetian

Printed and bound in Great Britain by
Biddles Ltd, Guildford and King's Lynn

Contents

THIRD JOURNEY 176

Acknowledgments

I am grateful to those who have so kindly helped me in the preparation of this book. My brother Martin de Bertodano has allowed me to rely on his expertise and he has done much to improve the text. Father Gerald O'Collins, SJ, kindly allowed me to draw on his excellent book *Second Journey* (Gracewing, Leominster, 1995) which was invaluable, and I would like to express my gratitude to those he acknowledges in his book.

I am grateful to Helena de Bertodano, Sister Philippa Edwards, OSB, Hon. William Jolliffe, Jane Gore-Booth, Shirley Harriott, Jill Hopkins, Helen Muller, Elizabeth Oliver, Sister Diane Szarfinski, OCD, and Mary Stewart. Mrs Joan Bond of the Catholic Central Library, the Reverend Alan Bond and their daughter Catherine Porter have been indefatigable in discovering books and references.

I am grateful to the Reverend James Curry for permission to use his account of the final days of Cardinal Hume; to Canon John Devane for reminding me of the story of 'Artaban'; to Alan and Verity Mitchell for allowing me to use Christopher's 'Letters'; to Sally Trench for permission to use an extract from *Bury Me in My Boots*; to Jean Vanier for allowing me to use an extract from *A Door of Hope* and for permission to use an extract from a recorded conversation between himself and Madame Pauline Vanier. Permission for the latter usage has also been obtained from Dr Thérèse Vanier, who has given me valuable assistance with this book. I am grateful to Terry Waite CBE for permission to use extracts from *Taken on Trust* and *Footfalls in Memory*. The community of the Adorers of the Sacred Heart of Montmartre at Tyburn Convent in London have been a constant source of spiritual support: in particular Mother M. Xavier McMonagle, OSB, and Mother M. Angela Stephens, OSB.

I am very grateful to Morag Reeve of Lion for inviting me to compile this anthology. I could not have had a more encouraging and supportive editor. I would also like to thank Jenni Dutton for her meticulous editing, Faith Cummins for clearing the permissions and Jonathan Roberts for the beautiful jacket design.

Every effort has been made to trace the source of each passage. These efforts have not always been successful and I would be grateful to know of errors or omissions so that suitable acknowledgment can be made in any future edition.

Introduction

This book gathers together stories that describe the journeying of the human spirit. From the beginning of human history men and women have known what it is to be pilgrims and travellers on the face of the earth. Stories of journeys resonate with some of the deepest experiences and yearnings of the human spirit.

In preparing this anthology for readers of all types and all ages, I have been struck by the fact that human and Christian experiences offer innumerable examples of spiritual journeying which may or may not involve physical displacement.

Some of these journeys bring us back to our starting-point. The mythical Greek hero Ulysses returned to his own hearth after years of wandering. To echo T.S. Eliot's lines from 'Little Gidding', the end of Ulysses' exploring came when he arrived back at his starting-point and knew his home in Ithaca and his wife Penelope 'for the first time'. In the world of Christian experience we read of Dante's imaginary journey from Hell to Purgatory to Heaven. He undertook the journey for the love of Beatrice, and it led him back to his starting-point in the sense that he became aware for the first time of the love of God which had, of course, always existed but which Dante had previously known only in theory: 'the love that moves the sun and the other stars'. In the 20th century the Governor General of Canada, Georges Vanier, underwent a similar experience on Good Friday 1938 when he became aware that God was a God of love as well as a God of transcendence and majesty.

Other journeys lead to altogether new destinations. In the biblical story, Abraham and Sarah were called forth from Ur of the Chaldees into a new destiny in a foreign place, where they were to become the ancestors of the Jewish people and of Jesus himself.

We may categorize journeys in different ways: by destination – a final homecoming like that of Ulysses, Dante or Georges Vanier – or by the awareness of a new destiny – like that of Abraham and Sarah.

In *Soul Searchers* I have divided the wealth of available material into three sections, according to whether the journey occurs at the beginning of life (First Journey), in the middle (Second Journey), or towards the end (Third Journey).

The First Journey takes us through the spiritual and psychological challenges of the first decades of life, from conception and birth, childhood and teenage years until we discover a measure of stability in 'who I am'.

Accounts of such journeys may be written from the perspective of mid-life or old age and tell us what happens as we begin to settle into a defined role in society, with the inevitable closing of options that this entails.

The Second Journey can occur at any time from the early twenties to the fifties or sixties – or even later. When Mahatma Gandhi was 24, and already a successful barrister, he experienced racial discrimination while travelling on a train in South Africa. This triggered his Second Journey, which in 1947 finally resulted in his becoming the father of Indian independence. In the biblical narrative of Genesis 12:1–9, we are told that Abraham was 75 years old when he was called, with his wife Sarah, into his Second Journey. In 1990 71-year-old Nelson Mandela was called to leave his South African prison in order to walk into history as the leader of his nation, marking the completion of a Second Journey at an age when many people are embarking upon their Third Journey.

A Second Journey can be initiated by bereavement, the loss of a job or the collapse of a marriage. Illness, the search for work, the upheaval of war and many other situations which we would not have chosen for ourselves can catapult us into new and frightening realities. The trigger can, however, be a gentler and subtler process, which nevertheless causes previous certainties to be questioned. The journey can take years, as in the case of Abraham and Sarah, or it may be completed in a matter of hours, as in the case of Cleopas and his companion meeting the risen Jesus on the road to Emmaus (Luke 24:13–35).

Dante was thrust into the path of his Second Journey by those who exiled him from his beloved city of Florence in 1301, so that he found himself 'in a dark wood, where the right road was wholly lost and gone'. Seemingly random misfortune or even wilful human actions which initiate a Second Journey can, in the long term, be seen as instances of God 'writing straight with crooked lines'. Sometimes abrupt divine intervention may lead directly to conversion and the call to undertake a Second Journey. The experience of Saul, who would become St Paul, is a case in point. The Pharisee Saul was on the road to Damascus, where he intended to persecute first-century Christians, when he found himself blinded and thrown to the ground. Then he heard the voice of Jesus asking, 'Saul, Saul, why are you persecuting me?' (Acts 9:1–4).

The Third Journey takes us into the final stage of life when we move towards death. On our First and Second Journeys we have guidelines or route maps in the shape of the experiences of those who have travelled the road before us and can assure us that we will come through and reach the other end. For the Third Journey we have no such clear and tangible certainty. For religious believers there is, however, the assurance that on the other side of death there is a glorious and everlasting state of being, in which 'neither eye has seen nor ear heard, nor has it entered into the heart of man or woman the things that God has prepared for those who love him' (1 Corinthians 2:9).

Yet the Third Journey is the only one we can be sure of completing. It is possible to decline the invitation to complete the First Journey. Most of us have met 'Peter Pan' characters who refuse to grow up and cannot take the step into maturity which involves the closing of some options in order to concentrate on others and make clear life choices. The refusal or inability to complete the First Journey can make it impossible to accept the invitation to greater maturity contained in the Second Journey.

For the terminology of First, Second and Third Journeys I have drawn on Gerald O'Collins' *Second Journey* which indicates the sources. This terminology provides the rationale for dividing *Soul Searchers* into three major sections. Within each section the extracts are ordered chronologically, in accordance with the dates of the journeys themselves, even though the accounts may actually have been written very much later. With regard to biblical quotations I have used various translations of the Bible, in particular the New International Version and the New Jerusalem Bible. With regard to dates and biographical details I have generally been guided by the 1998 revision of *The Oxford Dictionary of the Christian Church* and *The Cambridge Biographical Encyclopedia*.

Spiritual searching and journeying turn up everywhere in the sacred and secular stories of human beings. It is no surprise, therefore, to find such searching and journeying beginning and ending that most beautiful book, the Gospel of John. At the start the two disciples, hearing John the Baptist's words about Jesus ('Behold the lamb of God!'), began to follow Jesus down the road on what would prove to be a momentous mid-life journey (John 1:35–37). At the end of the Gospel, Peter is warned that following Jesus will lead him on his own Third Journey to death (John 21:18–19).

In compiling *Soul Searchers* I have tried to spread the net as widely as possible in terms of different countries and ways of life. It has been a privilege to work with this material and I welcomed the invitation to compile this anthology, not least because the themes of searching and journeying have helped me to understand my own human and spiritual existence, and to look back on the road I have travelled with greater understanding and appreciation of those who have accompanied me.

Teresa de Bertodano
October 2001

FIRST JOURNEY

The process of growing up and achieving adulthood constitutes our First Journey. Along the way we might be threatened with death, like Isaac and Nicholas Alkemade. Horrible things might happen to us, as Maya Angelou records. This initial journey often means leaving our parents' home and sometimes we make terrible mistakes, like the Prodigal Son. Years of education normally help to shape the intellectual and spiritual growth of young travellers, and sometimes there is a dramatic conclusion, as in the case of Edith Piaf.

First Journeys can be undertaken against the background of civil violence, as in the case of Mary McAleese in Belfast, or in the settings of brutal and genocidal war, as experienced by Anne Frank. By contrast, the initial search for human and spiritual maturity can take place in the relative tranquillity of peacetime, as with the young Florence Nightingale.

From the little information about the early years of Jesus that survives, it appears that his journey to adulthood largely unfolded at home in Nazareth. On the other hand, the First Journey of St Augustine of Hippo involved crossing the Mediterranean Sea, from North Africa to the glittering city of Rome.

Isaac

The Offering of Isaac

Abraham and Sarah, the ancestors of the Jewish people, lived in approximately 1800 BC. The growth to manhood of their son Isaac involved a remarkable testing of his father. Abraham's obedience brought God's blessing, not only on his descendants but on all the nations of the earth.

God tested Abraham. He said to him, 'Abraham!'
'Here I am,' he replied.

Then God said, 'Take your son, your only son, Isaac, whom you love, and go to the region of Moriah. Sacrifice him there as a burnt offering on one of the mountains I will tell you about.'

Early the next morning Abraham got up and saddled his donkey. He took with him two of his servants and his son Isaac. When he had cut enough wood for the burnt offering, he set out for the place God had told him about. On the third day Abraham looked up and saw the place in the distance. He said to his servants, 'Stay here with the donkey while I and the boy go over there. We will worship and then we will come back to you.'

Abraham took the wood for the burnt offering and placed it on his son Isaac, and he himself carried the fire and the knife. As the two of them went on together, Isaac spoke up and said to his father Abraham, 'Father?'

'Yes, my son?' Abraham replied.

'The fire and wood are here,' Isaac said, 'but where is the lamb for the burnt offering?'

Abraham answered, 'God himself will provide the lamb for the burnt offering, my son.' And the two of them went on together.

When they reached the place God had told him about, Abraham built an altar there and arranged the wood on it. He bound his son Isaac and laid him on the altar, on top of the wood. Then he reached out his hand and took the knife to slay his son. But the angel of the Lord called out to him from heaven, 'Abraham! Abraham!'

'Here I am,' he replied.

'Do not lay a hand on the boy,' he said. 'Do not do anything to him. Now I know that you fear God, because you have not withheld from me your son, your only son.'

Abraham looked up and there in a thicket he saw a ram caught by its horns. He went over and took the ram and sacrificed it as a burnt offering instead of his son. So Abraham called that place The Lord Will Provide. And to this day it is said, 'On the mountain of the Lord it will be provided.'

The angel of the Lord called to Abraham from heaven a second time and said, 'I swear by myself, declares the Lord, that because you have done this and have not withheld your son, your only son, I will surely bless you and make your descendants as numerous as the stars in the sky and as the sand on the seashore. Your descendants will take possession of the cities of their enemies, and through your offspring all nations on earth will be blessed, because you have obeyed me.'

Then Abraham returned to his servants, and they set off together for Beersheba. And Abraham stayed in Beersheba.

Genesis 22:1–19

Moses

The Birth of Moses

During the 13th century BC the Egyptian Pharaoh ordered his people to kill all the boys born to their Israelite captives. Ironically, it was Pharaoh's own daughter who rescued the Israelite baby Moses, who had been born into the tribe of Levi and was to grow up and become, under God, the liberator of the Israelites from their captivity.

Pharaoh gave this order to all his people: 'Every boy that is born you must throw into the Nile, but let every girl live.'

Now a man of the house of Levi married a Levite woman, and she became pregnant and gave birth to a son. When she saw that he was a fine child, she hid him for three months. But when she could hide him no longer, she got a papyrus basket for him and coated it with tar and pitch. Then she placed the child in it and put it among the reeds along the bank of the Nile. His sister stood at a distance to see what would happen to him.

Then Pharaoh's daughter went down to the Nile to bathe, and her attendants were walking along the river bank. She saw the basket among the reeds and sent her slave girl to get it. She opened it and saw the baby. He was crying, and she felt sorry for him. 'This is one of the Hebrew babies,' she said.

Then his sister asked Pharaoh's daughter, 'Shall I go and get one of the Hebrew women to nurse the baby for you?'

'Yes, go,' she answered. And the girl went and got the baby's mother. Pharaoh's daughter said to her, 'Take this baby and nurse him for me, and I will pay you.' So the woman took the baby and nursed him. When the child grew older, she took him to Pharaoh's daughter and he became her son. She named him Moses, saying, 'I drew him out of the water.'

Exodus 1:22 – 2:10

St John the Baptist

John's Birth Foretold

In order to introduce the story of Jesus' conception and birth, Luke tells the story of the conception and birth of Jesus' great precursor, John the Baptist. During his public ministry, Jesus was to say of John: 'Among those born of women there has not risen anyone greater than John the Baptist' (Matthew 11:11).

In the time of Herod king of Judea there was a priest named Zechariah, who belonged to the priestly division of Abijah, his wife Elizabeth was also a descendant of Aaron. Both of them were upright in the sight of God, observing all the Lord's commandments and regulations blamelessly. But they had no children, because Elizabeth was barren, and they were both well on in years.

Once when Zechariah's division was on duty and he was serving as priest before God, he was chosen by lot, according to the custom of the priesthood, to go into the temple of the Lord and burn incense.

And when the time for the burning of incense came, all the assembled worshippers were praying outside.

Then an angel of the Lord appeared to him, standing at the right side of the altar of incense. When Zechariah saw him, he was startled and was gripped with fear. But the angel said to him: 'Do not be afraid, Zechariah; your prayer has been heard. Your wife Elizabeth will bear you a son, and you are to give him the name John. He will be a joy and delight to you, and many will rejoice because of his birth, for he will be great in the sight of the Lord. He is never to take wine or other fermented drink, and he will be filled with the Holy Spirit even from birth. Many of the people of Israel will he bring back to the Lord their God. And he will go on before the Lord, in the spirit and power of Elijah, to turn the hearts of the fathers to their children and the disobedient to the wisdom of the righteous – to make ready a people prepared for the Lord.'

Zechariah asked the angel, 'How can I be sure of this? I am an old man and my wife is well on in years.'

The angel answered, 'I am Gabriel. I stand in the presence of God, and I have been sent to speak to you and to tell you this good news. And now you will be silent and not able to speak until the day this happens, because you did not believe my words, which will come true at their proper time.'

Meanwhile, the people were waiting for Zechariah and wondering why he stayed so long in the temple. When he came out, he could not speak to them. They realized he had seen a vision in the temple, for he kept making signs to them but remained unable to speak.

When his time of service was completed, he returned home. After this his wife Elizabeth became pregnant and for five months remained in seclusion. 'The Lord has done this for me,' she said. 'In these days he has shown his favour and taken away my disgrace among the people.'

Luke 1:5–25

The Birth of the Baptist

When it was time for Elizabeth to have her baby, she gave birth to a son. Her neighbours and relatives heard that the Lord had shown her great mercy, and they shared her joy.

On the eighth day they came to circumcise the child, and they were going to name him after his father Zechariah, but his mother spoke up and said, 'No! He is to be called John.'

They said to her, 'There is no one among your relatives who has that name.'

Then they made signs to his father, to find out what he would like to name the child. He asked for a writing tablet, and to everyone's astonishment he wrote, 'His name is John.' Immediately his mouth was opened and his tongue was loosed, and he began to speak, praising

God. The neighbours were all filled with awe, and throughout the hill country of Judea people were talking about all these things. Everyone who heard this wondered about it, asking, 'What then is this child going to be?' For the Lord's hand was with him.

His father Zechariah was filled with the Holy Spirit and prophesied:

'Praise be to the Lord, the God of Israel,
   because he has come and has redeemed his people.
He has raised up a horn of salvation for us
   in the house of his servant David
(as he said through his holy prophets of long ago),
salvation from our enemies
   and from the hand of all who hate us —
to show mercy to our fathers
   and to remember his holy covenant,
   the oath he swore to our father Abraham:
to rescue us from the hand of our enemies,
   and to enable us to serve him without fear
in holiness and righteousness before him all our days.
And you, my child, will be called a prophet of the Most High;
   for you will go on before the Lord to prepare the way for him,
to give his people the knowledge of salvation
   through the forgiveness of their sins,
because of the tender mercy of our God,
   by which the rising sun will come to us from heaven
to shine on those living in darkness
   and in the shadow of death,
   to guide our feet into the path of peace.'

And the child grew and became strong in spirit; and he lived in the desert until he appeared publicly to Israel.

Luke 1:57–80

Jesus

The Boy Jesus in the Temple

Luke records the visit the boy Jesus made to the Jerusalem temple with his parents when Jesus was 12 years old. It is in this passage that we learn the first recorded words of Jesus. Afterwards, he returned with his parents to Nazareth where he grew to full manhood.

The child grew and became strong; he was filled with wisdom, and the grace of God was upon him.

Every year his parents went to Jerusalem for the Feast of the Passover. When he was 12 years old, they went up to the Feast, according to the custom. After the Feast was over, while his parents were returning home, the boy Jesus stayed behind in Jerusalem, but they were unaware of it. Thinking he was in their company, they travelled on for a day. Then they began looking for him among their relatives and friends. When they did not find him, they went back to Jerusalem to look for him. After three days they found him in the temple courts, sitting among the teachers, listening to them and asking them questions. Everyone who heard him was amazed at his understanding and his answers. When his parents saw him, they were astonished. His mother said to him, 'Son, why have you treated us like this? Your father and I have been anxiously searching for you.'

'Why were you searching for me?' he asked. 'Didn't you know I had to be in my Father's house?' But they did not understand what he was saying to them.

Then he went down to Nazareth with them and was obedient to them. But his mother treasured all these things in her heart. And Jesus grew in wisdom and stature, and in favour with God and men.

Luke 2:40–52

The Prodigal Son

Parable of the Prodigal Son

In this parable Jesus tells the story of the younger son of a farmer who leaves home to squander his inheritance in a distant country, only to find himself falling on hard times and obliged to return to his father and his family. It is his father's merciful and all-embracing love that enables the boy to grow both humanly and spiritually.

There was a man who had two sons. The younger one said to his father, 'Father, give me my share of the estate.' So he divided his property between them.

Not long after that, the younger son got together all he had, set off for a distant country and there squandered his wealth in wild living. After he had spent everything, there was a severe famine in that whole country, and he began to be in need. So he went and hired himself out to a citizen of that country, who sent him to his fields to feed pigs. He longed to fill his stomach with the pods that the pigs were eating, but no one gave him anything.

When he came to his senses, he said, 'How many of my father's hired men have food to spare, and here I am starving to death! I will set out and go back to my father and say to him: Father, I have sinned against heaven and against you. I am no longer worthy to be called your son make me like one of your hired men.' So he got up and went to his father.

But while he was still a long way off, his father saw him and was filled with compassion for him; he ran to his son, threw his arms around him and kissed him.

The son said to him, 'Father, I have sinned against heaven and against you. I am no longer worthy to be called your son.'

But the father said to his servants, 'Quick! Bring the best robe and put it on him. Put a ring on his finger and sandals on his feet. Bring the fattened calf and kill it. Let's have a feast and celebrate. For this son of mine was dead and is alive again; he was lost and is found.' So they began to celebrate.

Meanwhile, the older son was in the field. When he came near the house, he heard music and dancing. So he called one of the servants and asked him what was going on. 'Your brother has come,' he replied, ' and your father has killed the fattened calf because he has him back safe and sound.'

The older brother became angry and refused to go in. So his father went out and pleaded with him. But he answered his father, 'Look! All these years I've been slaving for you and never disobeyed your orders. Yet you never gave me even a young goat so I could celebrate with my friends. But when this son of yours who has squandered your property with prostitutes comes home, you kill the fattened calf for him!'

'My son,' the father said, 'you are always with me, and everything I have is yours. But we had to celebrate and be glad, because this brother of yours was dead and is alive again; he was lost and is found.'

Luke 15:11–32

St Augustine

The Providence of God

The writings of St Augustine (354–430), bishop of Hippo, have been immensely influential in the development of Western Christianity. Augustine was born in North Africa to a pagan father and a Christian mother, St Monica (c. 331–387), who, in accordance with the custom of the time, enrolled him as a catechumen who would receive Christian training and instruction in preparation for baptism. As an adolescent, Augustine abandoned the Christianity of his mother and, at the age of 17, took a concubine by whom he had a son. The prayers of St Monica and St Ambrose were influential in drawing him back to Christianity, and Augustine was eventually baptized by St Ambrose in 387. In his *Confessions*, written soon after he had become bishop of Hippo in modern Algeria, Augustine addresses God, recalling his notorious life as a young man and his eventual decision to seek baptism. In this passage he recalls his difficult experiences as a young teacher in North Africa before his conversion.

You were at work in persuading me to go to Rome and to do my teaching there rather than at Carthage. The consideration which persuaded me I will not omit to confess to you because in this also your profoundly mysterious providence and your mercy very present to us are proper matters for reflection and proclamation. My motive in going to Rome was not that the friends who urged it on me promised higher fees and a greater position of dignity, though at that time these considerations had an influence on my mind. The principal and almost sole reason was that I had heard how at Rome the young men went quietly about their studies and were kept in order by a stricter imposition of discipline. They did not rush all at once and in a mob into the class of a teacher with whom they were not enrolled, nor were pupils admitted at all unless the teacher gave them leave. By contrast at

Carthage the licence of the students is foul and uncontrolled. They impudently break in and with almost mad behaviour disrupt the order which each teacher has established for his pupils' benefit. They commit many acts of vandalism with an astonishing mindlessness, which would be punished under the law were it not that custom protects them.

Thereby their wretched self-delusion is shown up. They act as if they were allowed to do what would never be permitted by your eternal law. They think they are free to act with impunity when by the very blindness of their behaviour they are being punished, and inflict on themselves incomparably worse damage than on others. When I was a student, I refused to have anything to do with these customs; as a professor I was forced to tolerate them in outsiders who were not my own pupils. So I decided to go where all informed people declared that such troubles did not occur. But it was you, 'my hope and my portion in the land of the living' (Psalm 141:6) who wished me to change my earthly home for 'the salvation of my soul' (Psalm 34:3). You applied the pricks which made me tear myself away from Carthage, and you put before me the attractions of Rome to draw me there, using people who love a life of death, committing insane actions in this world, promising vain rewards in the next. To correct my 'steps' (Psalm 36:23; Proverbs 20:20) you secretly made use of their and my perversity. For those who disturbed my serenity were blinded with a disgraceful frenzy. Those who invited me to go elsewhere had a taste only for this earth. I myself, while I hated a true misery here, pursued a false felicity there.

St Augustine of Hippo, *Confessions* V:8:14

St Joan of Arc

French Heroine

Joan of Arc (1412–31) was born in the French village of Domrémy in Lorraine. In 1425 she received the first of a series of·supernatural visitations in which St Michael, St Catherine, St Margaret and others revealed her mission to save France, which at that time was suffering under the Hundred Years' War with the English and civil war between the great houses of Orléans and Burgundy. In this extract, Joan describes her first experience of 'voices'.

Under her inspiring leadership the English army was forced to lift the siege of Orléans, but Joan was eventually sold to the English by the Duke of Burgundy and burnt as a heretic in 1431.

When I was 13 years old, I had a voice from God to help me govern my conduct. And the first time I was very fearful. And came this voice, about the hour of noon, in the summer-time, in my father's garden; I had not fasted on the eve preceding that day. I heard the voice on the right-hand side, towards the church; and rarely do I hear it without brightness. This brightness comes from the same side as the voice is heard. It is usually a great light. When I came to France, often I heard this voice… The voice was sent to me by God and, after I had thrice heard this voice, I knew that it was the voice of an angel. This voice has always guarded me well and I have always understood it clearly…

It has taught me to conduct myself well, to go habitually to church. It told me that I, Joan, should come into France… This voice told me, twice or thrice a week, that I, Joan, must go away and that I must come to France and that my father must know nothing of my leaving. The voice told me that I should go to France and I could not bear to stay where I was. The voice told me that I should raise the siege laid to the city of Orléans. The voice told me also that I should make my way to Robert de Baudricourt in the fortress of Vaucouleurs, the captain of that place, that he would give me people to go with me. And me, I answered it that I was a poor girl who knew not how to ride nor lead in war.

Régine Pernoud, *Joan of Arc: By Herself and Her Witnesses*

William Shakespeare

Infants and Schoolboys

In *As You Like It* William Shakespeare (1564–1616) presents human life as a play in seven acts. The human drama begins with the infant 'mewling and puking in his nurse's arms' and gives way to the schoolboy 'creeping like snail unwillingly to school'.

> All the world's a stage,
> And all the men and women merely players:
> They have their exits and their entrances;
> And one man in his time plays many parts,
> His acts being seven ages. At first the infant,
> Mewling and puking in the nurse's arms.
> And then the whining schoolboy, with his satchel,
> And shining morning face, creeping like snail
> Unwillingly to school. And then the lover,
> Sighing like furnace, with a woful ballad
> Made to his mistress' eyebrow. Then a soldier,
> Full of strange oaths, and bearded like the pard,
> Jealous in honour, sudden and quick in quarrel,
> Seeking the bubble reputation
> Even in the cannon's mouth. And then the justice.
> In fair round belly with good capon lined,
> With eyes severe, and beard of formal cut,
> Full of wise saws and modern instances;
> And so he plays his part. The sixth age shifts
> Into the lean and slippered pantaloon,
> With spectacles on nose and pouch on side,
> His youthful hose well saved a world too wide
> For his shrunk shank; and his big manly voice,

Turning again towards childish treble, pipes
And whistles in his sound. Last scene of all,
That ends this strange eventful history,
Is second childishness, and mere oblivion,
Sans teeth, sans eyes, sans taste, sans everything.

William Shakespeare, *As You Like It*, Act 2, Scene 7

John Wesley

The Young Mr Wesley

In his *Journal*, John Wesley (1703–91), the founder of the Methodist Movement, recalls his schooldays in England, his years at Oxford University and his early life and ministry as a priest of the Church of England.

I believe, till I was about 10 years old I had not sinned away that 'washing of the Holy Ghost' which was given me in baptism; having been strictly educated and carefully taught, that I could only be saved 'by universal obedience, by keeping all the commandments of God'; in the meaning of which I was diligently instructed. And those instructions, so far as they respected outward duties and sins, I gladly received, and often thought of. But all that was said to me of inward obedience, or holiness, I neither understood nor remembered. So that I was indeed as ignorant of the true meaning of the law, as I was of the gospel of Christ.

The next six or seven years were spent at school; where, outward restraints being removed, I was much more negligent than before, even of outward duties, and almost continually guilty of outward sins, which I knew to be such, though they were not scandalous in the eye of the world. However, I still read the scriptures and said my prayers, morning and evening. And what I now hoped to be saved by, was: I. Not being so bad as other people. 2. Having still a kindness for religion. And, 3. Reading the Bible, going to church, and saying my prayers.

Being removed to the University for five years, I still said my prayers, both in public and in private, and read with the scriptures, several other books of religion, especially comments on the New Testament. Yet I had not all this while so much as a notion of inward holiness; nay, went on habitually and, for the most part, very contentedly, in some or other known sin: indeed, with some intermission and short struggles, especially before and after the holy communion, which I was obliged to receive thrice a year. I cannot well tell what I hoped to be saved by now, when I was continually sinning against that little light I had, unless by those transient fits of what many divines taught me to call repentance.

When I was about 22, my father pressed me to enter into holy orders. At the same time, the providence of God directing me to Kempis's *Christian's Pattern*, I began to see, that true religion was seated in the heart, and that God's law extended to all our thoughts as well as words and actions. I was, however, very angry at Kempis, for being too strict; though I read him only in Dean Stanhope's translation. Yet I had frequently much sensible comfort in reading him, such as I was an utter stranger to before: and meeting likewise with a religious friend, which I never had till now, I began to alter the whole form of my conversation, and to set in earnest upon a new life. I set apart an hour or two a day for religious retirement. I communicated every week. I watched against all sin, whether in word or deed. I began to aim at, and pray for, inward holiness. So that now, 'doing so much, and living so good a life,' I doubted not but I was a good Christian.

Removing soon after to another college, I executed a resolution which I was before convinced was of the utmost importance – shaking off at once all my trifling acquaintance. I began to see more and more the value of time. I applied myself closer to study. I watched more carefully against actual sins; I advised others to be religious, according to that scheme of religion by which I modelled my own life. But meeting now with Mr Law's *Christian Perfection* and *Serious Call*, although I was much offended at many parts of both, yet they convinced me more than ever of the exceeding height and breadth and depth of the law of God. The light flowed in so mightily upon my soul, that everything appeared in a new view. I cried to God for help, and resolved not to prolong the time of obeying him as I had never done before. And by my continued endeavour to keep his whole law, inward and outward, to the utmost of my power, I was persuaded that I should be accepted of him, and that I was even then in a state of salvation.

In 1730 I began visiting the prisons; assisting the poor and sick in town; and doing what other good I could, by my presence, or my little fortune, to the bodies and souls of all men. To this end I abridged myself of all superfluities, and many that are called necessaries of life. I soon became a byword for so doing; and I rejoiced that my name was cast out as evil. The next spring I began observing the Wednesday and Friday fasts, commonly observed in the ancient church; tasting no food till three in the afternoon. And now I knew not how to go any farther. I diligently strove against all sin. I omitted no sort of self-denial which I thought lawful: I carefully used, both in public and in private, all the means of grace at all opportunities. I omitted no occasion of doing good: I for that reason suffered evil. And all this I knew to be nothing, unless as it was directed toward inward holiness. Accordingly this, the image of God, was what I aimed at in all, by doing his will, not my own. Yet when, after continuing some years in this course, I apprehended myself to be near death, I could not find that all this gave me any comfort, or any assurance of acceptance with God. At this I was then not a little surprised; not imagining I had been all this time building on the sand, nor considering that 'other foundation can no man lay, than that which is laid' by God, 'even Christ Jesus.'

Soon after, a contemplative man convinced me still more than I was convinced before, that outward works are nothing, being alone; and in several conversations instructed me, how to pursue inward holiness, or a union of the soul with God. But even of his instructions (though I then received them as the words of God) I cannot but now observe: 1. That he spoke so incautiously against trusting in outward works, that he discouraged me from doing them at all. 2. That he recommended (as it were, to supply what was wanting in them) mental prayer, and the like exercises, as the most effectual means of purifying the soul, and uniting it with God. Now these were, in truth, as much my own works as visiting the sick or clothing the naked; and the union with God, thus pursued, was as really my own righteousness, as any I had before pursued under another name.

In this refined way of trusting to my own works and my own righteousness (so zealously inculcated by the mystic writers), I dragged on heavily, finding no comfort or help therein, till the time of my leaving England. On shipboard, however, I was again active in outward works; where it pleased God of his free mercy to give me 26 of the Moravian brethren for companions, who endeavoured to show me 'a more excellent way.' But I understood it not at first. I was too learned and too wise. So that it seemed foolishness unto me. And I continued preaching, and following after, and trusting in, that righteousness whereby no flesh can be justified.

John Wesley, *John Wesley's Journal*

Florence Nightingale

Called by God

The First Journey of Florence Nightingale (1820–1910) was shaped by a call from God when she was 16 and preparing to leave home in England for a European pleasure trip with her family. In her acclaimed biography, *Florence Nightingale*, Cecil Woodham-Smith (1896–1977) indicates that the idea of nursing had not entered Florence's head at this stage. There was no inkling of the gifts that would lead to her renown as the heroine of the hospitals at Scutari during the Crimean War (1853–56) and the reformer of the hospital system.

> In the midst of bustle, plans, discussions, Miss Nightingale received a call from God.
>
> It is possible to know a very great deal about Miss Nightingale's inner life and feelings because she had the habit of writing what she called 'private notes'. She was unhappy in her environment, she had no one to confide in, and she poured herself out on paper... From time to time she also kept diaries; but it was in her private notes, written from girlhood to old age, that she recorded her true feelings, her secret experiences and her uncensored opinions.
>
> Her experience was similar to that which came to Joan of Arc. In a private note she wrote: 'On 7 February 1837, God spoke to me and called me to his service.' It was not an inward revelation. She heard, as Joan of Arc heard, an objective voice, a voice outside herself, speaking to her in human words.
>
> She was not quite 17 and she was already living largely in a dream world, which was often more actual to her than the real world. But the voices which spoke to her were not a phenomenon of adolescence. Nearly 40 years later, in a private note of 1874, she wrote that during her life her 'voices' had spoken to her four times. Once on

7 February 1837, the date of her call; once in 1853 before going to her first post at the Hospital for Poor Gentlewomen in Harley Street; once before the Crimea in 1854; and once after Sidney Herbert's death in 1861.

Her path was not made clear. The voices which spoke to Joan told her to take a definite course of action; Miss Nightingale was told nothing definite. God had called her, but what form that service was to take she did not know. The idea of nursing did not enter her mind. She doctored her dolls, she nursed sick pets, she was especially fond of babies. Her protective instincts were strong, but they had not yet led her to the knowledge that God had called her to the service of the sick.

Meanwhile she knew herself to be God's, and she was at peace. Her call had filled her with confidence and faith. God had spoken to her once; presently he would speak to her again.

Cecil Woodham-Smith, *Florence Nightingale*

Jo March

The Passing of Beth

In *Good Wives*, Louisa M. Alcott (1832–88) describes the death of Beth, the fragile sister of Meg, Jo and Amy. The sisters made their first appearance in Alcott's autobiographical novel *Little Women* (1868) as the daughters of an army chaplain during the American Civil War (1861–65). Beth's journey to death is a First Journey for her beloved sister Jo who decides that her literary ambitions are not, perhaps, the most important thing in her life.

Jo never left her for an hour since Beth had said, 'I feel stronger when you are here.' She slept on a couch in the room, waking often to renew the fire, to feed, lift, or wait upon the patient creature who seldom asked for anything, and 'tried not to be a trouble'. All day she haunted the room, jealous of any other nurse, and prouder of being chosen then than of any honour her life ever brought her. Precious and helpful hours for Jo, for now her heart received the teaching that it needed; lessons in patience were so sweetly taught her that she could not fail to learn them; charity for all, the lovely spirit that can forgive and truly forget unkindness, the loyalty to duty that makes the hardest easy, and the sincere faith that fears nothing, but trusts undoubtingly.

Often, when she woke, Jo found Beth reading in her well-worn little book, heard her singing softly, to beguile the sleepless night, or saw her lean her face upon her hands, while slow tears dropped through the transparent fingers; and Jo would lie watching her, with thoughts too deep for tears, feeling that Beth, in her simple, unselfish way, was trying to wean herself from the dear old life, and fit herself for the life to come, by sacred words of comfort, quiet prayers, and the music she loved so well.

Seeing this did more for Jo than the wisest sermons, the saintliest hymns, the most fervent prayers that any voice could utter; for, with eyes made clear by many tears, and a heart softened by the tenderest sorrow, she recognized the beauty of her sister's life – uneventful, unambitious, yet full of the genuine virtues which 'smell sweet, and blossom in the dust', the self-forgetfulness that makes the humblest on earth remembered soonest in heaven, the true success which is possible to all.

One night, when Beth looked among the books upon her table, to find something to make her forget the mortal weariness that was almost as hard to bear as pain, as she turned the leaves of her old favourite *Pilgrim's Progress*, she found a little paper, scribbled over in Jo's hand. The name caught her eye, and the blurred look of the lines made her sure that tears had fallen on it.

'Poor Jo! She's fast asleep, so I won't wake her to ask leave; she shows me all her things, and I don't think she'll mind if I look at this,' thought Beth, with a glance at her sister, who lay on the rug, with the tongs beside her, ready to wake up the minute the log fell apart.

My Beth

Sitting patient in the shadow
  Till the blessed light shall come,
A serene and saintly presence
  Sanctifies our troubled home.
Earthly joys and hopes and sorrows
  Break like ripples on the strand
Of the deep and solemn river
  Where her willing feet now stand.

O my sister, passing from me,
  Out of human care and strife,
Leave me, as a gift, those virtues
  Which have beautified your life.
Dear, bequeath me that great patience
  Which has power to sustain
A cheerful, uncomplaining spirit
  In its prison-house of pain.

Give me, for I need it sorely,
  Of that courage, wise and sweet,
Which has made the path of duty
  Green beneath your willing feet.
Give me that unselfish nature,
  That with charity divine
Can pardon wrong for love's dear sake —
  Meek heart, forgive me mine!

Thus our parting daily loseth
  Something of its bitter pain,
And while learning this hard lesson,
  My great loss becomes my gain.
For the touch of grief will render
  My wild nature more serene,
Give to life new aspirations,
  A new trust in the unseen.

Henceforth, safe across the river,
  I shall see for ever more
A beloved, household spirit
  Waiting for me on the shore.
Hope and faith, born of my sorrow,
  Guardian angels shall become,
And the sister gone before me
  By their hands shall lead me home.

Blurred and blotted, faulty and feeble, as the lines were, they brought a look of inexpressible comfort to Beth's face, for her one regret had been that she had done so little; and this seemed to assure her that her life had not been useless, that her death would not bring the despair she feared. As she sat with the paper folded between her hands, the charred log fell asunder. Jo started up, revived the blaze, and crept to the bedside, hoping Beth slept.

'Not asleep, but so happy, dear. See, I found this and read it; I knew you wouldn't care. Have I been all that to you, Jo?' she asked, with wistful, humble earnestness.

'O Beth, so much, so much!' and Jo's head went down upon the pillow, beside her sister's.

'Then I don't feel as if I'd wasted my life. I'm not so good as you make me, but I *have* tried to do right; and now, when it's too late to begin even to do better, it's such a comfort to know that someone loves me so much, and feels as if I'd helped them.'

'More than anyone in the world, Beth. I used to think I couldn't let you go; but I'm learning to feel that I don't lose you; that you'll be more to me than ever, and death can't part us, though it seems to.'

'I know it cannot, and I don't fear it any longer, for I'm sure I shall be your Beth still, to love and help you more than ever. You must take my place, Jo, and be everything to father and mother when I'm gone. They will turn to you, don't fail them; and if it's hard work alone, remember that I don't forget you, and that you'll be happier in doing that than writing splendid books or seeing all the world; for love is the only thing that we can carry with us when we go, and it makes the end so easy.'

'I'll try, Beth'; and then and there Jo renounced her old ambition, pledged herself to a new and better one, acknowledging the poverty of other desires, and feeling the blessed solace of a belief in the immortality of love.

So the spring days came and went, the sky grew clearer, the earth greener, the flowers were up fair and early, and the birds came back in time to say goodbye to Beth, who, like a tired but trustful child, clung to the hands that had led her all her life, as father and mother guided her tenderly through the Valley of the Shadow, and gave her up to God.

Seldom, except in books, do the dying utter memorable words, see visions, or depart with beatified countenances; and those who have sped many parting souls know that to most the end comes as naturally and simply as sleep. As Beth had hoped, the 'tide went out easily'; and in the dark hour before the dawn, on the bosom where she had drawn her first breath, she quietly drew her last, with no farewell but one loving look, one little sigh.

With tears and prayers and tender hands, mother and sisters made her ready for the long sleep that pain would never mar again, seeing with grateful eyes the beautiful serenity that soon replaced the pathetic patience that had wrung their hearts so long, and feeling, with reverent joy, that to their darling death was a benignant angel, not a phantom full of dread.

When morning came, for the first time in many months the fire was out, Jo's place was empty, and the room was very still. But a bird sang blithely on a budding bough, close by, the snowdrops blossomed freshly at the window, and the spring sunshine streamed in like a benediction over the placid face upon the pillow – a face so full of painless peace that those who loved it best smiled through their tears, and thanked God that Beth was well at last.

Louisa M. Alcott, *Good Wives*

St Katharine Drexel

An Unexpected Mission

St Katharine Drexel (1858–1955) of Philadelphia devoted her immense fortune to improving the circumstances of Native American and African American peoples. Katharine had originally wanted to join a contemplative religious order but found herself increasingly concerned about the situation of Native Americans and African Americans. In January 1887, 28-year-old Katharine was visiting Rome with her family and decided to consult Pope Leo XIII. His unexpected advice launched her on a journey which would lead her to found the Sisters of the Blessed Sacrament and, through them, a network of schools and missions across America. In her biography *The Life of Katharine Drexel*, Katherine Burton describes the momentous meeting with the Pope.

> When they knelt to receive Pope Leo's blessing and begged his blessing also for relatives and friends, the Holy Father nodded graciously and said, '*Tout – tout – est accordé.*' Then Kate asked if she might make a personal request, and he granted her the time to speak to him in private. Briefly and simply she told him of her desire to join a religious congregation vowed to contemplation. For some years she had been drawn to the religious life, she said, and now she felt that she had a true vocation. But a difficulty had arisen, for almost from the moment that she began to consider life in the convent she had also been led, through Bishop O'Connor, to take an increasing interest in the sad condition of the Indians in North America; she had aided both Bishop O'Connor and Father Stephan of the Indian Bureau in building and staffing various missions.
>
> 'It has seemed to me more than once, Your Holiness,' she said, 'that I ought to aid them by my personal work among them as well, and if I enter an enclosed congregation I might be abandoning those

whom God wants me to help. Perhaps Your Holiness will designate a congregation to which I could turn over my own income to carry on this work, some congregation that would give all its time and effort to the Indian missions.'

Leo XIII had listened very carefully. Then he looked thoughtfully at the beautifully dressed young woman before him, everything about her showing clearly her background of culture and wealth. She was obviously unmindful of anything except that she wanted to give her life to God and for souls. No doubt the Pope knew that she was a member of the extremely wealthy Drexel banking family, that her offering was no small thing, that these millions would do untold good among the Indians and would ease the heavy burdens of the missionaries and relieve their poverty. But he saw, too, that she was offering to God another gift – herself in a life of prayer.

For a full minute he said nothing. He was gazing at her with a thoughtful expression in his wise old eyes. 'But why not be a missionary yourself, my child?' he asked.

He said nothing more nor did he wait for an answer. Again he blessed her – 'and all your future works.'

Kate had kept calm all during the audience, but when she reached the antechamber she burst into tears. When she rejoined her sisters she had wiped away the tell-tale signs, but the perceptive Elizabeth thought she saw relief on her face and she wondered if the Holy Father had answered some question for Kate to which she had been unable to find the answer herself.

She was right: Kate was reassured. She was remembering the several times when she had spoken to Bishop O'Connor of becoming a cloistered nun, and he had said, 'Wait – wait a while,' and so she had delayed making any decision. Now the Pope himself had told her she need wait no longer. She had not received the answer she expected, yet deep in her heart she knew it was the one she must accept. She knew now why the bishop had told her to wait.

She need delay no longer. The Holy Father had shown her the road to her future.

Katherine Burton, *The Life of Katharine Drexel*

St Thérèse of Lisieux

Thérèse and the Pope

A few months after Katharine Drexel's successful visit to Pope Leo XIII another young woman came to Rome to seek his help with her future. But to all intents and purposes this papal audience was a disaster. In November 1887, 14-year-old Thérèse Martin (1873–97) was on pilgrimage to Rome with a group from the French diocese of Bayeux. Thérèse was determined to enter the Carmelite Order at the age of 15, but was meeting with setbacks at every turn, not least from the Vicar-General of Bayeux Diocese, Monsignor Révérony, who was accompanying the Bayeux pilgrims. Monsignor Révérony had forbidden anyone to speak to the Pope during the audience but Thérèse's sister Céline encouraged her to speak out! In this extract from her autobiography, Thérèse describes the disastrous day.

The Pope sat in a big armchair, in a white cassock and cape, wearing a *zucchetta*. I got a general impression of cardinals and archbishops and bishops standing round him, but I didn't try to distinguish because I had eyes for nothing but the Holy Father himself. We passed before him one by one, each pilgrim kneeling, kissing first his foot and then his hand, and receiving his benediction; then two members of the noble guard touched him lightly on the shoulder as a warning to get up – touched the pilgrim, I mean, not the Pope; how badly I tell my story! Before I went in, I had fully resolved to speak out; but my courage began to desert me when I found M. Révérony, of all people, standing close to his right hand! And at the same moment word was passed round, as from M. Révérony, that nothing must be said, because the interview was long enough as it was. I turned round to consult dear Céline and she said: 'Speak out.' A moment later, there I was at the Holy Father's feet, kissing his shoe: but when he held out his hand, I clasped mine together and looked up at him with the tears starting to my eyes: 'Most Holy Father,' I said, 'I've a great favour to ask of you.' He bent towards me till his head was nearly touching my face, and his dark, deep-set eyes seemed to look right down into the depths of my soul. 'Most Holy Father, ' I said, 'in honour of your jubilee, I want you to let me enter the Carmelite order at 15.' My voice must have been indistinct through emotion; so he turned to M. Révérony, who was looking at me in surprise and disapproval, and said: 'I can't quite understand.' If it had been God's will, M. Révérony could easily have made things all right; but no, it was all cross me this time, no crown. 'This child here,' said the Vicar-General, 'is anxious to enter Carmel at 15, and her superiors are looking into the matter at this moment.' The Holy Father looked at me with great kindness, but all he said was: 'Very well, my child, do what your superiors tell you.' I put both my hands on his knees, and had one more try: 'Yes, but if you'd say the word, Most Holy Father, everybody would agree.' He fixed his eyes on me, and said, emphasizing every syllable as he uttered it: 'All's well, all's well; if God wants you to enter, you will.' He spoke with such earnestness and such conviction that I can still hear him saying it.

His kindness gave me courage, and I wanted to go on; but the two members of the noble guard, finding that I paid no attention to their ceremonial touch, took me by the arms, and M. Révérony helped them to lift me up; I kept my arms on the Pope's knees, and they had to carry me away by main force. As they did so, His Holiness put his hand to my lips, and then raised it in blessing; he followed me with his eyes for quite a long time. As for my own eyes, they were full of tears, and M. Révérony got quite as many 'diamonds' as he'd had at Bayeux. Well, they carried me off (you might say) to the door, where another noble guard gave me a Papal medal. Céline, who came next to me, had witnessed the whole thing, and was almost as much distressed as I was, but she managed to ask the Holy Father to give Carmel his blessing. 'Carmel has had its blessing already,' said M. Révérony disapprovingly, and the Holy Father repeated, much more kindly: 'Yes, Carmel has had its blessing.'

St Thérèse of Lisieux, *The Autobiography of a Saint*

Although the papal audience ended in tears, Thérèse subsequently obtained permission to become a Carmelite nun at the age of 15.

Miles Franklin

Growing Up in Australia

Miles Franklin (1879–1954) achieved fame with her distinctively Australian autobiographical novel *My Brilliant Career*, in which Sybella Melvyn aspires to the cultivated life of a writer but feels hampered by the conventions of the society in which she lives. In this extract Sybella ends her story by inviting other young people to live courageously.

Christmas, only distinguished from the 52 slow Sundays of the year by plum-pudding, roast turkey, and a few bottles of home-made beer, has been once more; New Year, ushered in with sweet-scented midsummer wattle and bloom of gum- and box-tree has gone; February has followed, March is doing likewise, and my life is still the same.

What the future holds I know not, and am tonight so weary that I do not care.

Time rules us all. And life, indeed, is not
The thing we planned it out, ere hope was dead;
And then, we women cannot choose our lot.

Time is thorough in his work, and as that arch-cheat, Hope, gradually becomes a phantom of the past, the neck will grow inured to its yoke.

Tonight is one of the times when the littleness – the abject littleness – of all things in life comes home to me.

After all, what is there in vain ambition? King or slave, we all must die, and when death knocks at our door, will it matter whether our life has been great or small, fast or slow, so long as it has been true – true with the truth that will bring rest to the soul?

But the toughest lives are brittle,
  And the bravest and the best
Lightly fall — it matters little;
  Now I only long for rest.

To weary hearts throbbing slowly in hopeless breasts the sweetest thing is rest.

And my heart is weary. Oh, how it aches tonight — not with the ache of a young heart passionately crying out for battle, but with the slow dead ache of an old heart returning vanquished and defeated!

Enough of pessimistic snarling and grumbling! Enough! Enough! Now for a lilt of another theme:

I am proud that I am an Australian, a daughter of the Southern Cross, a child of the mighty bush. I am thankful I am a peasant, a part of the bone and muscle of my nation, and earn my bread by the sweat of my brow, as man was meant to do. I rejoice I was not born a parasite, one of the blood-suckers who loll on velvet and satin, crushed from the proceeds of human sweat and blood and souls.

Ah, my sunburnt brothers! — sons of toil and of Australia! I love and respect you well, for you are brave and good and true. I have seen not only those of you with youth and hope strong in your veins, but those with pathetic streaks of grey in your hair, large families to support, and with half a century sitting upon your work-laden shoulders. I have seen you struggle uncomplainingly against flood, fire, disease in stock, pests, drought, trade depression, and sickness, and yet have time to extend your hands and hearts in true sympathy to a brother in misfortune, and spirits to laugh and joke and be cheerful.

And for my sisters a great love and pity fills my heart. Daughters of toil, who scrub and wash and mend and cook, who are dressmakers, paperhangers, milkmaids, gardeners, and candle makers all in one, and yet have time to be cheerful and tasty in your homes, and make the best of the few oases to be found along the narrow dusty track of your existence. Would that I were more worthy to be one of you — more a typical Australian peasant — cheerful, honest, brave!

I love you, I love you. Bravely you jog along with the rope of class distinction drawing closer, closer, tighter, tighter around you: a few more generations and you will be as enslaved as were ever the *moujiks* of Russia. I see it and I know it, but I cannot help you. My ineffective life will be trod out in the same round of toil, — I am only one of yourselves, I am only an unnecessary, little, bush commoner, I am only a — woman!

The great sun is sinking in the west, grinning and winking knowingly as he goes, upon the starving stock and drought-smitten wastes of land. Nearer he draws to the gum-tree scrubby horizon, turns the clouds to orange, scarlet, silver flame, gold! Down, down he goes. The gorgeous, garish splendour of sunset pageantry flames out; the long shadows eagerly cover all; the kookaburras laugh their merry mocking goodnight; the clouds fade to turquoise, green, and grey; the stars peep shyly out; the soft call of the mopoke arises in the gullies! With much love and good wishes to all — goodnight! Goodbye! Amen.

Miles Franklin, *My Brilliant Career*

Ronald Knox

A Vow of Celibacy

The English Bible scholar and Roman Catholic apologist Ronald Knox (1888–1957) made a vow of celibacy as a 17-year-old schoolboy at Eton College when he was Captain of the School. Knox describes the circumstances surrounding the vow in his autobiography, *A Spiritual Aeneid*, in which he is characteristically modest about his abilities and achievements. According to Knox's biographer, Evelyn Waugh, he was considered to be 'the cleverest Etonian in human memory' as well as immensely popular.

I think I could still point to the precise place on 'Chamber Stairs' where I knelt down at the age of 17 one evening and bound myself by a vow of celibacy. The uppermost thought in my mind was not that of virginity: I was not fleeing from the wickedness of the world I saw round me. Without wishing to embark on a controversy, I must say here that I believe it possible at an ordinary house in an ordinary school for an ordinary boy, though he may hear much obscene conversation and much scandalous gossip, to go through his school time without having the moral evils which sometimes lie beneath the surface, thrust upon his notice. I knew people who were by repute immoral; the conventions of our society, as well as charity, demanded that I should give them the benefit of the doubt: I never heard a boy deliberately boast of his own sins. It was not, then, a sense of oppression about purity that influenced me. But at this time (as is common, I suppose, with many people) I was just beginning to form close and intimate friendships; I was just beginning also to realize that in many cases such friendships were likely to be dissolved through circumstances of separation after leaving school. And, conscious for the first time how much my nature craved for human sympathy and support, I thought it my obvious duty to deny myself that tenderest sympathy and support which a happy marriage would bring. I must have 'power to attend upon the Lord without impediment'.

I have no notion, humanly speaking, whence these ascetic impulses came. I cannot remember that any of my reading up till then would have suggested them to me... The aspiration must, I think, have been self-sown, and, poor as is my record of self-denial since then, I think the doctrine of merit is the most lucidly obvious to me still of all the truths of religion.

It will no doubt be supposed, from what I have written, that I was a shy, reserved, unpopular sort of boy, much given to self-communing and morbid imaginings. I can only say that the exact contrary was the case. This was just the time at which I was blossoming out into a sympathetic friend and a tolerable companion. I knew everybody round me, I wasted endless hours in talking, I watched matches, ate cake, scamped my work like anybody else. I was only exceptional as regards literary ability. I had won a Balliol scholarship a year earlier than I need have, and I wrote constantly for the *Eton College Chronicle*, which I finally edited, also once or twice for the *Cornhill* and the *World*. Yet neither the scholar nor the poet in any school story I ever read was anything but unpopular. I was quite hopeless at all games; yet nobody ever tried to 'crush my originality' or 'force me into a mould', or do any of the harm public schools are generally supposed to do in the case of unusual temperaments. I was supremely happy, and accepted everywhere at my own valuation as a very normal Etonian.

Ronald Knox, *A Spiritual Aeneid*

Edith Piaf

A Miracle

The French singer Edith Piaf (1915–63) spent part of her childhood with her grandmother who ran a brothel in Normandy. At the age of four Edith went blind and her grandmother took her on a pilgrimage to Lisieux to pray to St Thérèse for a cure. Apparently the girls who worked in the brothel joined in the pilgrimage and also prayed fervently for the tiny child. Their prayers were heard. Edith, her sight restored, went back to Lisieux to give thanks, accompanied by her grandmother and the girls. In this extract from her autobiography *The Wheel of Fortune*, Edith describes the roots of her devotion to St Thérèse and also the devastation she experienced on the death of her lover, world middleweight boxing champion Marcel Cerdan, in 1949.

I believe in God!

Quite early in my life I learnt the meaning of the word 'miracle'. When I was four years old, an attack of conjunctivitis blinded me. At the time I was living in Normandy, at the home of my grandmother. On 15 August 1919, she took me to Lisieux and we prayed together at the foot of the altar of little St Thérèse.

'Have pity on me,' I murmured. 'Give me back my sight.'

And 10 days later, at four o'clock in the afternoon, I saw again. Since that day, I have always carried the image of St Thérèse with me.

I have another talisman, a cross with seven emeralds which is just as precious to me. This I received from Marlene Dietrich one Christmas when I was in New York. With it, she sent a sheet of parchment with the words:

One must find God.
Marlene.
Rome.
Christmas.

Because I believe in God, I have no fear of death. There was a time, some years ago, when I even wished for it. My whole world had been shattered by the death of one I loved (Marcel Cerdan) and I thought I could never again know happiness or laughter. I had lost all hope and courage. Faith saved me.

   When the great champion to whom I was so closely bound was killed, I already knew that because others who loved him would suffer, I could never find a lasting happiness with him. His death was yet another blow. I was only saved by my faith.

Edith Piaf, *The Wheel of Fortune*

Billy Graham

A Gentle Call

Internationally renowned American evangelist Billy Graham (1918–) was an ordinary 16-year-old growing up in a farming family in North Carolina when he decided to accept the invitation to allow Christ to come into his life. The change was quiet and undramatic but it was the prelude to his ordination as a Southern Baptist minister and a career in Christian evangelism which has made Billy a household name. In his autobiography, *Just as I Am*, Billy Graham describes the gentle call from God that changed his life.

As a teenager, what I needed to know for certain was that I was right with God. I could not help but admit to myself that I was purposeless and empty-hearted. Our family Bible reading, prayer, psalm-singing, and churchgoing – all these had left me restless and resentful. I had even tried, guiltily, to think up ways of getting out of all those activities as much as I could. In a word, I was spiritually dead.

And then it happened, sometime around my 16th birthday. On that night, Dr Ham finished preaching and gave the Invitation to accept Christ. After all his tirades against sin, he gave us a gentle reminder: 'But God commendeth his love towards us, in that, while we were yet sinners, Christ died for us' (Romans 5:8, KJV). His song leader, Mr Ramsay, led us all in 'Just as I Am' – four verses. Then we started another song: 'Almost Persuaded, Now to Believe'.

On the last verse of that second song, I responded. I walked down to the front, feeling as if I had lead weights attached to my feet, and stood in the space before the platform. That same night, perhaps 300 or 400 other people were there at the front making spiritual commitments. The next night, my cousin Crook Stafford made his decision for Christ.

My heart sank when I looked over at the lady standing next to me with tears running down her cheeks. I was not crying. I did not feel any special emotion of any kind just then. Maybe, I thought, I was not supposed to be there. Maybe my good intentions to be a real Christian wouldn't last. Wondering if I was just making a fool of myself, I almost turned around and went back to my seat.

As I stood in front of the platform, a tailor named J.D. Prevatt, who was a friend of our family with a deep love for souls, stepped up beside me, weeping. Putting his arms around me, he urged me to make my decision. At the same time, in his heavy European accent, he explained God's plan for my salvation in a simple way. That explanation was addressed to my own mental understanding. It did not necessarily answer every question I had at that moment – and it certainly did not anticipate every question that would come to me in the months and years ahead – but it set forth simply the facts I needed to know in order to become God's child.

My tailor friend helped me to understand what I had to do to become a genuine Christian. The key word was *do*. Those of us standing up front had to decide to *do* something about what we knew before it could take effect.

He prayed for me and guided *me* to pray. I had heard the message, and I had felt the inner compulsion to go forward. Now came the moment to commit myself to Christ. Intellectually, I accepted Christ to the extent that I acknowledged what I knew about him to be true. That was mental assent. Emotionally, I felt that I wanted to love him in return for his loving me. But the final issue was whether I would turn myself over to his rule in my life.

I checked 'Recommitment' on the card I filled out. After all, I had been brought up to regard my baptism and confirmation as professions of faith too. The difference was that this time I was doing it on *purpose*, doing it with *intention*. For all my previous religious upbringing and church activity, I believe that that was the moment I made my real commitment to Jesus Christ.

No bells went off inside me. No signs flashed across the tabernacle ceiling. No physical palpitations made me tremble. I wondered again if I was a hypocrite, not to be weeping or something. I simply felt at peace. Quiet, not delirious. Happy and peaceful.

My father came to the front and put his arm around my shoulders, telling me how thankful he was. Later, back home, when we went to the kitchen, my mother put her arm around me and said, 'Billy Frank, I'm so glad you took the stand you did tonight.'

That was all.

I went upstairs to my room. Standing at the window, I looked out across one of the fields that was glowing in the moonlight.

Then I went over to my bed and for the first time in my life got down on my knees without being told to do so. I really wanted to talk to God. 'Lord, I don't know what happened to me tonight,' I prayed. '*You* know. And I thank you for the privilege I've had tonight.'

It took a while to fall asleep. How could I face school tomorrow? Would this action spoil my relationships with friends who were not interested in spiritual matters? Might Coach Eudy, who had publicly expressed his dislike of Dr Ham, make fun of me? Perhaps. I felt pretty sure, though, that the school principal, Connor Hutchinson, whose history lessons I enjoyed, would be sympathetic.

But the hardest question of all remained to be answered: What exactly, had happened to me?

All I knew was that the world looked different the next morning when I got up to do the milking, eat breakfast, and catch the school bus. There seemed to be a song in my heart, but it was mixed with a kind of pounding fear as to what might happen when I got to class.

The showdown at school was not too bad. For one thing, most of the students had not heard about what I had done at the Ham meeting the night before. Besides that, the change I felt so strongly inside me did not make me look or sound any different. I was still Billy Frank to them, and their attitude did not change. Studies and ball games and dates and chores on the farm – all these stayed pretty much the same. I was still just a high-spirited schoolboy.

I invited Sam Paxton, Wint Covington, and some of my other friends from high school to go with me to the Ham meetings. They did go once or twice, but somehow they did not respond as I had.

'I understand we have Preacher Graham with us today,' one of my teachers said to the class some days later. Everybody laughed. She was making fun of me, and I felt some resentment. Then I remembered what Dr Ham had said: when we come to Christ, we're going to suffer persecution.

It would take some time before I understood what had happened to me well enough to explain it to anybody else. There were signs, though, that my thinking and direction had changed, that I had truly been converted. To my own surprise, church activities that had bored me before seemed interesting all of a sudden – even Dr Lindsay's sermons (which I took notes on!). The choir sounded better to me. I actually wanted to go to church as often as possible.

The Bible, which had been familiar to me almost since infancy, drew me now to find out what it said besides the verses I had memorized through the years. I enjoyed the few minutes I could take when I was by myself each morning and evening for quiet talking to God in prayer. As one of Mr Ramsay's former choir members, I was even singing hymns while I milked the cows!

Billy Graham, *Just as I Am*

Maya Angelou

Childhood Horror

In the first volume of her autobiography *I Know Why the Caged Bird Sings*, the Black American writer Maya Angelou (1928–) describes the horrific experience of being raped as a child of eight by her mother's lover, Mr Freeman, who threatened to kill her brother Bailey if she told anyone. In this extract, Marguerite, as Maya was known, has been taken to hospital where she decides to confide in Bailey. Mr Freeman is tried, sentenced and released only to be lynched. The extract ends with Marguerite's conviction that in some way her voice in court has been responsible for Mr Freeman's death so she must become silent.

In the hospital, Bailey told me that I had to tell who did that to me, or the man would hurt another little girl. When I explained that I couldn't tell because the man would kill him, Bailey said knowingly, 'He can't kill me. I won't let him.' And of course I believed him. Bailey didn't lie to me. So I told him.

Bailey cried at the side of my bed until I started to cry too. Almost 15 years passed before I saw my brother cry again.

Using the old brain he was born with (those were his words later on that day) he gave his information to Grandmother Baxter, and Mr Freeman was arrested and was spared the awful wrath of my pistol-whipping uncles.

I would have liked to stay in the hospital the rest of my life. Mother brought flowers and candy. Grandmother came with fruit and my uncles clumped around and around my bed, snorting like wild horses. When they were able to sneak Bailey in, he read to me for hours.

The saying that people who have nothing to do become busybodies is not the only truth. Excitement is a drug, and people whose lives are filled with violence are always wondering where the next 'fix' is coming from.

The court was filled. Some people even stood behind the churchlike benches in the rear. Overhead fans moved with the detachment of old men. Grandmother Baxter's clients were there in gay and flippant array. The gamblers in pin-striped suits and their makeup-deep women whispered to me out of blood-red mouths that now I knew as much as they did. I was eight, and grown. Even the nurses in the hospital had told me that now I had nothing to fear. 'The worst is over for you,' they had said. So I put the words in all the smirking mouths.

I sat with my family (Bailey couldn't come) and they rested still on the seats like solid, cold grey tombstones. Thick and for evermore unmoving.

Poor Mr Freeman twisted in his chair to look empty threats over to me. He didn't know that he couldn't kill Bailey... and Bailey didn't lie... to me.

'What was the defendant wearing?' That was Mr Freeman's lawyer. 'I don't know.'

'You mean to say this man raped you and you don't know what he was wearing?' He snickered as if I had raped Mr Freeman. 'Do you know if you were raped?'

A sound pushed in the air of the court (I was sure it was laughter). I was glad that Mother had let me wear the navy-blue winter coat with brass buttons. Although it was too short and the weather was typical St Louis hot, the coat was a friend that I hugged to me in the strange and unfriendly place.

'Was that the first time the accused touched you?' The question stopped me. Mr Freeman had surely done something very wrong, but I was convinced that I had helped him to do it. I didn't want to lie, but the lawyer wouldn't let me think, so I used silence as a retreat.

'Did the accused try to touch you before the time he or rather you say he raped you?'

I couldn't say yes and tell them how he had loved me once for a few minutes and how he had held me close before he thought I had peed in the bed. My uncles would kill me and Grandmother Baxter would stop speaking, as she often did when she was angry. And all those people in the court would stone me as they had stoned the harlot in the Bible. And Mother, who thought I was such a good girl, would be so disappointed. But most important, there was Bailey. I had kept a big secret from him.

'Marguerite, answer the question. Did the accused touch you before the occasion on which you claim he raped you?'

Everyone in the court knew that the answer had to be No. Everyone except Mr Freeman and me. I looked at his heavy face trying to look as if he would have liked me to say No. I said No.

The lie lumped in my throat and I couldn't get air. How I despised the man for making me lie. Old, mean, nasty thing. Old, black, nasty thing. The tears didn't soothe my heart as they usually did. I screamed, 'Ole, mean, dirty thing, you. Dirty old thing.' Our lawyer brought me off the stand and to my mother's arms. The fact that I had arrived at my desired destination by lies made it less appealing to me.

Mr Freeman was given one year and one day, but he never got a chance to do his time. His lawyer (or someone) got him released that very afternoon.

In the living room, where the shades were drawn for coolness, Bailey and I played Monopoly on the floor. I played a bad game because I was thinking how I would be able to tell Bailey how I had lied and, even worse for our relationship, kept a secret from him. Bailey answered the doorbell, because Grandmother was in the kitchen. A tall white policeman asked for Mrs Baxter. Had they found out about the lie? Maybe the policeman was coming to put me in jail because I had sworn on the Bible that everything I said would be the truth, the whole truth, so help me, God. The man in our living room was taller than the sky and whiter than my image of God. He just didn't have the beard.

'Mrs Baxter, I thought you ought to know. Freeman's been found dead on the lot behind the slaughterhouse.'

Softly, as if she were discussing a church programme, she said, 'Poor man.' She wiped her hands on the dishtowel and just as softly asked, 'Do they know who did it?'

The policeman said, 'Seems like he was dropped there. Some say he was kicked to death.'

Grandmother's colour only rose a little. 'Tom, thanks for telling me. Poor man. Well, maybe it's better this way. He *was* a mad dog. Would you like a glass of lemonade? Or some beer?'

Although he looked harmless, I knew he was a dreadful angel counting out my many sins.

'No thanks, Mrs Baxter. I'm on duty. Gotta be getting back.'

'Well, tell your ma that I'll be over when I take up my beer and remind her to save some kraut for me.'

And the recording angel was gone. He was gone, and a man was dead because I lied. Where was the balance in that? One lie surely wouldn't be worth a man's life. Bailey could have explained it all to me, but I didn't dare ask him. Obviously I had forfeited my place in heaven for ever, and I was as gutless as the doll I had ripped to pieces ages ago. Even Christ himself turned his back on Satan. Wouldn't he turn his back on me? I could feel the evilness flowing through my body and waiting, pent up, to rush off my tongue if I tried to open my mouth. I clamped my teeth shut, I'd hold it in. If it escaped, wouldn't it flood the world and all the innocent people?

Grandmother Baxter said, 'Ritie and Junior, you didn't hear a thing. I never want to hear this situation nor that evil man's name mentioned in my house again. I mean that.' She went back into the kitchen to make apple strudel for my celebration.

Even Bailey was frightened. He sat all to himself, looking at a man's death – a kitten looking at a wolf. Not quite understanding it but frightened all the same.

In those moments I decided that although Bailey loved me he couldn't help. I had sold myself to the Devil and there could be no escape. The only thing I could do was to stop talking to people other than Bailey. Instinctively, or somehow, I knew that because I loved him so much I'd never hurt him, but if I talked to anyone else that person might die too. Just my breath, carrying my words out, might poison people and they'd curl up and die like the black fat slugs that only pretended.

I had to stop talking.

I discovered that to achieve perfect personal silence all I had to do was to attach myself leechlike to sound. I began to listen to everything. I probably hoped that after I had heard all the sounds, really heard them and packed them down, deep in my ears, the world would be quiet around me. I walked into rooms where people were laughing, their voices hitting the walls like stones, and I simply stood still – in the midst of the riot of sound. After a minute or two, silence would rush in to the room from its hiding place because I had eaten up all the sounds.

In the first weeks my family accepted my behaviour as a post-rape, post-hospital affliction. (Neither the term nor the experience was mentioned in Grandmother's house, where Bailey and I were again staying.) They understood that I could talk to Bailey, but to no one else.

Then came the last visit from the visiting nurse, and the doctor said I was healed. That meant that I should be back on the sidewalks playing handball or enjoying the games I had been given when I was sick. When I refused to be the child they knew and accepted me to be, I was called impudent and my muteness sullenness.

For a while I was punished for being so uppity that I wouldn't speak; and then came the thrashings, given by any relative who felt himself offended.

Maya Angelou, *I Know Why the Caged Bird Sings*

Jean Vanier

Called to Be a Leader

At the age of 13, Jean Vanier (1928–) knew that he wanted to leave his home in Canada and join the Royal Navy in war-torn England. His father, Georges Vanier (1888–1967), the future Governor General of Canada, allowed Jean to travel back across the Atlantic in order to spend just under four years in the Royal Navy. It was a brave decision, as a great many ships were being sunk by German U-boats on the Atlantic crossing, and Georges and Pauline Vanier were unable to find out for some time whether or not their son had reached England safely.

In 1964 Jean Vanier founded the communities of l'Arche for people with learning difficulties. In the introduction to *A Door of Hope* he writes about the importance of the permission he received from his parents as a 13-year-old. Pauline Vanier was not initially in favour of her son making the hazardous Atlantic crossing. She said that when she and her husband were discussing the matter Georges remarked, 'We must be careful not to clip Jean's wings. He may be called to be a leader.'

> Most of my early childhood was spent in England and France until 1940 when France fell and we left Europe for Canada.
>
> At the age of 13 I wanted to join the Royal Navy. When I asked my father's permission, he replied, 'If you feel that this is what you really want to do, then go, I trust you.' I have always been grateful to my parents for taking me seriously and for the trust they placed in me. Their confidence enabled me to trust myself and also gave me a sense of responsibility and an awareness that my own intuition was trustworthy.

Jean Vanier, *A Door of Hope*

Anne Frank

First Love

In her diary addressed to 'dearest Kitty' Anne Frank (1929–45) describes
the 26 months she and her family spent concealed in the 'Secret Annexe'
behind her father's office in Amsterdam. They shared the cramped
accommodation with another Jewish family: Mr and Mrs van Daan and their
shy 16-year-old son Peter. In this extract, 14-year-old Anne writes about her
sense of her dead grandmother's presence and reveals her feelings for Peter
van Daan. Five months later the inhabitants of the 'Secret Annexe' were
betrayed to the occupying German forces and captured. Anne died in the
concentration camp of Belsen in 1945 and Peter died in Mauthausen camp.

Friday, 3 March 1944

My dearest Kitty,

When I looked into the candle tonight, I felt calm and happy again.
It seems Grandma is in that candle, and it's Grandma who watches
over and protects me and makes me feel happy again. But... there's
someone else who governs all my moods and that's... Peter. I went to
get the potatoes today, and while I was standing on the stairway with
my pan full, he asked, 'What did you do during lunch break?'

I sat down on the stairs, and we began to talk. The potatoes
didn't make it to the kitchen until 5.15 (an hour after I'd gone to
get them). Peter didn't say anything more about his parents; we just
talked about books and about the past. Oh, he gazes at me with such
warmth in his eyes; I don't think it will take much for me to fall in
love with him.

He brought the subject up this evening. I went to his room after

59

peeling potatoes and remarked on how hot it was. 'You can tell the temperature by looking at Margot and me, because we turn white when it's cold and red when it's hot,' I said.

'In love?' he asked.

'Why should I be in love?' It was a pretty silly answer (or, rather, question).

'Why not?' he said, and then it was time for dinner.

What did he mean? Today I finally managed to ask him whether my chatter bothered him. All he said was, 'Oh, it's fine with me!' I can't tell how much of his reply was due to shyness.

Kitty, I sound like someone who's in love and can talk about nothing but her dearest darling. And Peter is a darling. Will I ever be able to tell him that? Only if he thinks the same of me, but I'm the kind of person you have to treat with kid gloves, I know that all too well. And he likes to be left alone, so I don't know how much he likes me. In any case, we're getting to know each other a little better. I wish we dared to say more. But who knows, maybe that time will come sooner than I think! Once or twice a day he gives me a knowing glance, I wink back, and we're both happy. It seems insane to talk about his being happy, and yet I have the overwhelming feeling he thinks the same way I do.

Yours, Anne M. Frank

Anne Frank, *The Diary of a Young Girl*

Nicholas Alkemade

Against All Odds

Nicholas Alkemade (1922–87) joined the Royal Air Force in 1940 at the age of 18 and served in Air Sea Rescue launches before transferring to Bomber Command because he 'wanted more excitement'! In Bomber Command Alkemade served as a rear gunner or 'tail-end Charlie' in a Lancaster bomber. In this extract from *Reader's Digest* he tells the story of his unique escape from death on 24 March 1944 when he bailed out over Germany at 21,000 feet without a parachute.

We were somewhere over the Ruhr when suddenly a series of shuddering crashes raked our aircraft from nose to tail, then two terrific thunderclaps as two cannon shells exploded on my turret ring mounting. The plexiglass blister shattered and vanished – one large fragment slicing into my right leg.

Luckily my turret had been facing astern. I quickly depressed my guns and stared out. Not more than 50 yards from me was the shadowy outline of a Junkers 88 fighter, his leading edge a line of brilliant white flashes as he blazed away at our wounded ship. I aimed point-blank and squeezed the trigger of my four banked 303 Brownings. They fired simultaneously and the Junkers was transfixed by four streams of fiery tracers. He peeled off, his port engine trailing flame. I did not watch to see his fate; I was too concerned about my own.

Flaming fuel from our tanks was streaking past me. On the intercom I started to report to the captain that the tail was on fire, but he cut me short with, 'I can't hold her for long, lads. You'll have to jump. Bale out! Bale out!'

Flicking the turret doors behind me open with my elbows, I turned and opened the fuselage door beyond – and stared for a horrified instant into a giant cauldron. Flame and smoke swept towards me. I recoiled, choking and blinded, into my turret. But I *had to get my chute*! I opened the doors again and lunged for the pack.

Too late! The case had been burnt off and the tightly packed silk was springing out, fold after fold, and vanishing in puffs of flame.

In the turret I took stock. Here I was, only 21 years old, and this was the end of the road. Already oil from the turret's hydraulic system was on fire and flames seared my face and hands. At any moment the doomed aircraft might explode.

Should I endure this roasting hell or should I jump? If I was to die, better a quick, painless end by diving into the ground... Quickly I hand-rotated my turret abeam, flipped the doors open and, in an agony of despair, somersaulted backwards into the night.

Oh, the blessed relief of being away from that shrivelling heat! Gratefully, I felt the cold air against my face. I had no sensation of falling. It was more like being at rest on an airy cloud. Looking down I saw the stars beneath my feet.

'Must be falling head first,' I thought.

If this was dying it was nothing to be afraid of. I only regretted that I should go without saying goodbye to my friends. I would never again see Pearl, my sweetheart back home in Loughborough. And I'd been due to go on leave the following Sunday.

Then – nothing. I must have blacked out.

In slow stages my senses returned. First there was an awareness of light above me, which gradually became a patch of starlit sky. The light was framed in an irregular opening that finally materialized as a hole in thickly interlaced boughs of fir trees. I seemed to be lying in a deep mound of underbrush heavily blanketed with snow.

It was bitterly cold. My head throbbed and there was terrible pain in my back. I felt all over my body. I found I could move my legs. I was all in one piece. In a sudden upwelling of unworthiness and delight, the very first thought to flash into my conscious mind was a heartfelt prayer of thanksgiving, of humble praise and utter wonderment. On the floor of the little patch of fir forest, into which I had hurtled parachuteless from a hell three and two-fifths miles above it, this was not blasphemy. 'Jesus Christ,' I said. 'I'm alive!'

I tried to sit up – but it hurt too much. Craning my neck I could see that my flying boots were gone and my clothes scorched and tattered. I began to be afraid of freezing to death. In the pocket of my tunic I found the flat tin, badly bent, in which I kept my cigarettes and my lighter. The cigarettes were unharmed; I lit up. My watch, I found, was still ticking. The luminous hands showed 3:20; it had been close to midnight when our aircraft was hit.

Attached to my collar was the whistle for use in case of ditching at sea to keep crew members in contact with one another.

'Here is one man who is happy to become a prisoner of war,' I said to myself. From time to time I blew the whistle. It seemed hours later I heard a far-off 'Hulloo!'

I kept whistling and the answering shouts grew closer. At last I could see flashlights approaching. Then some men and boys were standing over me. After relieving me of my cigarettes they growled, *''raus! Heraus!'* ('Get up!') When they saw I couldn't, they put a tarpaulin under me and dragged me across a frozen pasture to a cottage. There an old lady with a gnarled but kindly face gave me the finest egg nog I ever tasted.

As I lay on the floor I heard a car pull up outside. Two men in plain clothes clumped into the room. They looked me over carefully. Then, quite indifferent to my pain, they yanked me to my feet and bundled me out to their car. We seemed to hit all the bumps on our way to a hospital.

I was a long time in the operating room. Only later did I learn the sum of my injuries: burnt legs, twisted right knee, a deep splinter wound in my thigh, strained back, slight concussion and a deep scalp wound; first-, second- and third-degree burns on face and hands. Most of this damage I had sustained before jumping.

Finally, cleaned up and with most of the plexiglass fragments picked out of me, I was installed in a clean bed – but not to sleep! In came a tall, pompous character in a *Wehrmacht* uniform, thin as a hatchet in the face and wearing rimless glasses. Through an interpreter, a young convalescent soldier, he asked me the usual, probing questions. What targets did you attack? Where is your base? How many aircraft are there at your base?… and many others. I stated my name, rank and number. To the other questions I could only reply, 'I am not allowed to answer.'

Then they began asking about my parachute. 'Where did you hide it? Did you bury it? (Spies dropping into enemy territory commonly concealed their parachutes; airmen falling out of sky battles did not.)

'Parachute?' I said. 'I didn't use one!'

I thought Hatchet-Face would burst with rage. He let out a stream of oaths, then turned on his heel and stalked out. For three days the questioning was repeated. Finally I was left alone.

After three weeks, when my wounds were fairly healed, I was whisked off to Dulag Luft near Frankfurt and put into solitary confinement. The time gave me the opportunity to think out how I might convince my interrogators that my incredible story was true.

So I was ready when a week later a young *Luftwaffe* lieutenant led me into the office of the *Kommandant* of Dulag Luft. On the *Kommandant*'s desk I was amused to see a packet of English cigarettes and a bar of chocolate.

'We have to congratulate you, I understand, Sergeant,' the *Kommandant* said drily, in excellent English. 'Would you tell me all about your remarkable escape yourself, please? I have only a garbled account from the *Herr Leutnant*. I gather you claim to have jumped from a blazing bomber at a height of 6,000 metres without a parachute – a very tall story, Sergeant, *nicht wahr?*'

He could prove the story if he cared to, I told him. Hadn't a wrecked Lancaster fallen in the area on the night of March 24–25? If so, that would be the plane I had jumped from. The burnt remnants of my parachute pack could be found just forward of the rear fuselage door. Also, he could examine my parachute harness – to see for himself that *it had never been used.*

The *Kommandant* listened to me in silence. 'A really remarkable story,' he said – 'and I hear many!'

He fired some rapid German at the lieutenant, who saluted and left.

The *Kommandant* handed me a cigarette and we chatted pleasantly for the next quarter of an hour. Then the lieutenant, waving my parachute harness, burst into the office with three other officers, all shouting excitedly in German.

The lieutenant flung the harness on to the desk, pointed to the snap-hooks that were still in their clips and the lift webs still fastened down on the chest straps. The *Kommandant* soberly took in these facts, then leant back in his chair and studied each of us thoughtfully in turn. I'll never forget his next words; he spoke in English:

'Gentleman! A miracle – no less!'

He rose, came round his desk and offered me his hand. I took it. 'Congratulations, my boy, on being alive! What a story to tell your grandchildren!'

Nicholas Alkemade, *Reader's Digest*, August 1953

Leah Price

Travelling to the Congo

In *The Poisonwood Bible* by the American writer Barbara Kingsolver (1955–) we meet the evangelical Southern Baptist minister Nathan Price, who has decided to take his family on a mission from the United States to the Belgian Congo in 1959. The story is told by his wife and four daughters, who find that the reality of life in Central Africa is very far from their expectations. In this extract one daughter, Leah Price, describes their departure from Georgia.

We came from Bethlehem, Georgia, bearing Betty Crocker cake mixes into the jungle. My sisters and I were all counting on having one birthday apiece during our 12-month mission. 'And heaven knows,' our mother predicted, 'they won't have Betty Crocker in the Congo.'

'Where we are headed, there will *be* no buyers and sellers at all,' my father corrected. His tone implied that Mother failed to grasp our mission, and that her concern with Betty Crocker confederated her with the coin-jingling sinners who vexed Jesus till he pitched a fit and threw them out of church. 'Where we are headed,' he said, to make things perfectly clear, 'not so much as a Piggly Wiggly.' Evidently Father saw this as a point in the Congo's favour. I got the most spectacular chills, just from trying to imagine.

She wouldn't go against him, of course. But once she understood there was no turning back, our mother went to laying out in the spare bedroom all the worldly things she thought we'd need in the Congo just to scrape by. 'The bare minimum, for my children,' she'd declare under her breath, all the livelong day. In addition to the cake mixes, she piled up a dozen cans of Underwood devilled ham; Rachel's ivory plastic hand mirror with powdered-wig ladies on the back; a stainless-steel thimble; a good pair of scissors; a dozen number-2 pencils; a world of Band-Aids, Anacin, Absorbine Jr; and a fever thermometer.

And now we are here, with all these colourful treasures safely transported and stowed against necessity. Our stores are still intact, save for the Anacin tablets taken by our mother and the thimble lost down the latrine hole by Ruth May. But already our supplies from home seem to represent a bygone world: they stand out like bright party favours here in our Congolese house, set against a backdrop of mostly all mud-coloured things. When I stare at them with the rainy-season light in my eyes and Congo grit in my teeth, I can hardly recollect the place where such items were commonplace, merely a yellow pencil, merely a green bottle of aspirin among so many other green bottles upon a high shelf.

Mother tried to think of every contingency, including hunger and illness. (And Father does, in general, approve of *contingencies*. For it was God who gave man alone the capacity of foresight.) She procured a good supply of antibiotic drugs from our granddad Dr Bud Wharton, who has senile dementia and loves to walk outdoors naked but still can do two things perfectly: win at checkers and write out prescriptions. We also brought over a cast-iron frying pan, 10 packets of baker's yeast, pinking shears, the head of a hatchet, a fold-up army latrine spade, and all told a good deal more. This was the full measure of civilization's evils we felt obliged to carry with us.

Getting here with even the bare minimum was a trial. Just when we considered ourselves fully prepared and were fixing to depart, lo and behold, we learnt that the Pan American Airline would only allow 44 pounds to be carried across the ocean. Forty-four pounds of luggage per person, and not one iota more. Why, we were dismayed by this bad news! Who'd have thought there would be limits on modern jet-age transport? When we added up all our 44 pounds together, including Ruth May's – luckily she counted as a whole person even though she's small – we were 61 pounds over. Father surveyed our despair as if he'd expected it all along, and left it up to wife and daughters to sort out, suggesting only that we consider the lilies of the field, which have no need of a hand mirror or aspirin tablets.

'I reckon the lilies need *Bibles*, though, and his darn old latrine spade,' Rachel muttered, as her beloved toiletry items got pitched out of the suitcase one by one. Rachel never does grasp scripture all that well.

But considering the lilies as we might, our trimming back got us nowhere close to our goal, even without Rachel's beauty aids. We were nearly stumped. And then, hallelujah! At the last possible moment, saved. Through an oversight (or else probably, if you think about it, just plain politeness), they don't weigh the passengers. The Southern Baptist Mission League gave us this hint, without coming right out and telling us to flout the law of the 44 pounds, and from there we made our plan. We struck out for Africa carrying all our excess baggage on our bodies, under our clothes. Also, we had *clothes* under our clothes. My sisters and I left home wearing six pairs of underdrawers, two half-slips and camisoles; several dresses one on top of the other, with pedal pushers underneath; and outside of everything an all-weather coat. (The encyclopaedia advised us to count on rain.) The other goods, tools, cake-mix boxes and so forth were tucked out of sight in our pockets and under our waistbands, surrounding us in clanking armour.

We wore our best dresses on the outside to make a good impression. Rachel wore her green linen Easter suit she was so vain of, and her long whitish hair pulled off her forehead with a wide pink elastic hair band. Rachel is 15 – or, as she would put it, going on 16 – and cares for naught but appearances. Her full Christian name is Rachel *Rebeccah*, so she feels free to take after Rebekah, the virgin at the well, who is said in Genesis to be a 'damsel very fair' and was offered marriage presents of golden earbobs right off the bat, when Abraham's servant spied her fetching up the water. (Since she's my elder by one year, she claims no relation to the Bible's poor Rachel, Leah's younger sister, who had to wait all those years to get married.) Sitting next to me on the plane, she kept batting her white-rabbit eyelashes and adjusting her bright pink hair band, trying to get me to notice she had secretly painted her fingernails bubble-gum pink to match. I glanced over at Father, who had the other window seat at the opposite end of our entire row of Prices. The sun was a blood-red ball hovering outside his window, inflaming his eyes as he kept up a lookout for Africa on the horizon. It was just lucky for Rachel he had so much else weighing on his mind. She'd been thrashed with the strap for nail polish, even at her age. But that is Rachel to a T, trying to work in just one last sin before leaving civilization. Rachel is worldly and tiresome in my opinion, so I stared out the window, where the view was better.

Barbara Kingsolver, *The Poisonwood Bible*

Sally Trench

Getting to Know the Dossers

In her autobiographical bestseller *Bury Me in My Boots*, Sally Trench (1945–) recalls her first meeting with hungry and homeless men and women on London's Waterloo Station when she was 16. The experience led her to make regular late-night trips to the station, armed with coffee and cigarettes, and, ultimately, to leave her comfortable home to live alongside the people she wanted to help. As a result of her experiences in London Sally founded the charity Project Spark for children and young people.

I had always been a presumptuous child. I was the sort of ghastly kid that everyone dreaded having, the kind that if you said, 'Don't speak to strange men', would go in search of strangers to talk to, and the more weird and strange they were the better. A proper St Trinian's pupil!

My interest in the 'socially inadequate' developed from my hero-worshipping of tramps. How I envied their way of life, so free and wild, a world of their own. I loved to listen to their tales as much as I loved to tell my own, truth or fiction! When I left boarding school I went in search of a lost cause, determined to play a role in society. I found it on Waterloo Station.

I was coming home very late one night from the country, feeling weary and looking forward to a warm bed. Against a background noise of chamber music intermingled with the groans and sneezings of the engines, I passed the ticket office into the main hall. 'Oh, I beg your pardon!' I swung round to see who I had bumped into. She was an old lady, so wrapped up in moth-eaten scarves that her face was hardly visible. She wore a dress down to her ankles and a man's sweater, three times too big for her. She had no stockings, but a pair of disintegrating slippers covered part of her feet. She stood hunched over her brown paper parcels; I do not think she had noticed the impact as I had collided with her, not to mention my apology. I walked on. I noticed scruffy men bedded down under newspapers on the benches, others slouched dejectedly in the corners. They were all dirty and unshaven, a few of the lucky ones had overcoats to protect them against the winter nights, the rest just sat shivering. How easy it was to walk past. How easy it was to sympathize from a distance. How easy it was to pass by on the other side of the road like the Levite in the New Testament.

I stopped and turned back. I parked myself in the middle of a bench between two of the scruffiest men. All at once my Good Samaritan intentions left me and I became nervous. The men had not batted an eyelid. I could smell the alcohol. I fumbled in my pockets for cigarettes and, as I lit one, the two men seemed to wake up. One lurched sideways and leant against me. I was really frightened. 'Go' any to spare?' he slurred. I lit one and handed it to him and repeated the gesture for the bloke on my other side. The man was becoming heavy. If I edged away he might take offence, so I did the only thing possible. I took him by the shoulders and straightened him.

'Want any help, Missy?' A large West Indian, with his hands on his hips, a hat pushed to one side, and a most amiable grin on his round face, swayed before me. 'You don't belong here, Missy, not a high-class filly like you,' he reprimanded gently.

'I'm not a permanent, just passing through,' I said hastily.

'Just visiting. You're too pretty to be among us dirty drunks. You're not one of us. Go home.'

'I will. I just thought they might like a cigarette. What will happen to them? Will they go home?' He threw back his head and laughed.

'Home? Man, they got no home. This is their bedroom for tonight.' He bent down to me. 'Now you go home yourself, Missy, and don't you worry about us. Go home and thank the good Lord you got a home to go to.'

The background music had stopped, the engines were bedded down and the station porters were calling out their final farewells. The vast station, an active terminus during the day, was silent save for the periodical cooing of a sleepless pigeon. The homeless neglected and unwanted shivered under their newspapers. I shoved the packet of cigarettes into the West Indian's hands and did as I was told. I left the cold and hungry dossers to the night. But when I lay in my warm bed with my dog at my feet and a glass of hot chocolate in my hand, I did thank the kind Lord for having blessed me with a family and a home.

The following morning I was exercising my Afghan hound in the park when I came across a similar character to those of the previous night. He was prodding around in the litter bins in search of scraps. I smiled at him as I passed, and said 'Good morning'. He gave an inaudible grunt, picked up a dog-end and shuffled off in the opposite direction. I wondered where he had spent the night.

Just after midnight I dressed quickly in my jeans and placed the Thermos flask of coffee that I had made that evening in my haversack. The dog wagged his tail with excitement. 'Not this time,' I whispered, 'And don't you dare bark when I come back.' I patted him. Despondently, he jumped back on to my bed and watched me open the window and climb out on the windowsill. I wished that our stairs did not creak and that my father was not such a light sleeper. But he was, and the stairs did creak abominably, so there was only the drainpipe left. By the time I had reached the bottom and climbed down the wall, I was a nervous wreck. A car had passed with its headlights on, and a courting couple had inconveniently halted under the tree where I had intended to descend, so I had been forced to deviate from the route I had worked out in daylight. Trembling, I opened the garage and felt for my bicycle. It was as I had left it. I closed the door gently behind me and crossed to the other side of the road and waited. I expected the lights to come on in the house as father discovered his beloved daughter was not in bed. A full 10 minutes I waited. I was in the clear, no one had heard me. Relieved, I bicycled over to Waterloo Station.

Sally Trench, *Bury Me in My Boots*

Mary McAleese

Finding God Afresh

Mary McAleese was born in Belfast in 1951. In *Reconciled Being* she describes the experience of growing up as a Roman Catholic in Belfast and learning to move towards a truer and healthier image of God. Mary became a lawyer and went on to become President of Ireland in 1997.

Let me describe the pincer movement in which the warp and weft of my own life came to be shaped, some might say distorted by growing up in a world where to be a woman and a Catholic was to some extent at least, to be doubly excluded and marginalized if not doubly deviant!

I was born in Belfast between the Passionist monastery and the Orange Hall. In the former God was male, the altar was a male preserve, priests were heroes, and every mother wanted a son hero. 'My son the priest' had a cachet, which even 'my daughter the nun' could not hope to emulate. It was understood. God was male Father, male Son and male Holy Spirit. He was also by a happy coincidence Roman Catholic and probably Irish, his parents presumably having emigrated from Ireland to heaven during the Famine! The Catholic God had long since abandoned his 16th century teaching that outside Catholic walls there could be no salvation, but presumably since this was in the days before e-mail and faxes, the message had not quite reached all corners of his church. Rather grudgingly this God conceded that Protestants could be saved but it was generally understood this was in spite of their churches and not because of them. From the Orange Hall came another image of God, God the protector of Protestants, who had ordained that the corner of Northern Ireland would be Protestant and British in perpetuity, beginning 1921. This God believed the Pope was an anti-Christ, a deadly enemy and a man of sin. This God, to borrow an inelegant phrase used by one well-known Northern Christian minister, believed Catholic women were 'incubators for their papacy', and all Catholics were in error. These Gods carried their crosses like lances in a jousting tournament. Gods of appallingly narrow perspective and parochial obsessiveness. Fidgety Gods who brooded over small bits of the world with a warm embrace only for the chosen few and not the wide embrace of the God I came to know and need.

In the monastery there were over 40 men who, dressed in their flowing black habits, dominated the thinking and spiritual landscape of my childhood. I was taken aback to hear my daughter ask me some years ago if monks were examples of cross-dressers! Strange how a new vocabulary can shake your perspective! I owe those prayerful men a lot for their love of God was palpable but there was also a deficit. It was not deliberate or malintended but there was a deficit nonetheless. On the day I spoke out loud my desire to be a lawyer, the first to say 'You can't because you are a woman; you can't because no one belonging to you is in the law', was the Dublin born parish priest who weekly shared a whisky or three with my father. It was said with the kind of dismissive authority which is intended to silence protest or debate. The owner of superior knowledge, of real certitude had spoken and that was that. The same priest incidentally kept a double-entry scoreboard of the indignities heaped on Catholics by the Protestant government at Stormont many of which ironically involved keeping Catholics out of jobs for no reason other than the fact that they were Catholics. The irony of the similar group exclusion of women was unfortunately lost on him. My mother had inculcated into us a respect for the priesthood bordering on awe. I watched therefore in amazement as the chair was pulled out from under the cleric and he was propelled to the front door before the bottle of baby Powers had been uncorked. 'You — out' she roared at him 'and you' she said to me 'ignore him!' That was the only advice I ever received from either parent on the subject of career choice.

My schooling was all in convent schools so it would be untrue to say that there were no role models of working women for me. Between the nuns and my mother's own sisters there were many but there were also demarcation lines so clear, so defined that even now decades later, the same mother who so ably dispatched the sexist priest is able rather lamely to say, 'I don't support women priests but I don't know why.' I am saddened by the first part of her sentence but heartened by the second. If she knew why she opposed women priests I would really be worried! Those same demarcation lines on one side of which was authority and the other deference also allowed me many years later when the subject of women and priesthood was broached to say equally lamely, I do not understand the exclusion of women from the priesthood but then I am not a theologian. The historic parallels with the reasons why women could not be lawyers, could not be admitted to universities, could not be admitted to vote, had to surrender careers on marriage, did not escape me, I simply buried them. To challenge the awesome authority of the hierarchy seemed to open up an aptly named Pandora's box of things which might be difficult to swallow. If the church was wrong, on an issue on which it spoke with a chilling clarity and certainty, then how many other errors might lie buried in that theology. There was a comfort in burying myself inside the group consciousness and putting my hands over my ears so that I could not hear the doubts that were running about in my head. To pit myself against the group meant challenging, mother, father, family, parish, community and to live with some form of exclusion which, whether mild rebuke or subtle shunning, would inevitably follow.

The Dominican nuns to whom I owe my happy secondary education taught me about that great philosophical Colossus, St Thomas Aquinas. Unfortunately they did not teach me *all* about him. It was 20 years later that I discovered that I had been introduced to edited highlights only. Had I read what he had to say in the *Summa Theologica* about the inferiority of women, I might have begun to understand the connections through time, teaching and cultures which have shaped and circumscribed the roles permitted to women. But, before I knew, it was easier to feign ignorance than to face the doubt. The seed of doubt was planted nonetheless because one simple observation about truth is that it point-blank refuses to go away. It always finds a crevice to bubble through. It worries the minutest space until it pushes through to the light. As John Main and Thomas Merton both experienced, if the growth of the seed is suppressed, it festers until it eventually needs radical treatment.

In the political landscape of Northern Ireland separate identities and ambitions are shored up by conflicting versions of history, conflicting political ambitions and conflicting religious beliefs. Two separate sets of knowledge wrap people up, hermetically sealing them into systems of certainties and beliefs which resist contamination by doubt or updating. Inside one package resides all that is right and good. Inside the other resides all that is wrong and bad. The problem is of course that even if you and I occupy opposite packages we both believe we are in the one which monopolizes good and righteousness. Worse still our separate histories have taught us not only what to think but also crucially and much more intractably, how to think. What is true of the political landscape is if not exactly replicated at least mirrored in the sphere of gender and church and indeed in many spheres where relationships have broken down in a mire of mutual recrimination. The indicators are familiar – conflicting versions of the gospel, clashing theologies, claim and counterclaim, accusations of sedition, of grave error, of power-seeking, of lack of humility, of arrogance, threats of excommunication, accusations of fallibility and claims of infallibility. God is on my side says one. God is on mine says the other. The air is thick with the politics and the practice of exclusion.

And while the shouting match is going on, as each side rubbishes the other, what spiritual energy are we wasting, what richness are we denying to our world! What really would happen if both traditions in the North and both genders in the church embraced each other in a God-trusting compassion which abandons the need for definitive victories and definitive doctrines? Is it possible, as Merton believed, that only when you abandon the self do you abandon fear? We already know the dismal balance sheet of the gospel of exclusion. What of the balance sheet we have not yet seen but have had meagre yet exhilarating glimpses of, the balance sheet of the gospel of embrace?

Dr Anthony Padovano, who writes so powerfully on Merton, says:

'It is foolish for any culture to assume it is not profoundly influenced by a myth system. Such a denial is a myth itself.'

The Northern Irish poet Tom Paulin born into the Protestant community and culture describes his upbringing as puritan and anti-aesthetic. He was, he says, taught to be suspicious of what is rhetorical or ornate.

I, by contrast, raised in the same country but in the Roman Catholic tradition, was nurtured in the rhetoric of the doctrine of transubstantiation, the smell of incense, the plaster statues, and apparitions, the very things Paulin was taught to be suspicious of.

I grew up comfortable with them. He grew up uncomfortable with them. Already from early childhood in our two worlds we were learning to view each other not as interestingly different but as suspiciously, dangerously, different. We learnt early that we had nothing to learn from each other or to offer each other.

My mother grew up in a world where women left school young, married, gave up work and had nine children. The altar was her comfort in despair, the priest her ally in handing on the faith. Priests were men. Altar servers were boys. Feminism – what was that? 'Equal opportunities' might just as well have been a new television game show.

Mary McAleese, *Reconciled Being*

SECOND JOURNEY

The Bible yields some obvious examples of mid-life or Second Journeys set in train by an abrupt call from God. Abraham and Sarah were settled heads of a large rural household when the divine call broke into their lives and set them on the road to a new land (Genesis 12:1–9). Moses was a married man tending his father-in-law's flocks when God spoke to him from the burning bush, revealing the divine name, then sending Moses on a pilgrimage to liberate the suffering and enslaved people of God (Exodus 3).

Gnawing dissatisfaction with existing values and convictions puts many people, such as C.S. Lewis and Kathleen Norris, on the road to a deep spiritual discovery. A desire to do more for God and humanity can find a new focus, as when Mother Teresa of Calcutta heard a 'call within a call' to leave the sheltered and orderly life of a teacher in a middle-class school in order to walk out into the unknown and serve the poorest of the poor.

Illness may trigger a mid-life change of direction and mission – thus John Henry Newman recovered from a near-fatal sickness in Sicily and headed home to Oxford with a sense that 'God has created me to do him some definite service.' The experience of imprisonment and, in some cases, the threat of death sparked off the mid-life journeys of Sheila Cassidy, Charles Colson, Terry Waite and Nelson Mandela.

Some Second Journeys continue for years, as in the case of 'Weary' Dunlop's experience of wartime suffering – especially in the Japanese prisoner-of-war camps and on the Burma–Thailand 'Death Railway'. Other mid-life journeys last for a matter of hours or days, as with the Ethiopian eunuch in Acts 8:26–39 and Flannery O'Connor's fictional character Ruby Turpin in *Revelation*.

Abraham

The Call of Abram

Abram had no idea of his exalted destiny when the call of God broke into the settled life he was living with his wife Sarai at Haran in about 1800 BC. Their one sadness was that they were childless. Abram was 75 years old when he embarked on their extraordinary and life-changing Second Journey. Everything was to be different in the future, even their names. Abram was to become Abraham, meaning 'Father of Many', and Sarai was to become Sarah.

The Lord had said to Abram, 'Leave your country, your people and your father's household and go to the land I will show you.

'I will make you into a great nation
  and I will bless you;
I will make your name great,
  and you will be a blessing.
I will bless those who bless you,
  and whoever curses you I will curse;
and all peoples on earth
  will be blessed through you.'

So Abram left, as the Lord had told him; and Lot went with him. Abram was 75 years old when he set out from Haran. He took his wife Sarai, his nephew Lot, all the possessions they had accumulated and the people they had acquired in Haran, and they set out for the land of Canaan, and they arrived there.

Abram travelled through the land as far as the site of the great tree of Moreh at Shechem. At that time the Canaanites were in the land. The Lord appeared to Abram and said, 'To your offspring I will give this land.' So he built an altar there to the Lord, who had appeared to him.

From there he went on towards the hills east of Bethel and pitched his tent, with Bethel on the west and Ai on the east. There he built an altar to the Lord and called on the name of the Lord. Then Abram set out and continued towards the Negev.

Genesis 12:1–9

Moses

The Burning Bush

Moses was caring for his father-in-law Jethro's flocks in the desert of Midian, to the east of the Red Sea, when he received the call of Yahweh, the God of his ancestors, to lead the Israelite people out of their slavery to Pharaoh in Egypt. Moses lived in about the 13th century BC. He had been living as a shepherd for 40 years when he received the divine command to return to Egypt, confront Pharaoh and lead God's people into freedom.

Moses was looking after the flock of his father-in-law Jethro, the priest of Midian; he led it to the far side of the desert and came to Horeb, the mountain of God. The angel of Yahweh appeared to him in a flame blazing from the middle of a bush. Moses looked; there was the bush blazing, but the bush was not being burnt up. Moses said, 'I must go across and see this strange sight, and why the bush is not being burnt up.' When Yahweh saw him going across to look, God called to him from the middle of the bush. 'Moses, Moses!' he said. 'Here I am,' he answered. 'Come no nearer,' he said. 'Take off your sandals, for the place where you are standing is holy ground. I am the God of your ancestors,' he said, 'the God of Abraham, the God of Isaac and the God of Jacob.' At this Moses covered his face, for he was afraid to look at God.

Yahweh then said, 'I have indeed seen the misery of my people in Egypt. I have heard them crying for help on account of their taskmasters. Yes, I am well aware of their sufferings. And I have come down to rescue them from the clutches of the Egyptians and bring them up out of that country, to a country rich and broad, to a country flowing with milk and honey, to the home of the Canaanites, the Hittites, the Amorites, the Perizzites, the Hivites and the Jebusites. Yes indeed, the Israelites' cry for help has reached me, and I have also seen the cruel way in which the Egyptians are oppressing them. So now I am sending you to Pharaoh, for you to bring my people the Israelites out of Egypt.'

Moses said to God, 'Who am I to go to Pharaoh and bring the Israelites out of Egypt?' 'I shall be with you,' God said, 'and this is the sign by which you will know that I was the one who sent you. After you have led the people out of Egypt, you will worship God on this mountain.'

Moses then said to God, 'Look, if I go to the Israelites and say to them, "The God of your ancestors has sent me to you," and they say to me, "What is his name?" what am I to tell them?' God said to Moses, 'I am he who is.' And he said, 'This is what you are to say to the Israelites, "I am has sent me to you."' God further said to Moses, 'You are to tell the Israelites, "Yahweh, the God of your ancestors, the God of Abraham, the God of Isaac and the God of Jacob, has sent me to you." This is my name for all time, and thus I am to be invoked for all generations to come.

'Go, gather the elders of Israel together and tell them, "Yahweh, the God of your ancestors, has appeared to me – the God of Abraham, of Isaac and of Jacob – and has indeed visited you and seen what is being done to you in Egypt, and has said: I shall bring you out of the misery of Egypt to the country of the Canaanites, the Hittites, the Amorites, the Perizzites, the Hivites and the Jebusites, to a country flowing with milk and honey." They will listen to your words, and you and the elders of Israel are to go to the king of Egypt and say to him, "Yahweh, the God of the Hebrews, has encountered us. So now please allow us to make a three-days' journey into the desert and sacrifice to Yahweh our God." I am well aware that the king of Egypt will not let you go unless he is compelled by a mighty hand; he will not let you go until I have stretched out my arm and struck Egypt with all the wonders I intend to work there.

'I shall ensure that the Egyptians are so much impressed with this people that when you go, you will not go empty-handed. Every woman will ask her neighbour and the woman staying in her house for silver and golden jewellery, and clothing. In these you will dress your own sons and daughters, despoiling the Egyptians of them.'

Exodus 3

Jesus

The Baptism of Jesus

John the Baptist was about 30 years of age and living in the desert when he was called by God to baptize, to preach repentance and to announce the imminent arrival of the Messiah. The Second Journey of Jesus began with his baptism by John, which marked the beginning of his public life.

In the 15th year of the reign of Tiberius Caesar – when Pontius Pilate was governor of Judea, Herod, tetrarch of Galilee, his brother Philip, tetrarch of Iturea and Traconitis, and Lysanias, tetrarch of Abilene – during the high priesthood of Annas and Caiaphas, the word of God came to John son of Zechariah in the desert. He went into all the country around the Jordan, preaching a baptism of repentance for the forgiveness of sins. As is written in the book of the words of Isaiah the prophet:

A voice of one calling in the desert,
'Prepare the way for the Lord,
make straight paths for him.
Every valley shall be filled in,
every mountain and hill made low.
The crooked roads shall become straight,
the rough ways smooth.
And all mankind will see God's salvation.'

John said to the crowds coming out to be baptized by him, 'You brood of vipers! Who warned you to flee from the coming wrath? Produce fruit in keeping with repentance. And do not begin to say to yourselves, "We have Abraham as our father." For I tell you that out of these stones God can raise up children for Abraham. The axe is already at the root of the trees, and every tree that does not produce good fruit will be cut down and thrown into the fire.'

'What should we do then?' the crowd asked.

John answered, 'The man with two tunics should share with him who has none, and the one who has food should do the same.'

Tax collectors also came to be baptized. 'Teacher,' they asked, 'what should we do?'

'Don't collect any more than you are required to,' he told them.

Then some soldiers asked him, 'And what should we do?'

He replied, 'Don't extort money and don't accuse people falsely – be content with your pay.'

The people were waiting expectantly and were all wondering in their hearts if John might possibly be the Christ. John answered them all, 'I baptize you with water. But one more powerful than I will come, the thongs of whose sandals I am not worthy to untie. He will baptize you with the Holy Spirit and with fire. His winnowing fork is in his hand to clear his threshing-floor and to gather the wheat into his barn, but he will burn up the chaff with unquenchable fire.' And with many other words John exhorted the people and preached the good news to them.

But when John rebuked Herod the tetrarch because of Herodias, his brother's wife, and all the other evil things he had done, Herod added this to them all: he locked John up in prison.

When all the people were being baptized, Jesus was baptized too. And as he was praying, heaven was opened and the Holy Spirit descended on him in bodily form like a dove. And a voice came from heaven: 'You are my Son, whom I love; with you I am well pleased.'

Luke 3:1–22

The Road to Emmaus

The Two Disciples

The two disciples on the road to Emmaus are bewildered by the events of the last few days: the arrest and crucifixion of Jesus followed by the 'disappearance' of his body from the tomb. They are discussing it all as they walk along. They are joined by an 'anonymous' companion who appears to be ignorant of events which have been the talk of Jerusalem! The disciples don't know what to make of it all — and they don't seem to know what to make of their companion until he reveals himself as Jesus, their Lord and Master, only to disappear as suddenly as he had arrived.

Now that same day two of them were going to a village called Emmaus, about seven miles from Jerusalem. They were talking with each other about everything that had happened. As they talked and discussed these things with each other, Jesus himself came up and walked along with them; but they were kept from recognizing him.

He asked them, 'What are you discussing together as you walk along?'

They stood still, their faces downcast. One of them, named Cleopas, asked him, 'Are you the only visitor to Jerusalem who does not know the things that have happened there in these days?'

'What things?' he asked.

'About Jesus of Nazareth,' they replied. 'He was a prophet, powerful in word and deed before God and all the people. The chief priests and our rulers handed him over to be sentenced to death, and they crucified him, but we had hoped that he was the one who was going to redeem Israel. And what is more, it is the third day since all this took place. In addition, some of our women amazed us.

They went to the tomb early this morning but didn't find his body. They came and told us that they had seen a vision of angels, who said he was alive. Then some of our companions went to the tomb and found it just as the women had said, but him they did not see.'

He said to them, 'How foolish you are, and how slow of heart to believe all that the prophets have spoken! Did not the Christ have to suffer these things and then enter his glory?' And beginning with Moses and all the Prophets, he explained to them what was said in all the scriptures concerning himself.

As they approached the village to which they were going, Jesus acted as if he were going further. But they urged him strongly, 'Stay with us, for it is nearly evening; the day is almost over.' So he went in to stay with them.

When he was at the table with them, he took bread, gave thanks, broke it and began to give it to them. Then their eyes were opened and they recognized him, and he disappeared from their sight. They asked each other, 'Were not our hearts burning within us while he talked with us on the road and opened the scriptures to us?'

They got up and returned at once to Jerusalem. There they found the Eleven and those with them, assembled together and saying, 'It is true! The Lord has risen and has appeared to Simon.' Then the two told what had happened on the way, and how Jesus was recognized by them when he broke the bread.

Luke 24:13–35

The Ethiopian Eunuch

Philip and the Eunuch

The eunuch is travelling quietly home, reading from Isaiah, when he is joined by a fellow traveller who is unknown to him, but is in fact the apostle Philip. We know that the eunuch had been on a pilgrimage to Jerusalem – a long journey from Ethiopia – but we do not know the reason for his pilgrimage. He seems to be on a spiritual search and he is clearly a man of decision. As soon as Philip has explained the good news of Jesus to him, the eunuch requests baptism and his life is changed for ever.

The angel of the Lord spoke to Philip saying, 'Set out at noon and go along the road that leads from Jerusalem down to Gaza, the desert road.' So he set off on his journey. Now an Ethiopian had been on pilgrimage to Jerusalem; he was a eunuch and an officer at the court of the kandake, or queen, of Ethiopia; he was her chief treasurer. He was now on his way home; and as he sat in his chariot he was reading the prophet Isaiah. The Spirit said to Philip, 'Go up and join that chariot.' When Philip ran up, he heard him reading Isaiah the prophet and asked, 'Do you understand what you are reading?' He replied, 'How could I, unless I have someone to guide me?' So he urged Philip to get in and sit by his side. Now the passage of scripture he was reading was this:

Like a lamb led to the slaughter-house,
like a sheep dumb in front of its shearers,
he never opens his mouth.
In his humiliation fair judgement was denied him.
Who will ever talk about his descendants,
since his life on earth has been cut short?

The eunuch addressed Philip and said, 'Tell me, is the prophet referring to himself or someone else?' Starting, therefore, with this text of scripture, Philip proceeded to explain the good news of Jesus to him.

Further along the road they came to some water, and the eunuch said, 'Look, here is some water; is there anything to prevent my being baptized?' He ordered the chariot to stop, then Philip and the eunuch both went down into the water and he baptized him. But after they had come up out of the water again Philip was taken away by the Spirit of the Lord, and the eunuch never saw him again but went on his way rejoicing.

Acts 8:26–39

St Paul

The Road to Damascus

A classic Second Journey is perhaps that of the Pharisee Saul who was also called Paul. Saul was travelling from Jerusalem to Damascus when he found himself thrown to the ground and blinded. The object of Saul's journey had been to persecute the Christians of Damascus in the same way that he had persecuted the Christians of Jerusalem. Saul hears a voice asking, 'Saul, Saul, why are you persecuting me?' The voice then tells him to get up and go into the city where he will be told what he has to do. But Saul's reputation has preceded him to Damascus. When the Lord informs Ananias in a vision that he is to welcome Saul, his response is less than enthusiastic! In this extract from Acts 22, Saul tells his story to the Jews of Jerusalem.

I am a Jew… and was born at Tarsus in Cilicia. I was brought up here in this city. It was under Gamaliel that I studied and was taught the exact observance of the Law of our ancestors. In fact, I was as full of duty towards God as you all are today. I even persecuted this Way to the death and sent women as well as men to prison in chains as the high priest and the whole council of elders can testify. I even received letters from them to the brothers in Damascus, which I took with me when I set off to bring prisoners back from there to Jerusalem for punishment.

It happened that I was on that journey and nearly at Damascus when in the middle of the day a bright light from heaven suddenly shone round me. I fell to the ground and heard a voice saying, 'Saul, Saul, why are you persecuting me?' I answered, 'Who are you, Lord?' and he said to me, 'I am Jesus the Nazarene, whom you are persecuting.' The people with me saw the light but did not hear the voice which spoke to me. I said, 'What am I to do, Lord?' The Lord answered, 'Get up and go into Damascus, and there you will be told what you have been appointed to do.' Since the light had been so dazzling that I was blind, I got to Damascus only because my companions led me by the hand.

Someone called Ananias, a devout follower of the Law and highly thought of by all the Jews living there, came to see me; he stood beside me and said, 'Brother Saul, receive your sight.' Instantly my sight came back and I was able to see him. Then he said, 'The God of our ancestors has chosen you to know his will, to see the Upright One and hear his own voice speaking, because you are to be his witness before all humanity, testifying to what you have seen and heard. And now why delay? Hurry and be baptized and wash away your sins, calling on his name.'

'It happened that, when I got back to Jerusalem, and was praying in the Temple, I fell into a trance and then I saw him. 'Hurry,' he said, 'leave Jerusalem at once; they will not accept the testimony you are giving about me.' 'Lord,' I answered, 'they know that I used to go from synagogue to synagogue, imprisoning and flogging those who believed in you; and that when the blood of your witness Stephen was being shed, I, too, was standing by, in full agreement with his murderers, and in charge of their clothes.' Then he said to me, 'Go! I am sending you out to the Gentiles far away.'

Acts 22:3–21

Egeria

Egeria in Jerusalem

Egeria was a woman of the fourth century from either France or Spain. She may have been a nun and was possibly the Abbess of a community. In her letters home she describes what must have been the journey of a lifetime to Egypt, the Holy Land and Asia Minor. Egeria is a uniquely important witness to early Christian worship, and in this extract from her writings we hear about the lengthy Easter ceremonies in Jerusalem.

Loving sisters, I am sure it will interest you to know about the daily services they have in the holy places, and I must tell you about them. All the doors of the Anastasis are opened before cock-crow each day, and the '*monazontes* and *parthenae*', as they call them here, come in, and also some laymen and women, at least those who are willing to wake at such an early hour. From then until daybreak they join in singing the refrains to the hymns, psalms, and antiphons. There is a prayer between each of the hymns, since there are two or three presbyters and deacons each day by rota, who are there with the *monazontes* and say the prayers between all the hymns and antiphons.

As soon as dawn comes, they start the Morning Hymns, and the bishop with his clergy comes and joins them. He goes straight into the cave, and inside the screen he first says the Prayer for All (mentioning any names he wishes) and blesses the catechumens, and then another prayer and blesses the faithful. Then he comes outside the screen, and everyone comes up to kiss his hand. He blesses them one by one, and goes out, and by the time the dismissal takes place it is already day.

Again at midday everyone comes into the Anastasis and says psalms and antiphons until a message is sent to the bishop. Again he enters, and, without taking his seat, goes straight inside the screen in the Anastasis (which is to say into the cave where he went in the early morning), and again, after a prayer, he blesses the faithful and comes outside the screen, and again they come to kiss his hand.

At three o'clock they do once more what they did at midday, but at four o'clock they have *Lychnicon*, as they call it, or in our language, Lucernare. All the people congregate once more in the Anastasis, and the lamps and candles are all lit, which makes it very bright. The fire is brought not from outside, but from the cave — inside the screen — where a lamp is always burning night and day. For some time they have the Lucernare psalms and antiphons; then they send for the bishop, who enters and sits in the chief seat. The presbyters also come and sit in their places, and the hymns and antiphons go on. Then, when they have finished singing everything which is appointed, the bishop rises and goes in front of the screen (i.e. the cave). One of the deacons makes the normal commemoration of individuals, and each time he mentions a name a large group of boys responds *Kyrie eleison* (in our language, 'Lord, have mercy'). Their voices are very loud. As soon as the deacon has done his part, the bishops says a prayer and prays the Prayer for All. Up to this point the faithful and the catechumens are praying together, but now the deacon calls every catechumen to stand where he is and bow his head, and the bishop says the blessing over the catechumens from his place. There is another prayer, after which the deacon calls for all the faithful to bow their head, and the bishop says the blessing over the faithful from his place. Thus the dismissal takes place at the Anastasis, and they all come up one by one to kiss the bishop's hand.

Then, singing hymns, they take the bishop from the Anastasis to the Cross, and everyone goes with him. On arrival he says one prayer and blesses the catechumens, then another and blesses the faithful. Then again the bishop and all the people go Behind the Cross, and do there what they did Before the Cross; and in both places they come to kiss the bishop's hand, as they did in the Anastasis. Great glass lanterns are burning everywhere, and there are many candles in front of the Anastasis, and also Before and Behind the Cross. By the end of all this it is dusk. So these are the services held every weekday at the Cross and at the Anastasis.

But on the seventh day, the Lord's Day, there gather in the courtyard before cock-crow all the people, as many as can get in, as if it was Easter. The courtyard is the 'basilica' beside the Anastasis, that is to say, out of doors, and lamps have been hung there for them. Those who are afraid they may not arrive in time for cock-crow come early, and sit waiting there singing hymns and antiphons, and they have prayers between, since there are always presbyters and deacons there ready for the vigil, because so many people collect there, and it is not usual to open the holy places before cock-crow.

Soon the first cock crows, and at that the bishop enters, and goes into the cave in the Anastasis. The doors are all opened, and all the people come into the Anastasis, which is already ablaze with lamps. When they are inside, a psalm is said by one of the presbyters, with everyone responding, and it is followed by a prayer; then a psalm is said by one of the deacons, and another prayer; then a third psalm is said by one of the clergy, a third prayer, and the Commemoration of All. After these three psalms and prayers they take censers into the cave of the Anastasis, so that the whole Anastasis basilica is filled with the smell. Then the bishop, standing inside the screen, takes the Gospel book and goes to the door, where he himself reads the account of the Lord's resurrection. At the beginning of the reading the whole assembly groans and laments at all that the Lord underwent for us, and the way they weep would move even the hardest hearts to tears. When the Gospel is finished, the bishop comes out, and is taken with singing to the Cross, and they all go with him. They have one psalm there and a prayer, then he blesses the people, and that is the dismissal. As the bishop goes out, everyone comes to kiss his hand.

Then straight away the bishop retires to his house, and all the *monazontes* go back into the Anastasis to sing psalms and antiphons until daybreak. There are prayers between all these psalms and antiphons, and presbyters and deacons take their turn every day at the Anastasis to keep vigil with the people. Some laymen and women like to stay on there till daybreak, but others prefer to go home again to bed for some sleep.

Egeria, *Egeria's Travels*

St Augustine

The Conversion of Augustine

St Augustine of Hippo (354–430) wrestled for many years with the conflicting claims of Christianity and his own desires – a struggle which he expressed in the words, 'Grant me chastity and continence, but not yet.' Augustine's friend Alypius had been alongside him during the years of hesitation and searching and both young men eventually decided to seek baptism. In this extract from his *Confessions*, Augustine describes the final stages of his journey to faith and the joy he experienced once the decision was made.

From that direction where I had set my face and towards which I was afraid to move, there appeared the dignified and chaste Lady Continence, serene and cheerful without coquetry, enticing me in an honourable manner to come and not to hesitate. To receive and embrace me she stretched out pious hands, filled with numerous good examples for me to follow. There were large numbers of boys and girls, a multitude of all ages, young adults and grave widows and elderly virgins. In every one of them was Continence herself, in no sense barren but 'the fruitful mother of children' (Psalm 112:9), the joys born of you, Lord, her husband. And she smiled on me with a smile of encouragement as if to say: 'Are you incapable of doing what these men and women have done? Do you think them capable of achieving this by their own resources and not by the Lord their God? Their Lord God gave me to them. Why are you relying on yourself, only to find yourself unreliable? Cast yourself upon him, do not be afraid. He will not withdraw himself so that you fall. Make the leap without anxiety; he will catch you and heal you.'

I blushed with embarrassment because I was still listening to the mutterings of those vanities, and racked by hesitations I remained undecided. But once more it was as if she said: "'Stop your ears to your impure members on earth and mortify them" (Colossians 3:5). They declare delights to you, but "not in accord with the law of the Lord your God"' (Psalm 118:85). This debate in my heart was a struggle of myself against myself. Alypius stood quite still at my side, and waited in silence for the outcome of my unprecedented state of agitation.

From a hidden depth, a profound self-examination had dredged up a heap of all my misery and set it 'in the sight of my heart' (Psalm 18:15). That precipitated a vast storm bearing a massive downpour of tears. To pour it all out with the accompanying groans, I got up from beside Alypius (solitude seemed to me more appropriate for the business of weeping), and I moved further away to ensure that even his presence put no inhibition upon me. He sensed that this was my condition at that moment. I think I may have said something which made it clear that the sound of my voice was already choking with tears. So I stood up while in profound astonishment he remained where we were sitting. I threw myself down somehow under a certain fig tree, and let my tears flow freely. Rivers streamed from my eyes, a sacrifice acceptable to you (Psalm 50:19), and (though not in these words, yet in this sense) I repeatedly said to you: 'How long, O Lord? How long, Lord, will you be angry to the uttermost? Do not be mindful of our old iniquities' (Psalm 6:4). For I felt my past to have a grip on me. It uttered wretched cries: 'How long, how long is it to be?' 'Tomorrow, tomorrow.' 'Why not now? Why not an end to my impure life in this very hour?'

As I was saying this and weeping in the bitter agony of my heart, suddenly I heard a voice from the nearby house chanting as if it might be a boy or a girl (I do not know which), saying and repeating over and over again 'Pick up and read, pick up and read'. At once my countenance changed, and I began to think intently whether there might be some sort of children's game in which such a chant is used. But I could not remember having heard of one. I checked the flood of tears and stood up. I interpreted it solely as a divine command to me to open the book and read the first chapter I might find. For I had heard how Antony happened to be present at the gospel reading, and took it as an admonition addressed to himself when the words were read: 'Go, sell all you have, give to the poor, and you shall have treasure in heaven; and come, follow me' (Matthew 19:21). By such an inspired utterance he was immediately 'converted to you' (Psalm 50:15). So I hurried back to the place where Alypius was sitting. There I had put down the book of the apostle when I got up. I seized it, opened it and in silence read the first passage on which my eyes lit: 'Not in riots and drunken parties, not in eroticism and indecencies, not in strife and rivalry, but put on the Lord Jesus Christ and make no provision for the flesh in its lusts' (Romans 13:13–14).

I neither wished nor needed to read further. At once, with the last words of this sentence, it was as if a light of relief from all anxiety flooded into my heart. All the shadows of doubt were dispelled.

St Augustine of Hippo, *Confessions* **VIII:11:27–VIII:12:29**

St Gertrude the Great

A New Beginning

The German mystic St Gertrude (1256–c. 1302) was entrusted to the care of the Cistercian-inspired convent of Helfta in Thuringia at the age of five. Gertrude does not seem to have been particularly enamoured of the religious life until she came face to face with Jesus at the age of 25. In this extract from her writings she describes the transforming experience which turned a discontented young nun into a great contemplative.

I was in my 26th year. The day of my salvation was the Monday preceding the feast of the Purification of your most chaste Mother, which fell that year on the 27th of January. The desirable hour was after compline, as dusk was falling.

My God, you who are all truth, clearer than all light, yet hidden deeper in our hearts than any secret, when you resolved to disperse the darkness of my night, you began gently and tenderly by first calming my mind, which had been troubled for more than a month past. This trouble, it seems to me, served your purpose. You were striving to destroy the tower of vanity and worldliness which I had set up in my pride, although, alas, I was – in vain – bearing the name and wearing the habit of a religious. This was the way in which you sought to show me your salvation (Psalm 49:23).

At the stated hour, then, I was standing in the middle of the dormitory. An older nun was approaching and, having bowed my head with the reverence prescribed by our rule, I looked up and saw before me a youth of about 16 years of age, handsome and gracious. Young as I then was, the beauty of his form was all that I could have desired, entirely pleasing to the outward eye. Courteously and in a gentle voice (cf. Genesis 50:21) he said to me: 'Soon will come your salvation: why are you so sad? Is it because you have no one to confide in that you are sorrowful?'

While he was speaking, although I knew that I was really in the place where I have said, it seemed to me that I was in the choir, in the corner where I usually say my tepid prayers; and it was there that I heard these words: 'I will save you. I will deliver you. Do not fear.' With this, I saw his hand, tender and fine, holding mine, as though to plight a troth, and he added: 'with my enemies you have licked the dust (cf. Psalm 71:9) and sucked honey among thorns. Come back to me now, and I will inebriate you with the torrent of my divine pleasure' (Psalm 35:9).

As he was saying this, I looked and saw, between him and me, that is to say, on his right and on my left, a hedge of such length that I could not see the end of it, either ahead or behind. The top of this hedge was bristling with such large thorns that there seemed no way to get back to the youth. As I hesitated, burning with desire and almost fainting, suddenly he seized me and, lifting me up with the greatest ease, placed me beside him. But on the hand with which he had just given me his promise I recognized those bright jewels, his wounds, which have cancelled all our debts (Colossians 2:14).

I praise, adore, bless, and thank you to the best of my ability for your wise mercy and your merciful wisdom! For you, my Creator and my Redeemer, have sought to curb my stiff-necked obstinacy under you sweet yoke with the remedy best suited to my infirmity. From that hour, in a new spirit of joyful serenity, I began to follow the way of the sweet odour of your perfume (Song of Songs 1:3), and I found your yoke sweet and your burden light (Matthew 11:30) which a short time before I had thought to be unbearable.

St Gertrude the Great, *Gertrude of Helfta*

Dante Alighieri

The Inferno

In the three parts of his sacred poem *La Divina Commedia*, Dante (1265–1321) describes a vision, during which he travels for a week from Hell to Purgatory and finally to Heaven. In the first part, 'The Inferno', Dante travels from a dark forest down through Hell to Satan at the centre of the earth. The opening lines of 'The Inferno' portray a classic mid-life journey in which all previous certainties have disappeared. The 'right road' is lost and gone — and yet great good comes out of the apparent chaos and meaninglessness in which the traveller finds himself. Dante was in his forties when he began this great poem and he had been exiled from his beloved city of Florence — ingredients for a painful but ultimately fruitful Second Journey.

The Inferno

Midway this way of life we're bound upon,
I woke to find myself in a dark wood,
Where the right road was wholly lost and gone.

Ay me! How hard to speak of it — that rude
And rough and stubborn forest! The mere breath
Of memory stirs the old fear in the blood;

It is so bitter, it goes nigh to death;
Yet there I gained such good, that, to convey
The tale, I'll write what else I found therewith.

How I got into it I cannot say,
Because I was so heavy and full of sleep
When first I stumbled from the narrow way;

But when at last I stood beneath a steep
Hill's side, which closed that valley's wandering maze
Whose dread had pierced me to the heart-root deep,

Then I looked up, and saw the morning rays
Mantle its shoulder from that planet bright
Which guides men's feet aright on all their ways.

Dante Alighieri, 'The Inferno', Canto I

St Ignatius Loyola

A New Departure

St Ignatius Loyola (1491–1556) was a serving as Spanish knight at arms when, in 1521, he was severely wounded by a cannon while defending a Spanish citadel against an invading French army during the siege of Pamplona. To ease the boredom of a long convalescence in the family castle of Loyola, Ignatius found himself reading a life of Jesus and stories of the saints. He began to reflect on the change he experienced in his inner disposition after reading these books. This was the beginning of a Second Journey which led Ignatius to change his life radically and to found the Society of Jesus in 1540, popularly known as the Jesuits.

Ignatius was very addicted to reading aimless and exaggerated books about the illustrious deeds of the famous, and when he felt well again he asked for some to pass the time. But there were no books of that type in the house and he was given a book called *The Life of Christ* and another *The Flower of the Saints*...

By reading these regularly he developed a certain sympathy with what was written in them. Sometimes he took his mind off them and turned his thoughts to the type of story he used to read earlier on; sometimes, according as it occurred to him, he thought about those idle inclinations, and things of that nature, such as he used to think about formerly.

But divine mercy was at hand and, in place of these thoughts, it used to substitute others from what he had recently read. For when he had read the lives of Christ our Lord and the saints he would think to himself and ponder: 'What if I were to do what blessed Francis did or what blessed Dominic did?' And he used to meditate a good deal in this manner. This way of thinking lasted for some time, but then other things intervened, and he resumed his idle and worldly thoughts, and these persisted for a long time. He was involved in that succession of changes of mind for a considerable time.

But there was a difference in his two types of subject for thought. When he was intent on his worldly interests he got great pleasure at the time, but whenever he wearied of them and gave them up, he felt dejected and empty. On the other hand, when he thought about the austerities which he found that holy men practised, not only did he find joy in the account of them, but when he stopped thinking of them his joy remained unabated. However, he never noticed the difference or thought about it, until one day it dawned on him, and he began to wonder at it. He understood from experience that the one subject of thought left him dejection, while the other left him joy. This was the first conclusion which he reached concerning things of a supernatural nature. Afterwards, however, when he had undertaken spiritual exercises, this experience was the starting-point for teaching his followers the discernment of spirits.

The Acts of Saint Ignatius, taken down by Luis Gonzalez

John Wesley

Growing into Faith

John Wesley (1703–91) was in his thirties when he returned to London from an unsuccessful missionary journey to America. He had alienated his congregation in Savannah, Georgia, through the imposition of unduly severe pastoral discipline. In this extract from his *Journal*, Wesley laments his continuing bondage to sin. Eventually his friend, Peter Böhler of the Moravian Church, is able to convince him that he lacks saving faith. Wesley is now ready for the conversion experience, which takes place on 24 May 1738. During a reading of Luther's *Preface to the Romans* Wesley finds his heart is 'strangely warmed'. Although still a priest of the Church of England, Wesley discovers that the pulpits are closed to him, so he begins a preaching ministry which is to develop into the Methodist Movement.

All the time I was at Savannah I was thus beating the air. Being ignorant of the righteousness of Christ, which, by a living faith in him, bringeth salvation 'to every one that believeth', I sought to establish my own righteousness; and so laboured in the fire all my days. I was now properly 'under the law'; I knew that 'the law' of God was 'spiritual; I consented to it, that it was good'. Yea, 'I delighted in it, after the inner man.' Yet was I 'carnal, sold under sin'. Every day was I constrained to cry out, 'What I do, I allow not: for what I would, I do not; but what I hate, that I do. To will is' indeed 'present with me: but how to perform that which is good, I find not. For the good which I would, I do not; but the evil which I would not, that I do. I find a law, that when I would do good, evil is present with me': even 'the law in my members, warring against the law of my mind', and still 'bringing me into captivity to the law of sin'.

In this vile, abject state of bondage to sin, I was indeed fighting continually, but not conquering. Before, I had willingly served sin;

now it was unwillingly; but still I served it. I fell, and rose, and fell again. Sometimes I was overcome, and in heaviness: sometimes I overcame, and was in joy. For as in the former state I had some foretastes of the terrors of the law, so had I in this, of the comforts of the gospel. During this whole struggle between nature and grace, which had now continued about 10 years, I had many remarkable returns to prayer; especially when I was in trouble: I had many sensible comforts; which are indeed no other than short anticipations of the life of faith. But I was still 'under the law', not 'under grace' (the state most who are called Christians are content to live and die in); for I was only striving with, not freed from sin: neither had I the witness of the Spirit with my spirit, and indeed could not; for I 'sought it not by faith, but as it were by the works of the law'.

In my return to England, January, 1738, being in imminent danger of death, and very uneasy on that account, I was strongly convinced that the cause of that uneasiness was unbelief; and that the gaining a true, living faith was the 'one thing needful' for me. But still I fixed not this faith on its right object: I meant only faith in God, not faith in or through Christ. Again, I knew not that I was wholly void of this faith; but only thought I had not enough of it. So that when Peter Böhler, whom God prepared for me as soon as I came to London, affirmed of true faith in Christ (which is but one), that it had those two fruits inseparably attending it, 'dominion over sin, and constant peace from a sense of forgiveness', I was quite amazed, and looked upon it as a new gospel. If this was so, it was clear I had not faith. But I was not willing to be convinced of this. Therefore I disputed with all my might, and laboured to prove that faith might be where these were not; especially where the sense of forgiveness was not: for all the scriptures relating to this, I had been long since taught to construe away; and to call all Presbyterians who spoke otherwise. Besides, I well saw, no one could, in the nature of things, have such a sense of forgiveness, and not feel it. But I felt it not. If, then, there was no faith without this, all my pretensions to faith dropped at once.

When I met Peter Böhler again, he consented to put the dispute upon the issue which I desired, namely, scripture and experience. I first consulted the scripture. But when I set aside the glosses of men, and simply considered the words of God, comparing them together, endeavouring to illustrate the obscure by the plainer passages; I found they all made against me, and was forced to retreat to my last hold, 'that experience would never agree with the literal interpretation of those scriptures. Nor could I therefore allow it to be true, till I found some living witnesses of it.' He replied, he could show me such any time; if I desired it, the next day. And accordingly, the next day he came again with three others, all of whom testified, of their own personal experience, that a true, living faith in Christ is inseparable from a sense of pardon for all past, and freedom from all present, sins. They added with one mouth, that this faith was the gift, the free gift, of God; and that he would surely bestow it upon every soul who earnestly and perseveringly sought it. I was now thoroughly convinced; and by the grace of God, I resolved to seek it unto the end: 1. By absolutely renouncing all dependence in whole or in part, upon my own works or righteousness; on which I had really grounded my hope of salvation, though I knew it not, from my youth up. 2. By adding to the constant use of all the other means of grace, continual prayer for this very thing, justifying, saving faith, a full reliance on the blood of Christ shed for me; a trust in him as my Christ, as my sole justification, sanctification and redemption.

I continued thus to seek it (though with strange indifference, dullness and coldness, and unusually frequent relapses into sin), till Wednesday, May 24. I think it was about five this morning, that I opened my Testament on those words, 'There are given unto us exceeding great and precious promises, even that ye should be partakers of the divine nature' (2 Peter 1:4). Just as I went out, I opened it again on those words, 'Thou art not far from the kingdom of God.' In the afternoon I was asked to go to St Paul's. The anthem was, 'Out of the deep have I called unto Thee, O Lord: Lord, hear my voice. O let Thine ears consider well the voice of my complaint. If Thou, Lord, wilt be extreme to mark what is done amiss, O Lord, who may abide it? For there is mercy with Thee; therefore shalt Thou be feared. O Israel, trust in the Lord: for with the Lord there is mercy, and with him is plenteous redemption. And he shall redeem Israel from all his sins.'

In the evening I went very unwillingly to a society in Aldersgate Street, where one was reading Luther's preface to the Epistle to the Romans. About a quarter before nine, while he was describing the change which God works in the heart through faith in Christ, I felt my heart strangely warmed. I felt I did trust in Christ, Christ alone, for salvation: and an assurance was given me, that he had taken away my sins, even mine, and saved me from the law of sin and death.

I began to pray with all my might for those who had in a more especial manner despitefully used me and persecuted me. I then testified openly to all there, what I now first felt in my heart. But it was not long before the enemy suggested, 'This cannot be faith; for where is the joy?' Then was I taught, that peace and victory over sin are essential to faith in the Captain of our salvation; but that, as to the transports of joy that usually attend the beginning of it, especially in those who have mourned deeply, God sometimes giveth, sometimes withholdeth them, according to the counsels of his own will.

After my return home, I was much buffeted with temptations; but cried out, and they fled away. They returned again and again. I as often lifted up my eyes, and he 'sent me help from his holy place'. And herein I found the difference between this and my former state chiefly consisted. I was striving, yea, fighting with all my might under the law, as well as under grace. But then I was sometimes, if not often, conquered; now I was always conqueror.

John Wesley, *John Wesley's Journal*

Caroline Chisholm

A Harsh Reality

Caroline Chisholm (1808–77) was the contented mother of a young family living outside Sydney when, in 1839, she became aware of the needs of young women emigrating from Ireland and England to Australia. In *Caroline Chisholm: The Emigrant's Friend*, Joanna Bogle describes the meeting that was to change Caroline's life and make her one of Australia's heroines.

A visit into Sydney was quite an expedition from the Chisholms' home on the outskirts of the town. It made a busy day out, and Caroline would usually combine some shopping with a visit to friends. While news was exchanged and refreshments enjoyed, there was also an opportunity to see how the town was changing and what new buildings were going up or other developments were taking place. On town trips, Archibald also liked to buy a newspaper and to catch up on the controversies of the day. A walk around the port was also always exciting, especially for the small boys.

It was on one such visit that Caroline came across a forlorn group of girls, sitting together in the harbour, looking miserable, dirty, and hungry. It was impossible to pass by without making some enquiry about them. Caroline approached and asked them what was wrong. They turned out to be new arrivals from Britain, still ill from the horrors of the journey, and with nowhere to go and practically no money between them.

They were 'Bounty' migrants, shipped from Britain under the system through which ships' captains received money for the number of settlers they could bring. There had been pressure to bring out more single females, and so shiploads were now beginning to arrive. A harsh reality awaited these emigrants. There was no recognized job agency, and no accommodation on offer to those without funds.

Many of the girls were no more than children, not yet out of their teens. Most of them could not read or write. Their journey had been horrific – crammed together in filthy and smelly conditions, sometimes terrorized by members of the crew who knew them to be impoverished and without the protection of family or friends. They had seen death and disease on the journey, and now that they had finally arrived, it was only to find themselves completely abandoned while more fortunate passengers settled into hotels or lodgings. These girls desperately needed some basic security and assistance. Inevitably, Caroline ended up doing what her heart dictated – she took some of the most pitiful into her own home.

If she had believed half the stories told to her by long-time settlers she would have expected the girls to steal, cheat, lie, or turn the house into a brothel overnight. But none of this happened. Instead, the girls proved grateful for a chance to wash themselves and their clothes, to eat a decent meal, and to sleep in decent beds. Caroline made enquiries among her friends and acquaintances, and soon found that there was considerable demand for them in local families. There were plenty of jobs on offer. A colonial home needed all the help it could find, for cooking and cleaning and household tasks, laundry-work and helping a new mother with a baby. The girls themselves were only too anxious to work hard and prove themselves in return for good lodgings and modest wages. In no time, these Chisholm family visitors were setting off, their few belongings washed and re-packed, to new homes. Caroline was shortly to have the satisfaction of hearing that they had settled well, and even started a fashion locally, with other families seeking more like them. Suddenly, an emigrant girl newly-arrived from England or Ireland seemed to be an asset to a harassed housewife in the colony, rather than a problem to avoid.

Joanna Bogle, *Caroline Chisholm: The Emigrant's Friend*

John Henry Newman

Out of the Darkness

In 1833 the English theologian John Henry Newman (1801–90) undertook a Mediterranean trip which was to prove a life-changing experience for the young scholar. After an initial visit to Sicily, Newman returned there alone because he wanted to experience life as 'a solitary and a wanderer'. While on the island he collapsed with a fever, from which he was convinced he would not recover. His health was eventually restored, however, and on the journey back to England he wrote a poem, 'The Pillar of the Cloud', which is better known by its opening words, 'Lead, Kindly Light'. This poem, with its expression of the inner darkness through which the wanderer is eventually led to safety, contains the hallmarks of a Second Journey.

On Newman's return to England a new sphere of activity opened before him. He was convinced that 'God has still a work for me to do'. In 1843 he was to resign from his ministry in the Church of England to be received into the Roman Catholic Church in 1845 and ordained as a Roman Catholic priest. In 1879 he was made a cardinal.

Lead, Kindly Light

Lead, kindly Light, amid the encircling gloom,
Lead thou me on;
The night is dark, and I am far from home,
Lead thou me on.
Keep thou my feet; I do not ask to see
The distant scene; one step enough for me.

I was not ever thus, nor prayed that thou
Shouldst lead me on;
I loved to choose and see my path; but now
Lead thou me on.
I loved the garish day, and, spite of fears,
Pride ruled my will: remember not past years.

So long thy power hath blest me, sure it still
Will lead me on
O'er moor and fen, o'er crag and torrent, till
The night is gone.
And with the morn those Angel faces smile,
Which I have loved long since, and lost awhile.

John Henry Newman

Catherine Booth

A Social Reformer

Catherine Booth (1829–80) was highly influential in shaping the movement that was to become the Salvation Army and she made sure that her husband, William Booth, (1829–1912), was fully aware of the facts of deprivation. Catherine had been deeply affected by an encounter with a woman who had just given birth on a patch of waste ground. The experience inspired her to campaign for improvement in the position of women in 19th-century society and to ensure that the Army shared her concern. Former deputy leader of the British Labour Party Roy Hattersley describes the experience that changed Catherine's life and influenced the future of the Salvation Army.

> Catherine – the stronger, cleverer and certainly more attractive partner in the near-perfect Booth marriage – had understood the hard facts of deprivation ever since, walking across wasteland, she had found a bundle of rags which, on closer inspection, turned out to be a woman who had given birth a couple of hours earlier. That incident inspired her lifelong campaign to improve the position of women in 19th-century society. Combined with her defence of women's right to preach – supported by irrefutable scriptural evidence – her campaign to raise the age of consent and change the laws on prostitution and procuring made her one of the great social reformers of her age. Because of her, William Booth became a social reformer too.

Roy Hattersley, from an article in *The Tablet*, 16 September 2000

Francis Thompson

Pursued by God

In 'The Hound of Heaven' the English mystical poet Francis Thompson (1859–1907) describes the pursuit of the soul by God. Thompson's own spiritual journey included a period of near-destitution until his poetic gifts were discovered by Wilfred Meynell, husband of the poet Alice Meynell.

In these extracts from the poem, Thompson gives a powerful description of the inability of material goods to satisfy the soul, which is eventually forced to recognize that only God can assuage its thirst.

The Hound of Heaven

I fled Him, down the nights and down the days;
  I fled Him, down the arches of the years;
I fled Him, down the labyrinthine ways
  Of my own mind; and in the mist of tears
I hid from Him, and under running laughter.
    Up vistaed hopes I sped;
    And shot, precipitated,
Adown Titanic glooms of chasmèd fears,
  From those strong Feet that followed, followed after.

    But with unhurrying chase,
    And unperturbèd pace,
  Deliberate speed, majestic instancy,
    They beat — and a Voice beat
    More instant than the Feet —
'All things betray thee, who betrayest Me.' . . .

                    * * *

Now of that long pursuit
      Comes on at hand the bruit;
That Voice is round me like a bursting sea:
      'And is they earth so marred,
      Shattered in shard on shard?
   Lo, all things fly thee, for thou fliest Me!
      Strange, piteous, futile thing!
Wherefore should any set thee love apart?
Seeing none but I makes much of naught?' (He said),
'And human love needs human meriting:
      How hast thou merited —
Of all man's clotted clay the dingiest clot?
      Alack, thou knowest not
How little worthy of any love thou art!
Whom wilt thou find to love ignoble thee,
      Save Me, save only Me?
All which I took from thee I did but take,
      Not for thy harms,
But just that thou might'st seek it in My arms.
      All which thy child's mistake
Fancies as lost, I have stored for thee at home:
Rise, clasp My hand, and come!'

      Halts by me that footfall:
Is my gloom, after all,
   Shade of His hand, outstretched caressingly?
      'Ah, fondest, blindest, weakest,
I am He Whom thou seekest!
Thou dravest love from thee, who dravest Me.'

Francis Thompson

Mahatma Gandhi

The Struggle for Justice

Mahatma Gandhi (1869–1948) experienced racial prejudice for the first time in 1893 as a 24-year-old Indian barrister making his first visit to South Africa. Gandhi had come to South Africa to assist the merchant Abdulla Sheth in a lawsuit. Gandhi's experience in the first-class railway carriage was instrumental in persuading him to remain in South Africa in order to bring the plight of Indians there to the attention of the world. In this extract from his autobiography, *My Experiments with Truth*, he describes the railway journey which was to affect his life's direction. Gandhi emphasized the force of truth and the power of nonviolence (*ahimsa*) in the struggle against evil. He was to lead his country in its successful struggle for independence from Britain, which was achieved in 1947 – five months before Gandhi's assassination by a religious fanatic.

On the seventh or eighth day after my arrival, I left Durban. A first-class seat was booked for me. It was usual there to pay five shillings extra, if one needed a bedding. Abdulla Sheth insisted that I should book one bedding but, out of obstinacy and pride and with a view to saving five shillings, I declined. Abdulla Sheth warned me. 'Look, now,' said he 'this is a different country from India. Thank God, we have enough and to spare. Please do not stint yourself in anything that you may need.'

I thanked him and asked him not be anxious.

The train reached Maritzburg, the capital of Natal, at about 9 p.m. Beddings used to be provided at this station. A railway servant came and asked me if I wanted one. 'No,' said I, 'I have one with me.' He went away. But a passenger came next, and looked me up and down. He saw that I was a 'coloured' man. This disturbed him. Out he went and came in again with one or two officials. They all kept quiet, when another official came to me and said, 'Come along, you must go to the van compartment.'

'But I have a first-class ticket,' said I.

'That doesn't matter,' rejoined the other, 'I tell you, you must go to the van compartment.'

'I tell you, I was permitted to travel in this compartment at Durban, and I insist on going on in it.'

'No, you won't,' said the official. 'You must leave this compartment, or else I shall have to call a police constable to push you out.'

'Yes, you may. I refuse to get out voluntarily.'

The constable came. He took me by the hand and pushed me out. My luggage was also taken out. I refused to go to the other compartment and the train steamed away. I went and sat in the waiting room, keeping my hand-bag with me, and leaving the other luggage where it was. The railway authorities had taken charge of it.

It was winter, and winter in the higher regions of South Africa is severely cold. Maritzburg being at a high altitude, the cold was extremely bitter. My overcoat was in my luggage, but I did not dare to ask for it lest I should be insulted again, so I sat and shivered. There was no light in the room. A passenger came in at about midnight and possibly wanted to talk to me. But I was in no mood to talk.

I began to think of my duty. Should I fight for my rights or go back to India, or should I go on to Pretoria without minding the insults, and return to India after finishing the case? It would be cowardice to run back to India without fulfilling my obligation. The hardship to which I was subjected was superficial – only a symptom of the deep disease of colour prejudice. I should try, if possible, to root out the disease and suffer hardships in the process. Redress for wrongs I should seek only to the extent that would be necessary for the removal of the colour prejudice.

So I decided to take the next available train to Pretoria.

Mahatma Gandhi, *My Experiments with Truth*

The Titanic

The Wireless Operator's Story

Twenty-two-year-old Harold Bride (1890–1956) was serving as second wireless officer on the *Titanic* when she struck an iceberg on 14 April 1912 during her maiden voyage from England to the United States. Bride was serving under 25-year-old Jack Phillips who died in the disaster. In this extract from an interview in the *New York Times*, Bride describes the final hours of the *Titanic*.

I didn't have much to do aboard the *Titanic* except to relieve Phillips from midnight until some time in the morning, when he should be through sleeping. On the night of the accident I was not sending, but was asleep. I was due to be up and relieve Phillips earlier than usual. And that reminds me – if it hadn't been for a lucky thing, we never could have sent any call for help.

The lucky thing was that the wireless broke down early enough for us to fix it before the accident. We noticed something wrong on Sunday, and Phillips and I worked seven hours to find it. We found a 'secretary' burnt out, at last, and repaired it just a few hours before the iceberg was struck.

Phillips said to me as he took the night shift, 'You turn in, boy, and get some sleep, and go up as soon as you can and give me a chance. I'm all done for with this work of making repairs.'

There were three rooms in the wireless cabin. One was a sleeping room, one a dynamo room, and one an operating room. I took off my clothes and went to sleep in bed. Then I was conscious of waking up and hearing Phillips sending to Cape Race. I read what he was sending. It was traffic matter.

I remembered how tired he was, and I got out of bed without my clothes on to relieve him. I didn't even feel the shock. I hardly knew it had happened after the captain had come to us. There was no jolt whatever.

I was standing by Phillips telling him to go to bed when the captain put his head in the cabin.

'We've struck an iceberg,' the captain said, 'and I'm having an inspection made to tell what it has done for us. You better get ready to send out a call for assistance. But don't send it until I tell you.'

The captain went away and in 10 minutes, I should estimate the time, he came back. We could hear a terrible confusion outside, but there was not the least thing to indicate that there was any trouble. The wireless was working perfectly.

'Send the call for assistance,' ordered the captain, barely putting his head in the door.

'What call should I send?' Phillips asked.

'The regulation international call for help. Just that.'

Then the captain was gone. Phillips began to send 'C.Q.D.' [the general distress call]. He flashed away at it and we joked while he did so. All of us made light of the disaster.

We joked that way while he flashed signals for about five minutes. Then the captain came back.

'What are you sending?' he asked.

'C.Q.D.,' Phillips replied.

The humour of the situation appealed to me. I cut in with a little remark that made us all laugh, including the captain.

'Send "S.O.S.",' I said. 'It's the new call, and it may be your last chance to send it.'

Phillips with a laugh changed the signal to 'S.O.S.' The captain told us we had been struck amidships, or just back of amidships. It was 10 minutes, Phillips told me, after he had noticed the iceberg that the slight jolt that was the collision's only signal to us occurred. We thought we were a good distance away.

We said lots of funny things to each other in the next few minutes. We picked up first the steamship *Frankfurd*. We gave her our position and said we had struck an iceberg and needed assistance. The *Frankfurd* operator went away to tell his captain.

He came back, and we told him we were sinking by the head. By that time we could observe a distinct list forward.

The *Carpathia* answered our signal. We told her our position and said we were sinking by the head. The operator went to tell the captain, and in five minutes returned and told us that the captain of the *Carpathia* was putting about and heading for us.

Our captain had left us at this time and Phillips told me to run and tell him what the *Carpathia* had answered. I did so, and I went through an awful mass of people to his cabin. The decks were full of scrambling men and women. I saw no fighting, but I heard tell of it.

I came back and heard Phillips giving the *Carpathia* fuller directions. Phillips told me to put on my clothes. Until that moment I forgot that I was not dressed.

I went to my cabin and dressed. I brought an overcoat to Phillips. It was very cold. I slipped the overcoat upon him while he worked.

Every few minutes Phillips would send me to the captain with little messages. They were merely telling how the *Carpathia* was coming our way and gave her speed.

I noticed as I came back from one trip that they were putting off women and children in lifeboats. I noticed that the list forward was increasing.

Phillips told me the wireless was growing weaker. The captain came and told us our engine rooms were taking water and that the dynamos might not last much longer. We sent that word to the *Carpathia*.

I went out on deck and looked around. The water was pretty close up to the boat deck. There was a great scramble aft, and how poor Phillips worked through it I don't know.

He was a brave man. I learnt to love him that night, and I suddenly felt for him a great reverence to see him standing there sticking to his work while everybody else was raging about. I will never live to forget the work of Phillips for the last awful 15 minutes.

I thought it was about time to look about and see if there was anything detached that would float. I remember that every member of the crew had a special lifebelt and ought to know where it was. I remembered mine under my bunk. I went and got it. Then I thought how cold the water was.

I remembered I had some boots, and I put those on, and an extra jacket and I put that on. I saw Phillips standing out there still sending away, giving the *Carpathia* details of just how we were doing.

We picked up the *Olympic* and told her we were sinking by the head and were about all down. As Phillips was sending the message I strapped his lifebelt to his back. I had already put on his overcoat.

I wondered if I could get him into his boots. He suggested with a sort of laugh that I look out and see if all the people were off in the boats, or if any boats were left, or how things were.

I saw a collapsible boat near a funnel and went over to it. Twelve men were trying to boost it down to the boat deck. They were having an awful time. It was the last boat left. I looked at it longingly for a few minutes. Then I gave them a hand, and over she went. They all started to scramble in on the boat deck, and I walked back to Phillips. I said the last raft had gone.

Then came the captain's voice: 'Men you have done your full duty. You can do no more. Abandon your cabin. Now it's every man for himself. You look out for yourselves. I release you. That's the way of it at this kind of a time. Every man for himself.'

I looked out. The boat deck was awash. Phillips clung on sending and sending. He clung on for about 10 minutes, or maybe 15 minutes, after the captain had released him. The water was then coming into our cabin.

While he worked something happened I hate to tell about. I was back in my room getting Phillips' money for him, and as I looked out the door I saw a stoker, or somebody from below deck, leaning over Phillips from behind. He was too busy to notice what the man was doing. The man was slipping the lifebelt off Phillips's back.

He was a big man, too. I don't know what it was I got hold of. I remembered in a flash the way Phillips had clung on – how I had to fix that lifebelt in place because he was too busy to do it.

I knew that the man from below decks had his own lifebelt and should have known where to get it.

I suddenly felt a passion not to let that man die a decent sailors' death. I wished he might have stretched rope or walked a plank. I did my duty. I hope I finished him. I don't know. We left him on the cabin floor of the wireless room, and he was not moving.

From aft came the tunes of the band. It was a ragtime tune, I don't know what. Then there was 'Autumn'. Phillips ran aft, and that was the last I ever saw of him alive.

I went to the place I had seen the collapsible boat on the boat deck, and to my surprise I saw the boat and the men still trying to push it off. I guess there wasn't a sailor in the crowd. They couldn't do it. I went up to them and was just lending a hand when a large wave came awash of the deck.

The big wave carried the boat off. I had hold of an oarlock, and I went off with it. The next I knew I was in the boat.

But that was not all. I was in the boat, and the boat was upside down, and I was under it. And I remember realizing that I was wet through, and that whatever happened I must not breathe, for I was under water.

I knew I had to fight for it, and I did. How I got out from under the boat I do not know, but I felt a breath of air at last.

There were men all around me — hundreds of them. The sea was dotted with them, all depending on their lifebelts. I felt I simply had to get away from the ship. She was a beautiful sight then.

Smoke and sparks were rushing out of her funnel. There must have been an explosion, but we had heard none. We only saw the big stream of sparks. The ship was gradually turning on her nose — just like a duck does that goes down for a dive. I had only one thing on my mind — to get away from the suction. The band was still playing. I guess all of the band went down.

They were playing 'Autumn' then. I swam with all my might. I suppose I was 150 feet away when the *Titanic* on her nose, with her after-quarter sticking straight up in the air, began to settle — slowly.

When at last the waves washed over her rudder there wasn't the least bit of suction I could feel. She must have kept going just so slowly as she had been.

I forgot to mention that, besides the *Olympic* and *Carpathia*, we spoke to some German boat, I don't know which, and told them how we were. We also spoke to the *Baltic*. I remembered those things as I began to figure what ships would be coming towards us.

I felt, after a little while, like sinking. I was very cold. I saw a boat of some kind near me and put all my strength into an effort to swim to it. It was hard work. I was all done when a hand reached out from the boat and pulled me aboard. It was our same collapsible. The same crowd was on it.

There was just room for me to roll on the edge. I lay there, not caring what happened. Somebody sat on my legs. They were wedged in between slats and were being wrenched. I had not the heart left to ask the man to move. It was a terrible sight all around — men swimming and sinking.

I lay where I was, letting the man wrench my feet out of shape. Others came near. Nobody gave them a hand. The bottom-up boat already had more men than it would hold and it was sinking.

At first the larger waves splashed over my clothing. Then they began to splash over my head, and I had to breathe when I could.

As we floated around on our capsized boat, and I kept straining my eyes for a ship's lights, somebody said, 'Don't the rest of you think we ought to pray?' The man who made the suggestion asked what the religion of the others was. Each man called out his religion. One was a Catholic, one a Methodist, one a Presbyterian.

It was decided the most appropriate prayer for all was the Lord's Prayer. We spoke it over in chorus with the man who first suggested that we pray as the leader.

Some splendid people saved us. They had a right-side-up boat, and it was full to its capacity. Yet they came to us and loaded us all into it. I saw some lights off in the distance and knew a steamship was coming to our aid.

Harold Bride, from an article in the *New York Times*, 28 April 1912

C.S. Lewis

Checkmate

In *Surprised by Joy* the English scholar and Christian apologist C.S. Lewis (1893–1963) describes the moment of free choice in his journey to faith which came during a bus journey in Oxford. Lewis, a Fellow of Magdalen College, had begun his journey from atheism. He was now finding that most of the people he admired had joined 'the other side' and God was closing in on him!

The odd thing was that before God closed in on me, I was in fact offered what now appears a moment of wholly free choice. In a sense. I was going up Headington Hill on the top of a bus. Without words and (I think) almost without images, a fact about myself was somehow presented to me. I became aware that I was holding something at bay, or shutting something out. Or, if you like, that I was wearing some stiff clothing, like corsets, or even a suit of armour, as if I were a lobster. I felt myself being, there and then, given a free choice. I could open the door or keep it shut; I could unbuckle the armour or keep it on. Neither choice was presented as a duty; no threat or promise was attached to either, though I knew that to open the door or to take off the corset meant the incalculable. The choice appeared to be momentous but it was also strangely unemotional. I was moved by no desires or fears. In a sense I was not moved by anything. I chose to open, to unbuckle, to loosen the rein. I say, 'I chose,' yet it did not really seem possible to do the opposite. On the other hand, I was aware of no motives. You could argue that I was not a free agent, but I am more inclined to think that this came nearer to being a perfectly free act than most that I have ever done. Necessity may not be the opposite of freedom, and perhaps a man is most free when, instead of producing motives, he can only say, 'I am what I do.' Then came the repercussion on the imaginative level. I felt as if I were a man of snow at long last beginning to melt. The melting was starting in my back – drip-drip and presently trickle-trickle, I rather disliked the feeling.

The fox had been dislodged from Hegelian Wood and was now running in the open… bedraggled and weary, hounds barely a field behind. And nearly everyone was now (one way or another) in the pack; Plato, Dante, MacDonald, Herbert, Barfield, Tolkien, Dyson, Joy itself. Everyone and everything had joined the other side. Even my own pupil Griffiths – now Dom Bede Griffiths – though not yet himself a believer, did his share. Once, when he and Barfield were lunching in my room, I happened to refer to philosophy as 'a subject'. 'It wasn't a *subject* to Plato,' said Barfield, 'it was a way.' The quiet but fervent agreement of Griffiths, and the quick glance of understanding between these two, revealed to me my own frivolity. Enough had been thought, and said, and felt, and imagined. It was about time that something should be done.

For of course there had long been an ethic (theoretically) attached to my Idealism. I thought the business of us finite and half-unreal souls was to multiply the consciousness of Spirit by seeing the world from different positions while yet remaining qualitatively the same as Spirit; to be tied to a particular time and place and set of circumstances, yet there to will and think as Spirit itself does. This was hard; for the very act whereby Spirit projected souls and a world gave those souls different and competitive interests, so that there was a temptation to selfishness. But I thought each of us had it in his power to discount the emotional perspective produced by his own particular selfhood, just as we discount the optical perspective produced by our position in space. To prefer my own happiness to my neighbour's was like thinking that the nearest telegraph post was really the largest. The way to recover, and act upon, this universal and objective vision was daily and hourly to remember our true nature, to reascend or return into that Spirit which, in so far as we really were at all, we still were. Yes; but I now felt I had better try to do it. I faced at last (in MacDonald's words) 'something to be neither more nor less nor other than *done*'. An attempt at complete virtue must be made.

Really, a young Atheist cannot guard his faith too carefully. Dangers lie in wait for him on every side. You must not do, you must not even try to do, the will of the Father unless you are prepared to 'know of the doctrine'. All my acts, desires, and thought were to be brought into harmony with universal Spirit. For the first time I examined myself with a seriously practical purpose. And there I found what appalled me; a zoo of lusts, a bedlam of ambitions, a nursery of fears, a harem of fondled hatreds. My name was legion.

Of course I could do nothing – I could not last out one hour – without continual conscious recourse to what I called Spirit. But the fine, philosophical distinction between this and what ordinary people call 'prayer to God' breaks down as soon as you start doing it in earnest. Idealism can be talked, and even felt; it cannot be lived. It became patently absurd to go on thinking of 'Spirit' as either ignorant of, or passive to, my approaches. Even if my own philosophy were true, how could the initiative lie on my side? My own analogy, as I now first perceived, suggested the opposite: if Shakespeare and Hamlet could ever meet, it must be Shakespeare's doing.* Hamlet could initiate nothing. Perhaps, even now, my Absolute Spirit still differed in some way from the God of religion. The real issue was not, or not yet, there. The real terror was that if you seriously believed in even such a 'God' or 'Spirit' as I admitted, a wholly new situation developed. As the dry bones shook and came together in that dreadful valley of Ezekiel's, so now a philosophical theorem, cerebrally entertained, began to stir and heave and throw off its graveclothes, and stood upright and became a living presence. I was to be allowed to play at philosophy no longer. It might, as I say, still be true that my 'Spirit' differed in some way from 'the God of popular religion'. My Adversary waived the point. It sank into utter unimportance. He would not argue about it. He only said, 'I am the Lord'; 'I am that I am'; 'I am.'

People who are naturally religious find difficulty in understanding the horror of such a revelation. Amiable agnostics will talk cheerfully about 'man's search for God'. To me, as I then was, they might as well have talked about the mouse's search for the cat. The best image of my predicament is the meeting of Mime and Wotan in the first act of *Siegfried; hier brauch' ich nicht Spärer noch Späher, Einsam will ich…* (I've no use for spies and snoopers. I would be private…)

Remember, I had always wanted, above all things, not to be 'interfered with'. I had wanted (mad wish) 'to call my soul my own'. I had been far

* i.e. Shakespeare could, in principle, make himself appear as Author within the play, and write a dialogue between Hamlet and himself. The 'Shakespeare' within the play would of course be at once Shakespeare and one of Shakespeare's creatures. It would bear some analogy to Incarnation. [C.S. Lewis note.]

more anxious to avoid suffering than to achieve delight. I had always aimed at limited liabilities. The supernatural itself had been to me, first, an illicit dram, and then, as by a drunkard's reaction, nauseous. Even my recent attempt to live my philosophy had secretly (I now knew) been hedged round by all sorts of reservations. I had pretty well known that my ideal of virtue would never be allowed to lead me into anything intolerably painful; I would be 'reasonable'. But now what had been an ideal became a command; and what might not be expected of one? Doubtless, by definition, God was Reason itself. But would he also be 'reasonable' in that other, more comfortable, sense? Not the slightest assurance on that score was offered me. Total surrender, the absolute leap in the dark, were demanded. The reality with which no treaty can be made was upon me. The demand was not even 'All or nothing'. I think that stage had been passed, on the bus stop when I unbuckled my armour and the snowman started to melt. Now, the demand was simply 'All'.

You must picture me alone in that room in Magdalen, night after night, feeling, whenever my mind lifted even for a second from my work, the steady, unrelenting approach of him whom I so earnestly desired not to meet. That which I greatly feared had at last come upon me. In the Trinity Term of 1929 I gave in, and admitted that God was God, and knelt and prayed: perhaps, that night, the most dejected and reluctant convert in all England. I did not then see what is now the most shining and obvious thing; the Divine humility which will accept a convert even on such terms. The Prodigal Son at least walked home on his own feet. But who can duly adore that Love which will open the high gates to a prodigal who is brought in kicking, struggling, resentful, and darting his eyes in every direction for a chance of escape? The words *compelle intrare*, compel them to come in, have been so abused by wicked men that we shudder at them; but, properly understood, they plumb the depth of the Divine mercy. The hardness of God is kinder than the softness of men, and his compulsion is our liberation.

C.S. Lewis, *Surprised by Joy*

Dorothy Day

Radical Commitment

The American peace campaigner, social activist and journalist Dorothy Day (1897–1980) left the Communist Party when she joined the Roman Catholic Church. In this extract from her autobiography, *The Long Loneliness*, she describes the Communist-inspired hunger marchers who came to Washington in 1932 to present the plight of the destitute to their legislators. Dorothy was covering the march for a Roman Catholic journal and she tells of her growing awareness of the lack of Catholic involvement in the struggle for social justice. The hunger march marked the start of a Second Journey which would lead Dorothy to found the Catholic Worker Movement with French social activist Peter Maurin and thus inspire the leaders of her Church to adopt a more radical approach to issues of peace and justice.

On a bright sunny day the ragged horde triumphantly with banners flying, with lettered slogans mounted on sticks, paraded 3,000 strong though the tree-flanked streets of Washington. I stood on the curb and watched them, joy and pride in the courage of this band of men and women mounting in my heart, and with it a bitterness too that since I was now a Catholic, with fundamental philosophical differences, I could not be out there with them. I could write, I could protest, to arouse the conscience, but where was the Catholic leadership in the gathering of bands of men and women together, for the actual works of mercy that the comrades had always made part of their technique in reaching the workers?

How little, how puny my work had been since becoming a Catholic, I thought. How self-centred, how ingrown, how lacking in sense of community! My summer of quiet reading and prayer, my self-absorption seemed sinful as I watched my brothers in their struggle, not for themselves but for others. How our dear Lord must love them, I kept thinking to myself. They were his friends, his comrades, and who knows how close to his heart in their attempt to work for justice. I remembered that the first public act of our Lord recorded in the New Testament was the overthrowing of the money-changers' tables in the temple. The miracle at Cana, when Christ was present at the wedding feast and turned water into wine, has been written of as the first public act of our Lord. It was the first miracle, it was the sanctifying of marriage, but it was not the social act of overturning the tables of the money-changers, a divine courage on the part of this obscure Jew, going into the temple and with bold scorn for all the riches of this world, scattering the coins and the traffickers in gold.

The demands of the marchers were for social legislation, for unemployment insurance, for old-age pensions, for relief for mothers and children, for work. I remember seeing one banner on which was inscribed, 'Work, not wages,' a mysterious slogan having to do with man's dignity, his ownership of and responsibility for the means of production.

The years have passed, and most of the legislation called for by those workers is on the books now. I wonder how many realize just how much they owe the hunger marchers, who endured fast and cold, who were like the Son of man, when he said, 'The foxes have holes, and the birds of the air have nests but the Son of man hath not where to lay his head.'

When the demonstration was over and I had finished writing my story, I went to the national shrine at the Catholic University on the feast of the Immaculate Conception. There I offered up a special prayer, a prayer which came with tears and with anguish, that some way would open up for me to use what talents I possessed for my fellow workers, for the poor.

As I knelt there, I realized that after three years of Catholicism my only contact with active Catholics had been through articles I had written for one of the Catholic magazines. Those contacts had been brief, casual. I still did not know personally one Catholic layman.

And when I returned to New York, I found Peter Maurin — Peter the French peasant, whose spirit and ideas... dominated the rest of my life.

Dorothy Day, *The Long Loneliness*

Georges Vanier

A Meeting with Jesus

Georges Vanier (1888–1967) was the 19th Governor General of Canada and a distinguished soldier and diplomat. Between 1931 and 1939 Vanier served as First Secretary to the Canadian High Commission in London. On Good Friday 1938 he accompanied his wife Pauline to a three-hour liturgy in the Jesuit church where he underwent an experience of conversion that was to transform his spiritual life. Pauline Vanier (1898–1991) describes the experience.

My husband was very much a practising Catholic but at the same time somewhat puritanical and very scrupulous. Although he only received communion and made his confession once a year, his life was nevertheless one of remarkable purity. Georges' conversion was perhaps due to the fact that I sometimes went to hear a Jesuit friend when he was preaching or giving talks at the church in Farm Street. And I know that I got on my husband's nerves if I talked about him too much. One day Georges said to me 'It's Good Friday and your friend Father Steuart is going to be preaching.' (At that time there was a Good Friday service lasting from midday until 3.00 p.m. which included the final words of Christ on the Cross.) So my husband said, 'Do you want to go because I can let you have the car?' I replied, 'I'm not going unless you come with me.' He was a bit put out but said 'Very well, we'll go.' So we went and the sermon was on the last words of Christ which were so extraordinary in the ardour of their love.

When we came out of the church my husband turned to me and said, 'I never realized that God was love. I had always thought of him as a God of justice, a God of majesty and of transcendence – but not as a God of love.' He was obviously deeply moved and from that day forward he received communion every Sunday and very soon – probably not much more than a month later – he started to go to communion every day and his spiritual life became much deeper.

He never asked Father Steuart to be his director. I don't think he ever had a spiritual director. I think that God was directing him – the Holy Spirit. Georges was a true contemplative.

Pauline Vanier, from a recorded conversation with her son, Jean Vanier

Thomas Merton

Going to Mass for the First Time

In August 1938 Thomas Merton (1915–68) was in New York working on his thesis at Columbia University. His subject was 'Nature and Art in William Blake' and the background reading was drawing him inexorably closer to the Roman Catholic Church. One Sunday morning in August he heeded an inner prompting to attend Mass and found himself embarked on a Second Journey which would lead him to enter the strictly contemplative Cistercians of the Strict Observance at the Abbey of Gethsemani in Kentucky. Paradoxically, his attempt to 'leave the world' was to bring him international renown through his autobiography *The Seven Storey Mountain*. In this extract from the book Merton describes his first visit to a Roman Catholic church.

Every week, as Sunday came around, I was filled with a growing desire to stay in the city and go to some kind of a church.

At first, I had vaguely thought I might try to find some Quakers, and go and sit with them. There still remained in me something of the favourable notion about Quakers that I had picked up as a child, and which the reading of William Penn had not been able to overcome.

But, naturally enough, with the work I was doing in the library, a stronger drive began to assert itself, and I was drawn much more imperatively to the Catholic Church. Finally the urge became so strong that I could not resist it. I called up my girl and told her that I was not coming out that weekend, and made up my mind to go to Mass for the first time in my life.

The first time in my life! That was true. I had lived for several years on the continent, I had been to Rome, I had been in and out of a thousand Catholic cathedrals and churches, and yet I had never heard Mass. If anything had ever been going on in the churches I visited, I had always fled, in wild Protestant panic.

I will not easily forget how I felt that day. First, there was this sweet, strong, gentle, clean urge in me which said: 'Go to Mass! Go to Mass!' It was something quite new and strange, this voice that seemed to prompt me, this firm, growing interior conviction of what I needed to do. It had a suavity, a simplicity about it that I could not easily account for. And when I gave into it, it did not exult over me, and trample me down in its raging haste to land on its prey, but it carried me forward serenely and with purposeful direction.

That does not mean that my emotions yielded to it altogether quietly. I was really still a little afraid to go to a Catholic church, of set purpose, with all the other people, and dispose myself in a pew, and lay myself open to the mysterious perils of that strange and powerful thing they called their 'Mass'.

God made it a very beautiful Sunday. And since it was the first time I had ever really spent a sober Sunday in New York, I was surprised at the clean, quiet atmosphere of the empty streets uptown. The sun was blazing bright. At the end of the street, as I came out of the front door, I could see a burst of green, and the blue river and the hills of Jersey on the other side.

Broadway was empty. A solitary trolley came speeding down in front of Barnard College and past the School of Journalism. Then, from the high, grey, expensive towers of the Rockefeller Church, huge bells began to boom. It served very well for the 11 o'clock Mass at the little brick Church of Corpus Christi, hidden behind Teachers College on 121st Street.

How bright the little building seemed. Indeed, it was quite new. The sun shone on the clean bricks. People were going in the wide open door, into the cool darkness and, all at once, all the churches of Italy and France came back to me. The richness and fullness of the atmosphere of Catholicism that I had not been able to avoid apprehending and loving as a child, came back to me with a rush: but now I was to enter into it fully for the first time. So far, I had known nothing but the outward surface.

It was a gay, clean church, with big plain windows and white columns and pilasters and a well-lighted, simple sanctuary. Its style was a trifle eclectic, but much less perverted with incongruities than the average Catholic church in America. It had a kind of a 17th-century, oratorian character about it, though with a sort of American colonial tinge of simplicity. The blend was effective and original: but although all this affected me, without my thinking about it, the thing

129

that impressed me most was that the place was full, absolutely full. It was full not only of old ladies and broken-down gentlemen with one foot in the grave, but of men and women and children young and old – especially young: people of all classes, and all ranks on a solid foundation of working men and women and their families.

I found a place that I hoped would be obscure, over on one side, in the back, and went to it without genuflecting, and knelt down. As I knelt, the first thing I noticed was a young girl, very pretty too, perhaps 15 or 16, kneeling straight up and praying quite seriously. I was very much impressed to see that someone who was young and beautiful could with such simplicity make prayer the real and serious and principal reason for going to church. She was clearly kneeling that way because she meant it, not in order to show off, and she was praying with an absorption which, though not the deep recollection of a saint, was serious enough to show that she was not thinking at all about the other people who were there.

What a revelation it was, to discover so many ordinary people in a place together, more conscious of God than of one another: not there to show off their hats or their clothes, but to pray, or at least to fulfil a religious obligation, not a human one…

Since it was summer time, the 11 o'clock Mass was a Low Mass: but I had not come expecting to hear music. Before I knew it, the priest was in the sanctuary with the two altar boys, and was busy at the altar with something or other which I could not see very well, but the people were praying by themselves, and I was engrossed and absorbed in the thing as a whole: the business at the altar and the presence of the people. And still I had not got rid of my fear. Seeing the late-comers hastily genuflecting before entering the pew, I realized my omission, and got the idea that people had spotted me for a pagan and were just waiting for me to miss a few more genuflections before throwing me out or, at least, giving me looks of reproof.

Soon we all stood up. I did not know what it was for. The priest was at the other end of the altar, and, as I afterwards learnt, he was reading the Gospel. And then the next thing I knew there was someone in the pulpit.

It was a young priest, perhaps not much over 33 or 34 years old. His face was rather ascetic and thin, and its asceticism was heightened with a note of intellectuality by his horn-rimmed glasses, although he was only one of the assistants, and he did not consider himself an intellectual, nor did anyone else apparently consider him so. But anyway, that was the impression he made on me: and his sermon, which was simple enough, did not belie it.

It was not long: but to me it was very interesting to hear this young man quietly telling the people in language that was plain, yet tinged with scholastic terminology, about a point in Catholic Doctrine. How clear and solid the doctrine was: for behind those words you felt the full force not only of scripture but of centuries of a unified and continuous and consistent tradition. And above all, it was a vital tradition: there was nothing studied or antique about it. These words, this terminology, this doctrine, and these convictions fell from the lips of the young priest as something that was most intimately part of his own life. What was more, I sensed that the people were familiar with it all, and that it was also, in due proportion, part of their life also: it was just as much integrated into their spiritual organism as the air they breathed or the food they ate worked into their blood and flesh.

What was he saying? That Christ was the Son of God. That, in him, the second Person of the Holy Trinity, God, had assumed a human nature, a human body and soul, and had taken flesh and dwelt among us, full of grace and truth: and that this man, whom men called the Christ, was God. He was both man and God: two natures hypostatically united in one Person or suppositum, one individual who was a divine Person, having assumed to himself a human nature. And his works were the works of God: his acts were the acts of God. He loved us: God, and walked among us: God, and died for us on the Cross, God of God, light of light, true God of true God.

Jesus Christ was not simply a man, a good man, a great man, the greatest prophet, a wonderful healer, a saint: he was something that made all such trivial words pale into irrelevance. He was God. But nevertheless he was not merely a spirit without a true body, God hiding under a visionary body: he was also truly a man, born of the flesh of the most pure Virgin, formed of her flesh by the Holy Spirit. And what he did, in that flesh, on earth, he did not only as man but as God. He loved us as God, he suffered and died for us, God.

And how did we know? Because it was revealed to us in the scriptures and confirmed by the teaching of the church and of the powerful unanimity of Catholic Tradition from the First Apostles, from the first Popes and the early Fathers, on down through the Doctors of the Church and the great scholastics, to our own day. *De Fide Divina.* If you believed it, you would receive light to grasp it, to understand it in some measure. If you did not believe it, you would never understand: it would never be anything but scandal or folly.

And no one can believe these things merely by wanting to, of his own volition. Unless he receive grace, an actual light and impulsion of the mind and will from God, he cannot even make an act of living faith. It is God Who gives us faith, and no one cometh to Christ unless the Father draweth him.

I wonder what would have happened in my life if I had been given this grace in the days when I had almost discovered the Divinity of Christ in the ancient mosaics of the churches of Rome. What scores of self-murdering and Christ-murdering sins would have been avoided – all the filth I had plastered upon his image in my soul during those last five years that I had been scourging and crucifying God within me?

It is easy to say, after it all, that God had probably foreseen my infidelities and had never given me the grace in those days because he saw how I would waste and despise it: and perhaps that rejection would have been my ruin. For there is no doubt that one of the reasons why grace is not given to souls is because they have so hardened their wills in greed and cruelty and selfishness that their refusal of it would only harden them more... But now I had been beaten into the semblance of some kind of humility by misery and confusion and perplexity and secret, interior fear, and my ploughed soul was better ground for the reception of good seed.

The sermon was what I most needed to hear that day. When the Mass of the Catechumens was over, I, who was not even a catechumen, but only a blind and deaf and dumb pagan as weak and dirty as anything that ever came out of the darkness of Imperial Rome or Corinth or Ephesus, was not able to understand anything else.

It all became completely mysterious when the attention was refocused on the altar. When the silence grew more and more profound, and little bells began to ring, I got scared again and, finally, genuflecting hastily on my left knee, I hurried out of the church in the middle of the most important part of the Mass. But it was just as well. In a way, I suppose I was responding to a kind of liturgical instinct that told me I did not belong there for the celebration of the Mysteries as such. I had no idea what took place in them: but the fact was that Christ, God, would be visibly present on the altar in the Sacred Species. And although he was there, yes, for love of me: yet he was there in his power and his might, and what was I? What was on my soul? What was I in his sight?

132

It was liturgically fitting that I should kick myself out at the end of the Mass of the Catechumens, when the ordained *ostiarii* should have been there to do it. Anyway, it was done.

Now I walked leisurely down Broadway in the sun, and my eyes looked about me at a new world. I could not understand what it was that had happened to make me so happy, why I was so much at peace, so content with life for I was not yet used to the clean savour that comes with an actual grace – indeed, there was no impossibility in a person's hearing and believing such a sermon and being justified, that is, receiving sanctifying grace in his soul as a habit, and beginning, from that moment, to live the divine and supernatural life for good and all. But that is something I will not speculate about.

All I know is that I walked in a new world. Even the ugly buildings of Columbia were transfigured in it, and everywhere was peace in these streets designed for violence and noise. Sitting outside the gloomy little Childs restaurant at 111th Street, behind the dirty, boxed bushes, and eating breakfast, was like sitting in the Elysian Fields.

Thomas Merton, *The Seven Storey Mountain*

Chiune Sugihara

A Japanese Schindler

The German industrialist Oskar Schindler (1908–74) is rightly remembered for saving thousands of Jewish lives during the Second World War. Among less-publicized heroes was the Japanese Consul General in Lithuania Chiune Sugihara (1900–86) and his wife Yukiko (1913–). In 1940 Sugihara defied the direct order of the Japanese Foreign Ministry, which had forbidden him to give travel documents to anyone who did not possess an onward visa from Japan. He and his wife knew that this action might cost them their lives and the lives of their children. They nevertheless wrote and signed thousands of transit visas which would enable Polish Jews who had escaped into Lithuania to continue their journey eastwards through the Soviet Union and Japan and thus escape the German invasion of Lithuania in the following year.

For 29 days from 31 July to 28 August 1940 Chiune and Yukiko Sugihara sat writing and signing visas – over 300 each day. Chiune Sugihara did not stop to eat – his wife brought him sandwiches and at the end of each day she massaged his hands when he could no longer write. People were standing in front of the consulate day and night. When some began climbing the compound wall Sugihara came out to calm them down and assure them that he would do his best to help them all. Hundreds of applicants became thousands as he worked to grant as many visas as possible before being obliged to close the consulate and leave Lithuania for Germany. Consul Sugihara continued issuing documents from his train window until it departed for Berlin. As the train pulled out of the station he gave the visa stamp to a refugee who was able to use it to save more Jewish lives.

Despite his disobedience, the Japanese government found Sugihara's skills useful for the remainder of the war, but in 1945 he was dismissed from the diplomatic service. Once a rising star in the Japanese Foreign Service, Sugihara found work as a part-time translator and interpreter and then as the manager of an export company.

After the war Chiune Sugihara never mentioned his extraordinary deed. It was not until 1969 that he was discovered by a man he had helped to save. Hundreds of others then came forward and testified to the Yad Vashem Martyrs' Remembrance Authority in Jerusalem. In 1985 Chiune Sugihara was recognized as 'Righteous Among the Nations' – Israel's highest honour. It is estimated that there may be as many as 40,000 people who owe their lives to the actions of Chiune and Yukiko Sugihara.

When asked why he had defied his government Mr Sugihara liked to give two reasons: 'They were human beings and they needed help. I'm glad I found the strength to make the decision to give it to them.' He was also fond of saying, 'I may have had to disobey my government, but if I had not done so I would have been disobeying God.'

Ron Greene, *Visas for Life: The Remarkable Story of Chiune and Yukiko Sugihara*

'Weary' Dunlop

The Christ of the Burma Road

Sir Edward 'Weary' Dunlop (1907–93) was a surgeon in the Australian army during the Second World War. About two years after enlisting he was posted to Indonesia and was in Java when the Japanese took control of the island in 1942. In this extract from *Weary: The Life of Sir Edward Dunlop*, Sue Ebury describes an example of the heroism which characterized 'Weary' Dunlop's care for the sick. The wounded prisoners were subsequently taken from Java to Thailand where their Japanese captors forced them to work on the construction of a railway from West Thailand into Burma. 'Weary' Dunlop ministered to the sick in appalling conditions and was described as the 'Christ of the Burma Road'. He was regarded as a national hero at the time of his death and his ashes were scattered over the Burma railway by Australian Prime Minister Paul Keating.

Captain Nakazawa, who seemed to have acquired complete responsibility for the hospital, became increasingly 'trying'. Finally, early on the morning of Friday 17 April, he clashed violently with Weary over the division of patients and staff: Weary and a few staff were to stay with the more seriously ill, the rest of the patients and medical staff would be removed immediately to prison camp 'the same… as other soldiers'. They were to be sorted into three categories: lying, sitting and walking cases. Weary protested at the inclusion of a group 'whose lives would be endangered by movement'. Nakazawa contemptuously brushed aside the lists and stamped off with his escort to inspect some 10 surgical patients in the resuscitation ward.

Weary led him across to the two boys with shattered faces who had been blinded by the mine explosion. Nakazawa motioned a guard towards Bill Griffiths. From a nearby bed, John Denman saw the guard 'put one up the spout'.

Weary moved swiftly between Griffiths and the rifle as the guard, yelling threateningly, thrust the bayonet towards the motionless man in the bed. Griffiths knew none of this – only sensed danger – before Weary's voice rang out: 'If you are going to do that, you must go through me first.' He glared at Nakazawa, who moved his gaze after a few tense moments and gestured towards a paraplegic. Without taking his eyes off the Japanese, Weary placed himself between this patient and the soldiers. The ward was still, the paraplegics' eyes dark with fright in their sweating faces. It seemed a long time before the staff captain moved on, striking contemptuously the legs of other patients: 'Man walk.'

Griffiths was a sitting patient, the first blind boy a walking one. Nakazawa refused to look at X-ray film and strolled round the ward; classifications were arrived at by throwing back the blankets and inspecting men's legs, occasionally feeling their calves.

Weary now weighed into him about the rights of medical personnel under the Geneva Convention, but he waved this aside airily... Their conversation became increasingly heated on Nakazawa's part, steely with controlled anger on Weary's, who told Nakazawa that the British, Dutch and Australian governments would ultimately hold him responsible for such illegal actions, and he had no doubt he would be hanged.

'Good!' spat Nakazawa. 'Now you will lead the march to gaol.'

Sue Ebury, *Weary: The Life of Sir Edward Dunlop*

Mother Teresa of Calcutta

Following Jesus

In 1946 the future Mother Teresa (1910–97) was a young nun in Calcutta, teaching in a middle-class school. She was happy in her work and, when she set off for Darjeeling to make her retreat, she had no idea that she was about to experience a Second Journey which would lead to international acclaim. Malcolm Muggeridge recounts the life-changing experience in *Something Beautiful for God*.

In Skopje in Yugoslavia I lived at home with my parents; we children used to go to a non-Catholic school but we also had very good priests who were helping the boys and the girls to follow their vocation according to the call of God. It was then that I first knew I had a vocation to the poor.

At the beginning, between 12 and 18, I didn't want to become a nun. We were a very happy family. But when I was 18, I decided to leave my home and become a nun. I wanted to be a missionary, I wanted to go out and give the life of Christ to the people in the missionary countries. At that time some missionaries had gone to India from Yugoslavia. They told me the Loreto nuns were doing work in Calcutta and other places. I offered myself to go out to the Bengal Mission, and they sent me to India in 1929.

I took the first vows in Loreto in 1931. Then in 1937 I took final vows in Loreto. At Loreto I was in charge of a school in the Bengali department. At that time many of the girls that are now with me were girls in school. I was teaching them.

In 1946 I was going to Darjeeling, to make my retreat. It was in that train, I heard the call to give up all and follow Jesus into the slums to serve him among the poorest of the poor. I knew it was his will, and that I had to follow him. There was no doubt that it was going to be his work. But I waited for the decision of the church.

I had first to apply to the Archbishop of Calcutta. Then, with his approval, the Mother General of the Loreto nuns gave me permission to write to Rome. I had to do this because I was a nun who had taken final vows and nuns cannot be allowed to leave the convent. I wrote to the Holy Father, Pope Pius XII, and by return post I got the answer on the 12th of April. He said that I could go out and be an unenclosed nun under obedience to the Archbishop of Calcutta.

Malcolm Muggeridge, *Something Beautiful for God*

Ruby Turpin

Revelation

Most of the short stories of the American writer Flannery O'Connor (1925–64) are set in the Southern United States. In *Revelation* she presents Ruby Turpin and her husband Claud who are small-time farmers. Ruby has been attacked and insulted in the doctor's surgery by a young woman who calls her a wart hog! Back home on the farm, Ruby goes to the pig parlour and screams out her rage to God or to anyone who will listen. The results are very unexpected.

The pig parlour commanded a view of the back pasture where their 20 beef cows were gathered around the hay-bales Claud and the boy had put out. The freshly cut pasture sloped down to the highway. Across it was their cotton field and beyond that a dark green dusty wood which they owned as well. The sun was behind the wood, very red, looking over the paling of trees like a farmer inspecting his own hogs.

'Why me?' she rumbled. 'It's no trash around here, black or white, that I haven't given to. And break my back to the bone every day working. And do for the church.'

She appeared to be the right size woman to command the arena before her. 'How am I a hog?' she demanded. 'Exactly how am I like them?' and she jabbed the stream of water at the shoats. 'There was plenty of trash there. It didn't have to be me.

'If you like trash better, go get yourself some trash then,' she railed. 'You could have made me trash. Or a nigger. If trash is what you wanted why didn't you make me trash?' She shook her fist with the hose in it and a watery snake appeared momentarily in the air. 'I could quit working and take it easy and be filthy,' she growled. 'Lounge about the sidewalks all day drinking root beer. Dip snuff and spit in every puddle and have it all over my face. I could be nasty.

'Or you could have made me a nigger. It's too late for me to be a nigger,' she said with deep sarcasm, 'but I could act like one. Lay down in the middle of the road and stop traffic. Roll on the ground.'

In the deepening light everything was taking on a mysterious hue. The pasture was growing a peculiar glassy green and the streak of highway had turned lavender. She braced herself for a final assault and this time her voice rolled out over the pasture. 'Go on,' she yelled, 'call me a hog! Call me a hog again. From hell. Call me a wart hog from hell. Put that bottom rail on top. There'll still be a top and a bottom!'

A garbled echo returned to her.

A final surge of fury shook her and she roared, 'Who do you think you are?'

The colour of everything, field and crimson sky, burnt for a moment with a transparent intensity. The question carried over the pasture and across the highway and the cotton field and returned to her clearly like an answer from beyond the wood.

She opened her mouth but no sound came out of it.

A tiny truck, Claud's, appeared on the highway, heading rapidly out of sight. Its gears scraped thinly. It looked like a child's toy. At any moment a bigger truck might smash into it and scatter Claud's and the niggers' brains all over the road.

Mrs Turpin stood there, her gaze fixed on the highway, all her muscles rigid, until in five or six minutes the truck reappeared, returning. She waited until it had had time to turn into their own road. Then like a monumental statue coming to life, she bent her head slowly and gazed, as if through the very heart of mystery, down into the pig parlour at the hogs. They had settled all in one corner around the old sow who was grunting softly. A red glow suffused them. They appeared to pant with a secret life.

Until the sun slipped finally behind the tree line, Mrs Turpin remained there with her gaze bent to them as if she were absorbing some abysmal life-giving knowledge. At last she lifted her head. There was only a purple streak in the sky, cutting through a field of crimson and leading, like an extension of the highway, into the descending dusk. She raised her hands from the side of the pen in a gesture hieratic and profound. A visionary light settled in her eyes. She saw the streak as a vast swinging bridge extending upward from the earth through a field of living fire. Upon it a vast horde of souls were rumbling toward heaven. There were whole companies of white-trash,

141

clean for the first time in their lives, and bands of black niggers in white robes, and battalions of freaks and lunatics shouting and clapping and leaping like frogs. And bringing up the end of the procession was a tribe of people whom she recognized at once as those who, like herself and Claud, had always had a little of everything and the God-given wit to use it right. She leant forward to observe them closer. They were marching behind the others with great dignity, accountable, as they had always been for good order and common sense and respectable behaviour. They alone were on key. Yet she could see by their shocked and altered faces that even their virtues were being burnt away. She lowered her hands and gripped the rail of the hog pen, her eyes small but fixed unblinkingly on what lay ahead. In a moment the vision faded but she remained where she was, immobile.

At length she got down and turned off the faucet and made her slow way on the darkening path to the house. In the woods around her the invisible cricket choruses had struck up, but what she heard were the voices of the souls climbing upward into the starry field and shouting hallelujah.

Flannery O'Connor, *Revelation*, from *The Complete Stories*

Michael Bourdeaux

Religious Persecution

In 1964 Michael Bourdeaux (1934–) was a young Anglican priest living with his family in a London parish. Michael had studied at Moscow University and was becoming increasingly concerned at the plight of Christians in the USSR. He was unable to obtain concrete information until a letter from two Ukrainian Christians describing heartbreaking persecution fell into his hands. In *Risen Indeed* he describes the astonishing series of events which confirmed his suspicions and led him to abandon the security of parish ministry to found the Keston Institute, which monitors freedom of religion and researches religious affairs in Communist and post-Communist countries.

There was serious, perhaps increasing, persecution of the church in the Soviet Union. Of that I was sure. But it was virtually impossible to uncover details of it. I had gone to Moscow for a second visit, three weeks as an interpreter at the British Exhibition in 1961, but had learnt scarcely anything new. People were as terrified to talk as they had been during my student year. Stalin had been dead for less than a decade still. Now at the beginning of 1964 I had no money to go to Moscow again and even if I had there was no guarantee the expense would be justified.

As I was thinking all this through, God's timing was perfect once again. An envelope arrived containing a short duplicated letter on green paper, an English translation of a letter from a Ukrainian Christian. It was accompanied by a note from my old friend and teacher at Oxford, the late Dr Nicholas Zernov. He said a document had come to him from a school-teacher friend in Paris, a girl of Russian origin who had recently been in Moscow. There she had met some Orthodox Christians from the distant west of the Soviet Union who had given her an appeal to the outside world, begging people to intervene with the Soviet government and prevent the imminent closure of the Pochaev Monastery, one of the greatest Christian shrines of the country. Dr Zernov could not vouch for the authenticity of the letter, nor did he know whether it should be publicized, but he had translated it so that at least it could be shown privately to some interested people.

The appeal recounted heartbreaking persecutions: monks beaten up by the KGB, subjected to humiliating medical examinations, thrown out onto the streets; if they came back into their quarters from which the local authorities were trying to evict them, they were rounded up, pushed into lorries, taken hundreds of kilometres into the countryside, far from the nearest house, and just dumped. The authors wrote with absolute simplicity, just listing the facts to which they claimed to be eyewitnesses. There were two names at the end, Varavva and Pronina, surnames unadorned even by an initial.

Moved by what I read, I had the gut feeling that I was for the first time in my life hearing the true voices of the persecuted church. But what should I do? With whom should I talk? By the 1980s there were reported to be as many as 150 missionary societies, large and small, setting out in some way to help Christians in Eastern Europe. But except for a handful, they were all of very recent provenance. The two or three which did already exist (the Slavic Gospel Association in Chicago, Slaviska Missionen in Stockholm, Aid to the Church in Need in Belgium) had so little work in Britain that their existence was unknown to me during the 1980s.

If the words of the document were true, then the persecution had become much worse, far more physical and brutal, than I had imagined. There was clearly more to do than just to write. I really had to become more personally involved and see whether there was something I could actively do to help. It was now a priority to return to the Soviet Union.

1964 provided not one but two opportunities. First in April I managed to obtain a very cheap trip with a group of teachers. On the few occasions that I could break free from the group, conversations were inhibited by the all-pervading fear. I talked to some warm and wonderful people, but on new information my sheet of paper remained blank. Hardly was I back from this than an invitation came to accompany a group of Americans as leader – a free trip and an offer I could not refuse. It was on this second visit in August that God wrenched the steering wheel out of my grasp.

On my first evening in Moscow I went to see some old friends. They were delighted to see me unexpectedly a second time that year and immediately began answering the questions I had put four months previously. 'It's providential you've come back again. The persecution has become so much worse since you were last here in April. By then we had heard rumours that it was very bad in the provinces, but now it's started to affect us right here in Moscow. Do you know that Church of St Peter and St Paul, that beautiful one standing on its own in the centre of a square? Well, they demolished it last week, despite protests. A ring of people standing round it after the authorities had closed it didn't stop the soldiers moving in, fixing a dynamite charge and detonating it. You'd better go and see for yourself.'

I took a taxi at once, so that I could be there in order to catch the last of the daylight. There were several churches of St Peter and Paul in Moscow, but my friends had told me the exact location of this one. I stopped the taxi short of the square, so that no suspicions should be aroused, and I walked on alone. From my student days I remembered the beautiful church with its one central large and four smaller surrounding cupolas. But now the great square was empty, except for a circular wooden fence about 12 feet high, totally blocking any view of what lay inside it. I was afraid to go too close, feeling sure that the square must be under constant observation. From a slight hill up one side street I could just see some twisted metal on top of a pile of masonry, the remains of what had been the crosses on the cupolas. My attention was attracted by two dumpy black figures across the road. Standing right by the fence, one was trying to hoist the other up by her elbows to peer in or over – not very successfully, I guessed, in view of the girth and short stature of both. But now I could see the point of the exercise. There was a chink between two of the boards forming the fence and this became broader the higher it went.

I must talk to these women, I said to myself; they could tell me more details of what has happened. I waited until they had left the square, followed them quietly for 100 yards, caught up with them and said, 'Skazhitye, pozhaluista... Tell me, please, do you know what's happened here?'

They jumped back, terrified as I thought. 'Who are you?'

I did not know what to say, but I answered: 'I'm a foreigner, just come to find out more about the church here in the Soviet Union – but if you're afraid to talk to me I'll leave you alone.'

'No you won't. You're a foreigner? We need you.' As she said this, one of them put her hand forward and placed it firmly on my shoulder. 'Come with us, we need to talk to you.'

I followed discreetly behind them, not talking any more for fear of attracting attention. We walked, boarded a bus, then a tram. We were on the very edge of Moscow, where country villages, their little wooden houses nestling among the trees, were already being consumed by the square solid blocks of Khrushchev's new Moscow.

Ahead of me, the two women walked into an old wooden building and straight up a flight of stairs, where there was another woman just like them waiting.

'See what God has brought us – a young man from abroad', said one.

'Yes, but who are you really?' asked the other who had come in with me.

'I'm an Englishman. I used to study at Moscow University. I met many Christians here. Then recently I heard that the persecution of the church was getting worse in the Soviet Union. I decided I must come back to see if this were true and whether I could do anything at all to help my Christian friends.'

'Wonderful, wonderful... but why precisely did you come?' asked the third, the woman whose flat this was.

'I received a document...'

'What document?'

'It was from Ukraine, from Pochaev, sent via a schoolteacher from Paris.'

'Who wrote it?'

'Two women...'

'What were their names?'

'Mm... Varavva and – oh, yes – Pronina.'

Suddenly the silence was total. I wondered if I'd said something wrong. Then a deep sob from the third woman. 'My guests... this is Feodosia Varavva.'

'Yes, I wrote that appeal. This is Pronina who signed it, too.'

'When we'd written it we came to Moscow, nearly 1,300 kilometres, to find a foreigner. We searched for days unsuccessfully, but eventually we met a French school-teacher who happened to speak Russian. She took the letter for us.'

'I never met her,' I said, 'but I got it through a friend a few weeks later. I came back to find out more.'

'It was over six months ago that we last came to Moscow. But

146

since then so much has happened. Things have got much worse. They're putting our monks into psychiatric prisons. We wrote several new documents and so did the monks themselves. We arrived here this afternoon to look for another foreigner, but before we had time to start our search, our friend here sent us out to see the terrible things which have been happening in Moscow itself. That's where we met you.'

From that moment the direction of my life was set. I could see that I had to find some way of serving the persecuted church full time. As there were no existing organizations I knew doing this, it would mean giving up personal security and branching out on my own. Perhaps 30 was the right age for this, yet my responsibility to provide for my family was daunting. I felt totally impotent then to respond to the hand on my shoulder, to the commission, 'We need you.' How could I, a lone voice who scarcely had a voice, respond to the needs of millions of suffering Christians? Yet I could never even contemplate ignoring such a call.

Michael Bourdeaux, *Risen Indeed*

Charles Colson

Prison Sentence

From 1969 to 1973 Charles Colson (1931–) served as Special Counsel to Richard Nixon, Republican President of the United States from 1969 to 1974. Although Colson was known as the White House 'hatchet man', he was not directly involved in the attempted break-in at the Democratic Party headquarters in the Watergate building in Washington. Watergate led to Nixon's resignation – the only way the President could avoid impeachment. In 1974, however, Colson pleaded guilty to a Watergate-related charge and served seven months of a one-to-three-year sentence in Maxwell Prison, Alabama. He had become a Christian the previous year. In his autobiography, *Born Again*, Colson describes his initial experience of imprisonment in Fort Holabird high-security detention facility in the Baltimore–Washington area, where he was required to remain as a potential witness in the event of President Nixon's impeachment. Watergate and its aftermath marked the beginning of an extraordinary Second Journey for Colson and his wife Patty. His experiences in prison and his conversion to Christianity led to a worldwide mission to improve the circumstances of prisoners, and the foundation of Prison Fellowship Ministries and the associated organizations, Justice Fellowship and Neighbours Who Care.

> The Army-style barracks was as depressing inside as it appeared on the outside. Paint was peeling from the walls, steam pipes ran down the long corridor through the centre of the building which was illuminated only by dim light bulbs dangling every 30 feet from the ceiling. A stale, greasy odour seeped from a tiny kitchen on the right. A small dining room was on the left immediately inside the hole-riddled front screen door.
>
> The chief deputy led me to the Control Room, a glassed-in office in the centre of the first-floor corridor. Processing began: more

finger-prints, Polaroid snapshots, inspection of my luggage and person effects, a thorough shakedown for drugs and contraband, and the filling out of endless forms.

'What is your number?' the deputy asked.

'I don't have a number.'

'What do you mean you don't have a number? Every federal prisoner has a number.'

'Maybe you're supposed to give me one, sir.'

'Those people in Washington,' grumbled the deputy. 'Don't they know what kind of an establishment I'm running here?'

Then I made the mistake of asking, 'I don't. Can you tell me something about this place?'

'No! The important thing for you to remember is that you remember nothing. No one knows this place exists. You will meet some very unusual men here. Don't discuss your business with them and don't ask them about theirs. When you leave here forget you ever met them. You will only know them by their first names anyway. Obey the rules and mind your own business.'

I was then turned over to Joe, a swarthy man with shaggy black hair who spoke little English. He showed me to my room, a 9-by-12 cubicle tucked under the eaves on the second floor, furnished with a maple bed, a battered dresser, and a small wooden desk. The desktop was etched with graffiti by the generations who had passed through this room – from young Army lieutenants to federal prisoners. The temperature was over 100 degrees. Baltimore was in the grip of the worst hear wave of the year.

As other inmates drifted by, Joe introduced me. Pete, a young Italian, reported that he, too, had been a Marine; Angie, an outgoing, genial sort, was from New York's 'Little Italy'. Pat and Andy, I learnt, were ex-syndicate operatives and central figures in a big narcotics ring. I was told that two young men named Eddie and Jimmy were kept apart from the others for the good reason that both were ex-Baltimore policemen. Former cops and gangsters crammed into the same little building made a strange mix.

There was Mike, a muscular brute with long, flowing blonde hair and an unmistakable Boston accent. There were others representing a variety of nationalities: Italians, Cubans, Frenchmen, including one whose hairy body was colourfully tattooed from top to bottom.

When I asked Joe how to lock my door, he leant back and roared with laughter. 'No locks here; just one happy family.' I had not seen

149

the movie *The Godfather* – or his term 'family' would have been even more unnerving.

There was one man at Holabird I had known before – Herb Kalmbach, the President's personal lawyer, who had surrendered the week before I did and like me was awaiting his turn to testify at the impeachment hearings. Joe pointed out his room. When I looked in, Herb, a tall, urbane, and handsome man in his fifties, bounded from his chair. 'Am I glad to see you! Not here, of course, but it's so great to greet an old friend.' It was the renewal of a friendship that was to become important to us both.

I took the deputy's warning seriously and suppressed my curiosity about the other inmates. With no facilities for exercise, time dragged. The heat was oppressive… Jimmy the young ex-cop who was in prison for taking bribes, helped lift the oppressiveness with his chatter, particularly at meals.

During dinner one night little Pete was quite noisy, his high-pitched voice reverberating through the room that 20 of us were crowded into. Jimmy whispered to me, 'Don't fool with him; he goes off his rocker once in a while. He was one of the top narcotics men in New York.'

'That little kid?' I asked.

'That little kid', Jimmy responded, 'was one of the bosses. They say his testimony will bring down 100 people. Leave him alone. He would think nothing of putting one of those knives right through your gut.' Jimmy nodded to the large bread knife in the centre of the table, glistening in the late-afternoon sun. Jimmy pointed to Mike. 'He was one of their "hit men", you know.'

'That one who never says anything? The big guy from Boston?' Mike across the room ate without expression, his eyes cold and steel-hard.

'I thought you knew all about Mike,' he continued. 'You're from Boston, aren't you? It was a big thing when he was pinched. They say he's knocked off 28.'

I stared at Jimmy in disbelief. 'People – 28 people?'

'That's what a hit man does, you know. Kills people.' Jimmy's tone indicated I was not with it.

I had trouble suppressing a grin. The hit man and the hatchet man – what a vaudeville team Mike and I would make! Serious again I asked, 'Why isn't anyone with 28 murders on death row somewhere?'

Jimmy shrugged. 'They've got him here to protect him. He's more valuable to the government alive than dead.'

While trying to keep from staring at Mike, I began to long for a cell with a lock on it.

As the days dragged by, visits by Patty and the brothers were my faith strengtheners, even though the visiting conditions were awkward and restrictive. It was especially hard for Patty and me – the long days of separation interrupted by a few hours of make-believe normality, one eye always on the clock, then the pain of parting. Yet slowly over the months our conversations about faith had become more meaningful. We were making progress in our understanding of the Bible, but still I held back from asking her to pray with me.

One day late in July after a tense visit, Patty wrote me a letter: 'Darling, I prayed most of the way home for both of us and I think it might be nice if from now on we prayed together, before leaving each other in the evening...'

I received the letter the next day and wanted to shout for joy! All that night I felt that tingling sensation, the worth-it-all feeling I had known before in some of my darkest hours. From that day forward we held hands and prayed aloud together every time she visited, whether in public or private. This spiritual unity would sustain us through harder days to come.

Charles Colson, *Born Again*

John Bradburne

Faithful to the End

The life of John Bradburne (1921–79) was a ceaseless quest for God which took him from England to India and Israel and finally to Zimbabwe, where he found his true home among men and women suffering from leprosy. Bradburne's biography, *Strange Vagabond of God* by his Jesuit friend John Dove, includes a description of the daily routine at Mtemwa camp as observed by another Jesuit, David Gibbs. As the Zimbabwe war for independence gathered momentum it became increasingly dangerous for John to remain at Mtemwa as a solitary white man, but he refused to consider leaving. In September 1979 John Bradburne was abducted by guerrillas and tried on the charge of being 'an informer'. Despite the fact that the case was dismissed John Bradburne was shot while attempting to return to Mtemwa. His murderers have never been brought to justice.

John's day began in a sense at dusk with the chanting of the evening office in his hut. The night hours were his, unless there was a death or a very sick leper in the compound, to be spent in prayer and meditation and, 'When the Muse came', in writing poetry. In the early hours of the morning he would run a mile, 'just to keep fit', have a quick wash in the plastic basin outside his front door, and then set off for the compound to open the church in preparation for the morning communion service. A priest would visit Mtemwa each week for Mass and on the other days John would hold the morning service, reading from the Bible, reciting the morning prayers, administering the Blessed Sacrament and playing the organ.

The voices die away, the organ stops, the doors are opened and the lepers file out led by 'Baba' (father) John carrying a basket. As the lepers come out of the chapel, having just received the Body of Christ, they stop to chat to 'Baba' John. Some just say 'hello', others ask for medicine for a headache, a cough, a cold, malaria, itching body or sore eyes. 'Baba' delves into his basket and produces a bottle, a tube, a few capsules, an ointment, a cream or just a few sweets for those who need cheering up. There is something for everybody. Spiritually fulfilled, materially helped, the lepers move off to their huts happy, cared for and at peace with God and with each other. Some walk, others crawl and still others are wheeled away in wheelchairs.

After the last leper has gone to his hut, 'Baba' John puts away his basket, closes the harmonium, shuts the church and makes his way slowly down the avenue towards his hut to have his breakfast.

John lived on bread, cheese, coffee, lactogen (powdered milk), orange juice and the occasional egg, giving away most of what he was given to the lepers. 'After all,' he said, 'the lepers need these things more than I do.' He didn't believe in saving anything. The lepers were always needing something and John was always receiving just what they needed at the time they needed it, or else money would find its way to Mtemwa in time to buy what was wanted in the compound. 'Help', John was fond of saying, 'always comes from somebody.' He received clothing, food, medicines, and numerous of other gifts which he used to make the lives of the lepers more bearable – snuff, pipes, sweets, sacks of nuts, powdered milk and fresh meat. All sorts of gifts came from all sorts of people – all were passed on to the lepers and all were used to help them.

Once breakfast was over, John went back to the compounds for his 'rounds'. He visited every leper every day just to make sure that all was well. If anybody needed any help, John was there to give it. He would bath those who needed bathing, build fires, make beds, change dressings and give out whatever he had received or bought for his people. At the beginning of the 'round' his wheelbarrow was always full – full of sugar, tea, sweets, onions, vegetables, nuts, tomatoes, bread, meat – anything he had to give out. By the time he reached the chapel for the midday Angelus, the barrow was empty and each leper had been helped in some small way.

After a period of quiet in the presence of the Lord, the afternoon would be spent in much the same way – cutting firewood, cleaning out the cattle grid, collecting reeds for making hats, making tea or coffee for the sick or just popping in to chat and cheer up the people. Once or twice a week John would go up to the village to do the shopping for the lepers. For those really ill or dying, John would buy something special at the village – perhaps fresh oranges, an egg or two, an extra portion of milk or a pint of 'real' milk. On his return from the shopping he would visit his 'special' patients – those seriously ill at the time – and help them to get their fire lit, bed made, pipe filled, coffee boiled or whatever other small tasks needed to be done. Sometime he would simply crouch on his haunches and chatter away, trying to help and encourage.

At a death John was always present to give comfort to the dying and to all the lepers who were losing a dear friend. In a small community like Mtemwa a death affects everybody very deeply and John helped the lepers, even those who had no beliefs, to see that death was, in most cases, a blessed relief from many years of suffering and the opening of the door to joy, peace and happiness.

At about four o'clock the bell rang for the saying of the rosary and evening prayers in the church – held early so as not to coincide with the lepers' evening meal at five o'clock. After the last leper had left the church, John would lock up, pop in to see anybody who might need help to settle down for the night and then make his way down the avenue back to his hut to spend the night alone with his God, singing, praying, writing or just sitting quietly in the presence of his Maker.

David Gibbs in *Strange Vagabond of God* **by John Dove**

Sheila Cassidy

Interrogation and Torture

In 1971 Dr Sheila Cassidy (1937–) resigned from her job in England to work in Santiago, Chile, where she found herself increasingly involved in the work of nuns and priests struggling for justice against a repressive military dictatorship. In 1975 Sheila was arrested for treating a wounded guerrilla, Nelson Gutierrez. In this extract from her best-selling autobiography, *Audacity to Believe*, she describes the first of several experiences of torture. Charges were never brought and, after 59 days of imprisonment, Sheila was expelled from the country.

I was told to get out of the car and was led stumbling across what I think was a courtyard. We paused as metal gates were opened and then slammed shut behind us. I was led into a room and without any further ado was ordered to remove my clothes.

I was incredulous. There must be some mistake. I told them quickly that I was a British doctor and that this would cause an international incident. Then came the reply that brought home to me the appalling truth of the reality of my situation for they said, and I quote

'Nuestra imagen en el exterior es tan mal que no nos importa.' – 'Our image in the exterior is so bad that we don't care.'

Again they told me to undress and, searching desperately for something to convince them that they could not do this to me I said, 'My father is an Air Vice Marshal,' but there was no reply.

Frantically I said, 'I'm going to be a nun.' This brought a rapid response, 'You're not one, are you?' to which I replied, 'No.'

Again came the order to undress. Slowly I removed my sweater and could not bring myself to go further. Then I felt a rough hand grab my shirt and one of the buttons came off. Realizing that they meant what they said and wanting to avoid further manhandling I removed the remainder of my clothes. The handkerchief around my eyes was by this time a little loose and I saw that I was in a small room which contained a double metal bunk and a table and chair. On the wall hung a street plan of Santiago and crowded into the room, for it was quite small, were about five men in plain clothes and a woman.

They told me then to lie on the bed and quickly they secured me to the bottom half of the bunk, tying my wrists and ankles and upper arms and placing a wide band across my chest and abdomen. Then it began. I felt an electric shock pass through me and then another and another.

I made to scream, but found there was a gag in my mouth.

Then the questions began.

'Where did you treat Gutierrez?'

'Who asked you to treat him?'

[My brain was very clear and the implications of this question were immediately apparent: if they didn't know where I'd treated Nelson they didn't know of the involvement of the priests and nuns and perhaps they never need to know.]

'Arturo.'

'Where does he work?'

'The Hospital Salvador.' This was a hospital near my home and the only doctor I knew there was a woman.

'Why did they ask you?' Again I hesitated and again I felt the shocks. Mercifully the answer came: so logical that they were in no doubt.

'He was afraid.'

They changed tack. 'Where did you meet him?' That was more difficult. Where could I have met him and yet not have names to give away? The electricity spurred me on. 'At a party.' That fitted. Now they were on to him and soon they'd have him and with him all his friends.

'Where does he live?'

'I don't know.'

The sharp pain told me they were angry.

'You're lying.' O God, how could I tell them where he lived when he didn't exist? Again the pain, and again.

Frantically: 'He told me he had a beach house in Algarrobo. He invited me there.'

'Where?' They believed me. They could see it all: the soft lights, the music, the invitation for a weekend out of Santiago.

'Where?' Where indeed. I'd never been to Algarrobo, just passed it in the bus.

'I don't know. I never went. I don't go out with married men.'

Thwarted, they tried another tack.

'Where did you treat Gutierrez?'

'In a private house.' That at least was true.

'Who owned the house?'

'Miguel Rojas.'

'What does he do?'

'He's an architect.'

'Where does he live?'

'I don't know.' Again I knew their anger, and again, and again, as I tried desperately to think what to say.

'It was night. I didn't see the name of the street.'

'How did you get there?'

'I was taken by car.'

'What sort of a car?'

'A Peugeot.' (The convent car had been a Peugeot.)

'What colour?'

'White.'

'What colour was the upholstery?'

'Blue.'

I heard them repeat it: 'A white Peugeot. Blue upholstery.' Now they were getting somewhere. They began to look up Rojas in the telephone book and I heard them turn the pages in excitement.

'How did they contact you?' Dear God, was there no end to it?

'They phoned me.'

'Who phoned you?'

'The doctor phoned me.'

'What did he say?'

'He told me to wait at the garage on the corner of Vicuña Mackenna and Rancagua.' (Vicuña Mackenna is a main street near my house.)

'Who was in the car?'

'A man.'

'What did he look like?'

'He had a moustache.'

'What else?'

'I didn't notice.'

'What was his name?'

'I don't know. He didn't tell me.'

'Where did you go?'

'I don't know.' This wouldn't do and, the stepped-up current told me clearly that I must do better.

'Where did you go?'

'He told me not to look.'

'You must have looked. Women always look.' How right they were.

'I didn't. He told me not to. He said it wasn't in my interest to know where I was going.' This seemed plausible enough but they were determined.

'Which direction did the car take?' Quickly I thought and chose the direction that led furthest away from Helen's house.

'Towards the Central Station.'

'And then?'

'Below the station.'

'And?'

There was no answer. This was an area that I didn't know at all, a big highway leading out to the airport. There were residential areas on either side. Or were there? Was it only wasteland? I didn't know.

'Where did you turn off?'

So we must have turned off. But where.

'I don't know.'

This was the answer they didn't like and I knew it at once. I heard them looking at the map and they were obviously plotting my route. I heard the words '*Obispo Subercaseaux*' and latched on to them.

'Where did you turn?'

Mentally I tossed for it. 'Right.'

'What was the street called?'

'I don't know.'

'Of course you know.'

'*Obispo no sé cuánto.*' (Bishop something or other.)

'You said you couldn't see.' Dear God, was there no pleasing them?

'I think it was called Bishop something.'

'Bishop what?'

'I don't know.'

'You do know.'

'I don't.'

'You do.'

'I don't.' This was dicey. If I named the street they could prove me wrong and if I didn't it seemed they'd never stop. I stuck to my guns.

'*Obispo no sé cuánto.*'

They tried a different tack.

'What was the house like?'

'A big house.'

'What colour?'

'White.'

'What style?'

'Colonial.'

'What colour were the gates?'

This was money for jam. 'Black.'

'Sheet metal or railings?'

'Sheet metal.'

'Who was in the house?'

'Rojas.'

'Who else?'

'His wife.'

'Who else?'

'The maid.' There would have to be a maid. There always was.

'Who else?'

'Nobody.'

'What's the name of the street?' Again it began.

'I don't know.'

They shoved the gag in my mouth. 'Raise your fingers when you remember.' Again it came, wave after wave, and I raised my fingers.

'Well?'

'I'll take you there. I'll show you.'

'What's the name of the street?'

'I don't know but I'll show you.'

I had no plan but anything must be better than this. There could be no future in going to look for a house which didn't exist, but by now I could see no future, only a haze of pain from which I must escape.

Suddenly it stopped. A voice said, 'Untie her,' and I heard them move out.

I felt the bands on my wrists and ankles go slack and there was a new surge of pain as the circulation returned. I tried to sit up but couldn't lift my head. Gentle hands pulled me up and I sat blind and giddy on the edge of the bunk. They stood me up and caught me as I fell. I felt a chair pushed under me and then I heard a new voice.

This was a kind voice, educated and almost fatherly. 'Poor *gringa*,' it said. 'How do you feel?' For a moment I was overwhelmed with relief.

This must be a senior officer who had come to take me away to the consul.

'How did you get mixed up in this, *gringa*?'

'I was asked to by a friend.'

'A fine friend to let you in for this!'

I was silent.

'You were very stupid to get involved.'

This was a friendly man who thought I was a stupid foreigner and I said pathetically, 'I was a fool.' He was pleased. 'Poor, stupid *gringa*. But now you are going to help us, eh?' So that was it. I was being softened up. Anger gave me courage.

'Oh yes, I'll do anything. Anything to stop this.'

'Good. Good *gringa*.'

Suddenly he stopped and I felt him touch my chest. 'What's that scar, *gringa*?' Of course! The scar. I'd forgotten. In Chile many young people have valve lesions following rheumatic fever and undergo operations to free valves that are stuck together or replace ones that are badly damaged. My scar was the legacy of an operation on my sternum but it could just as well have been the result of cardiac surgery. I said as convincingly as I could, 'They operated on my heart.'

'What was wrong with it?' He was obviously shaken. Here was my way out. If they thought I had a bad heart they wouldn't give me the shocks again. But quickly: what could I say it had been? What operation would leave me without a murmur? My mind went blank and I couldn't think of a heart lesion which would leave no signs. Lamely I said, 'I was very young. I don't know.'

'What could the electricity do to you?'

This was hopeful. 'It could give me ventricular fibrillation.'

'What?'

'It could make my heart go very fast.'

'And?'

'It could kill me.'

There was a pause while he thought. Then he said '*Gringa*, you're lying. Get dressed. You'd better help us or you'll be in trouble.'

He went and the men who had helped me off the bed now handed me my clothes and helped me as I fumbled with buttons and hooks and shoes that I could not see. They were gentle and patient with me and, helpless and unseeing, I felt the contrast so great that they seemed like friends.

(It was only after my return to England that I learnt that the warmth of the friendly interrogator is part of a highly developed interrogation technique. After a session with aggressive interrogators, when the victim is shaken and demoralized, a new, apparently kindly 'father figure' is brought and the relaxation in defences so produced is often effective where the first method has failed.)

My captors led me out and I asked to go to the bathroom: they let me go but stood outside and when I went to drink from the tap shouted at me that I mustn't. (I learnt later that drinking after the electrical 'treatment' can cause convulsions.)

We went outside and it was cold. They removed the bandage and taped my eyes shut with scotch tape, so that I could no longer see even the ground I walked on. I was led across the yard and pushed into a car. The gates opened and the car turned out and I felt the bump as we went over the bridge and drove down towards the town.

Sheila Cassidy, *Audacity to Believe*

Nelson Mandela

Walking into Freedom

On 11 February 1990 Nelson Mandela (1918–) walked out of prison on South Africa's Robben Island at the age of 71, having been imprisoned since 1962. Mandela was embarking on a Second Journey which would take him to the presidency of his country and a role as an internationally respected statesman at an age when many people are firmly embarked on their Third and final Journey. Although Mandela had realized that his wife Winnie, along with members of the African National Congress (ANC) and the United Democratic Front (UDF), would meet him on his release from prison, he had not appreciated the extent to which the eyes of the world would be focused upon him. In Mandela's autobiography, *Long Walk to Freedom*, he describes the experience.

> I awoke on the day of my release after only a few hours' sleep at 4.30 a.m. 11 February was a cloudless, end-of-summer Cape Town day. I did a shortened version of my usual exercise regimen, washed and ate breakfast. I then telephoned a number of people from the ANC and the UDF in Cape Town to come to the cottage to prepare for my release and work on my speech. The prison doctor came by to give me a brief check-up. I did not dwell on the prospect of my release, but on all the many things I had to do before then. As so often happens in life, the momentousness of an occasion is lost in the welter of a thousand details.
>
> There were numerous matters that had to be discussed and resolved with very little time to do so. A number of comrades from the Reception Committee, including Cyril Ramaphosa and Trevor Manuel, were at the house bright and early. I wanted initially to address the people of Paarl, who had been very kind to me during my incarceration, but the reception committee was adamant that that would not be a good idea: it would look curious if I gave my first

speech to the prosperous white burghers of Paarl. Instead, as planned, I would speak first to the people of Cape Town at the Grand Parade in Cape Town.

One of the first questions to be resolved was where I would spend my first night of freedom. My inclination was to spend the night in the Cape Flats, the bustling black and Coloured townships of Cape Town, in order to show my solidarity with the people. But my colleagues and, later, my wife argued that for security reasons I should stay with Archbishop Desmond Tutu in Bishopscourt, a plush residence in a white suburb. It was not an area where I would have been permitted to live before I went to prison, and I thought it would send the wrong signal to spend my first night of freedom in a posh white area. But the committee explained that Bishopscourt had become multiracial under Tutu's tenure, and symbolized an open, generous non-racialism.

The prison service supplied me with boxes and crates for packing. During my first 20 or so years in prison, I accumulated very few possessions, but in the last few years I had amassed enough property – mainly books and papers – to make up for previous decades. I filled over a dozen crates and boxes.

My actual release time was set for 3 p.m., but Winnie and Walter and the other passengers from the chartered flight from Johannesburg did not arrive until after two. There were already dozens of people at the house, and the entire scene took on the aspect of a celebration. Warrant Officer Swart prepared a final meal for all of us and I thanked him not only for the food he had provided for the last two years but also the companionship. Warrant Officer James Gregory was also there at the house, and I embraced him warmly. In the years that he had looked after me from Pollsmoor to Victor Verster, we had never discussed politics, but our bond was an unspoken one and I would miss his soothing presence. Men like Swart, Gregory and Warrant Officer Brand reinforced my belief in the essential humanity even of those who had kept me behind bars for the previous 27 and a half years.

There was little time for lengthy farewells. The plan was that Winnie and I would be driven in a car to the front gate of the prison. I had told the authorities that I wanted to be able to say goodbye to the guards and warders who had looked after me and I asked that they and their families wait for me at the front gate, where I would be able to thank them individually.

163

At a few minutes after three, I was telephoned by a well-known SABC presenter who requested that I get out of the car a few hundred feet before the gate so that they could film me walking towards freedom. This seemed reasonable, and I agreed. This was my first inkling that things might not go as smoothly as I had imagined.

By 3.30, I began to get restless, as we were already behind schedule. I told the members of the Reception Committee that my people had been waiting for me for 27 years and I did not want to keep them waiting any longer. Shortly before four, we left in a small motorcade from the cottage. About a quarter of a mile in front of the gate, the car slowed to a stop and Winnie and I got out and began to walk towards the prison gate.

At first I could not really make out what was going on in front of us, but when I was within 150 feet or so, I saw a tremendous commotion and a great crowd of people: hundreds of photographers and television cameras and news people as well as several thousand well-wishers. I was astounded and a little bit alarmed. I had truly not expected such a scene; at most, I had imagined that there would be several dozen people, mainly the warders and their families. But this proved to be only the beginning; I realized we had not thoroughly prepared for all that was about to happen.

Within 20 feet or so of the gate, the cameras started clicking, a noise that sounded like some great herd of metallic beasts. Reporters started shouting questions; television crews began crowding in; ANC supporters were yelling and cheering. It was a happy, if slightly disorienting, chaos. When a television crew thrust a long, dark and furry object at me, I recoiled slightly, wondering if it were some newfangled weapon developed while I was in prison. Winnie informed me that it was a microphone.

When I was among the crowd I raised my right fist, and there was a roar. I had not been able to do that for 27 years and it gave me a surge of strength and joy. We stayed among the crowd for only a few minutes before jumping back into the car for the drive to Cape Town. Although I was pleased to have such a reception, I was greatly vexed by the fact that I did not have a chance to say goodbye to the prison staff. As I finally walked through the gates to enter a car on the other side, I felt — even at the age of 71 — that my life was beginning anew. My 10,000 days of imprisonment were at last over.

Nelson Mandela, *Long Walk to Freedom*

Terry Waite

Into Captivity

In January 1987 Terry Waite (1939–) was in Lebanon as Special Envoy of the Archbishop of Canterbury in order to negotiate the release of American hostages Terry Anderson and Tom Sutherland. Waite had been promised the opportunity to visit the hostages on 20 January but the short car journey across Beirut aroused his suspicions, which proved to be well founded. This was the first of the 1,763 days which Waite was to spend in captivity – most of them in solitary confinement without either books or writing materials. Much of the time was spent working out in his head the autobiography, *Taken on Trust*, which was published to international acclaim two years after his release. In the prologue Waite describes his final days of freedom and the first intimations that he was to join the hostages.

> When I awoke, it was dusk. For a moment I lay still, slowly, reluctantly returning to the conscious world. It was unusually quiet. A gentle breeze stirred the faded hotel curtains, bringing with it a hint of the sea. Somewhere in the building a tap was turned on, sending the pipes in my bathroom into spasm. I swung my legs over the edge of the bed and walked to the window. On the pavement below, the street vendors had gone for the day. The only people left were the journalists. They sat on the seawall, smoking, chatting, waiting like pilgrims for a miracle. I closed the window and drew the curtains, shutting out the last of the dying light. I had already packed to depart for London, and now I checked my pockets: one blank memo pad, one ballpoint pen. Nothing more. I debated with myself whether to wear my wedding ring or lock it in my briefcase. I decided to wear it and my watch. I tuned my small radio in to the World Service of the BBC. World News would be broadcast on the hour; it was a link with home. While I balanced the radio on my briefcase and waited for the familiar

strains of 'Lillibullero' there was a knock at the door. I opened it just enough to see who was there. As I had expected, it was one of my Druze bodyguards.

'Are you ready, sir?'

I invited him in, switched off the radio and made a final check. Everything was packed. It would be a matter of minutes to collect my bags and leave for the airport. I picked up a black leather jacket from the back of a chair. My bodyguards had spent several days searching Beirut before they found one large enough to fit me. Again I checked my pockets – nothing but a pen and a notepad. My guard pointed to a bullet-proof vest lying on the bed.

'Aren't you going to wear that?'

I shook my head. If one of the kidnappers wanted to kill me, he would be near enough to shoot me in the head; a bullet-proof vest would be useless. I took a last look around the room and moved towards the door. Several more guards were standing in the corridor, each with an automatic weapon. We walked towards the lift. A guard with a chest like a beer barrel propped open the door.

'We leave by the basement.'

The antiquated lift descended slowly through the faded glory of the Riviera Hotel. With a gentle groan it touched down, and the gates were cranked open. Two men went before me, two behind. We threaded our way through the subterranean maze, emerging in a side street. I turned up my collar and hunched down into my jacket. The road was full of potholes and strewn with bricks and slabs of broken concrete. It was raining when we reached the car. I squeezed into the back, totally surrounded by protective Druze. As we drove away from the hotel, I saw the journalists still watching and waiting and hoping. In a few minutes we were in a street close to the American University of Beirut (AUB). The car stopped, and I shook hands with the guards.

'Thanks for your help. Whatever happens, don't try to follow me.'

They smiled, large, friendly, roguish smiles. 'Be careful.'

I slipped out of the car and watched them drive away. It was dark, and apart from a few parked cars, the street was deserted. In the distance I could hear the sound of shellfire as Beirut warmed up to yet another night of carnage. By now a steady rain was falling. I walked briskly up the street, looking neither left nor right, past the petrol station, past the apartments, straight to my rendezvous. As agreed, the main door was left ajar. I pushed it open and went in. In the shadows, a pair of eyes peered at me from behind the barely open door of the porter's room. I looked straight back at them, and slowly, as if by remote control, the door closed. I stepped inside the lift and ascended to the apartment of my intermediary, Dr Mroueh. He occupied two apartments in the block. One he used as his consulting rooms, the other as his residence. He opened the door as soon as I rang the bell and invited me into his study.

'Hello, Terry, good to see you again.'

He smiled nervously and lit his pipe while I looked around. Nothing had changed. The same chromium-and-glass desk, leather chairs, framed certificates on the walls. He gestured to me to sit. We chatted inconsequentially until the telephone rang. He spoke softly in Arabic for a few moments and then stood.

'I am so sorry, but I have to leave.'

'Why?'

'A patient is in labour. I am needed urgently.'

'Can't you wait a little longer?'

'That is not possible – I am sorry.'

Somewhere in the back of my head a bell, which had been ringing gently for days, increased in volume.

'I have to go to the hospital. I'll leave the door on the latch. When you leave, please lock it behind you.'

We shook hands, and he left. I crossed to the window and stared down at the empty street. It was not too late to walk away. Within a few minutes I could be back at the hotel. I turned and looked at the bookcase. Nothing but medical tomes. I walked down the corridor to the surgery, slipped off my shoes and stood on the scales: 236 pounds – almost 17 stone. Too heavy; I ought to be 15 stone, probably less. I returned to the other room and paced up and down, trying to quell my mounting anxiety. I thought of Terry Anderson and Tom Sutherland and for a moment wondered what it was like to be imprisoned for month after month. I had been alone in this room for less than an hour, and already I felt the walls and ceiling pressing in on me. I sat in one of the leather chairs and tried to regain my composure. Then I heard it: the gentle hum of an electric motor. Someone was coming up in the lift. I stood and crossed the room. There was a faint thud as the lift came to an abrupt halt. I heard the lift door open, and a second later the doorbell rang. A small stocky man wearing a single-breasted suit stood on the landing. He was my principal contact with the kidnappers, and we had met previously. I could feel his nervousness.

'Are you alone?'

'Yes.'

He stepped into the apartment. 'Are you armed?'

'No.'

'Please, I shall have to search you.' He patted my body and turned towards the door. 'We must leave right now.'

We got into the lift and silently descended. In the lobby the porter's door was firmly closed. We walked into the empty street and found it was still raining. After a few paces, the man halted beside a large car.

'You sit in the back. If we are stopped, you must say I am responsible for driving you around Beirut.'

I climbed into the back seat, and we drove out into the night. As we went through the battered streets I remembered a similar journey I had made years ago in Tehran. Then, as now, there were no reliable guarantees. I got into a car totally at the mercy of kidnappers and was driven to a secret location. The Iranian Revolutionary Guards had kept their word: they took me to the hostages they were holding and returned me to Tehran a few hours later. Now, I had been given a promise that I would be allowed to see Terry Anderson and Tom Sutherland, who, according to their captors, were depressed and ill. The kidnappers knew it was an invitation I could not refuse. It was because my contact gave me his word 'as a Muslim' that I had decided to trust him. I peered through the side windows of the car. Every minute or two a brilliant flash of light illuminated the surrealistic landscape. Only an El Greco could have captured the stark drama of the scene. The pain, the horror, the light, the shadows, the beauty, and behind it all a people suffering, weeping, dying. Suddenly, without warning, the driver pulled the car to the side of the road.

'Why do we stop here?'

'You must get out — we have a puncture.'

I knew he was lying. It was obvious that we would change cars at some point. Why tell such a stupid and pointless lie? There was another car in front of us now, with two men in police uniforms sitting inside.

'Get into the back quickly.'

The man in the suit sat beside me. 'Now, I am sorry, I must blindfold you.'

He produced a strip of curtain material and covered my eyes. It wasn't the change of car that worried me or the blindfold. I had expected both. It was the lie. From that point on I began to prepare myself for capture. We drove for half an hour or so. My companions exchanged words in Arabic. I said nothing. It was as though I had walked on to a track and all I could do now was to follow it wherever it led. I have no memory at all of my thoughts and feelings during that half-hour of darkness.

Suddenly the car slowed. We turned into a side road, lurched through water-filled potholes and stopped. The door opened. 'Get out please.'

I stepped out of the car, guided by one of the party. From under my blindfold I could see an old apartment block. The southern suburbs? We walked a few paces towards the building and began to climb a flight of stairs. At the second floor we stopped. A door was unlocked, and I was led through. I was conscious of other people in the room into which I was taken. As we crossed the floor and entered a side room, I could see several pairs of feet in the rough, homemade sandals worn by the poorer members of the Muslim community.

'Mr Waite, I must ask you to change your clothes.'

Again, I had expected this. It would probably be followed by another body search – even an examination of each of my teeth. They were looking for locator devices, minute electronic instruments which, I am told, can be implanted in the body to enable an individual to be tracked. I removed my clothes and subjected myself to a search. A long Islamic gown and a pair of slippers were then handed to me.

'You must now wait some time. You can sleep.'

They guided me back to the main room.

'Some people will stay with you tonight. You must not speak.'

I sat down on the couch. Someone brought me a blanket. I swung my legs up, turned to face the wall and loosened my blindfold. Within a few moments I was asleep. I slept fitfully. Throughout the night I was conscious of people coming and going. Other people were sleeping in the room. Someone was always awake. I spent the whole of the next day blindfolded, sitting or lying on the couch. In the evening the man in the suit returned.

'Mr Waite, how are you?'

'I am well. When will you take me to see the hostages?'

'Later.'

'How much later?'

'Not long now.'

He handed me a sandwich bought from a street trader.

'Eat, Mr Waite. It's good.'

It was good. Pieces of chicken wrapped in unleavened bread. I ate it all.

'Now, Mr Waite, we must go. Please stand up.'

I stood.

'You must do exactly what I tell you. You must not speak – understand?'

'Yes.'

Several people surrounded me, and someone tightened my blindfold and pulled it down over my nose. People on either side of me took hold of my arms and led me across the room. The apartment door was opened. I felt a cool draught of night air. It was very still – so still that I could hear the breathing of the people around me. We waited – one minute, two, longer. Someone whispered. I was guided forward, at first slowly and then faster as we crossed a corridor. Within a moment we had entered another apartment. I was led to a couch and told to sit.

'You can sleep, Mr Waite.'

'How long do I wait here?'

'Not long.'

I heard some of the party leave the room. Others settled in a far corner. I put up my feet and slept.

During the whole of the next day I dozed. More sandwiches were brought. Once I was given some hot tea. I tried to assess my position. When I had agreed to visit the hostages I knew that I was taking a very high risk. I took it because I felt I must do everything within my power to help them and their families. If anything went wrong, I would have to carry the full responsibility. Up to now everyone had been polite. I had suffered no violence. I had been blindfolded for a couple of days but had not been chained or secured in any other way. However, something was amiss. The whole 'feel' of the situation told me so.

'You sleep a lot.'

Someone was standing behind me.

'I am very tired.'

'It is good to sleep.'

'When will you take me to see the hostages?'

'I don't know.'

'Who does know?'

'I speak little English – sorry.'

It was late evening of the second day. I sat blindfolded, waiting, wondering, hoping. The door opened.

'Stand up, Mr Waite.'

I rose.

'We are now going to take you.'

I made no reply.

'You must do as you are told. No speak.'

Once again I was surrounded by guards. No one spoke.

A voice whispered behind me, 'I am going to take the cover off your eyes. You must keep your eyes closed. Understand?'

'Yes.'

A door opened. Again a wait. A hand pushed me gently from behind. 'Walk.'

I moved gingerly down two flights of stairs. Someone guided me into a large van. A sliding door clicked shut and was locked.

'Sit down, Mr Waite. You can open your eyes.'

It was the man in the single-breasted suit. He stood by the door, holding a two-way radio in one hand and an automatic pistol in the other.

The van was littered with building materials, and the front compartment was completely sealed off from the back so that I could not see the driver or see out of the window.

'Are you taking me to the hostages?'

'Do not speak.'

I sat on a sack of cement. The van lurched forward, crashing through potholes like a drunken elephant. The radio telephone crackled into life. To my surprise it was a woman's voice. The man in the suit replied. Finally, we came to an unsteady halt, and I could hear voices. A road block? The driver was conversing with someone outside the van. The man in the suit looked anxious. Suddenly, the conversation ceased, a door slammed, we moved forward.

Again we must have driven for about half an hour. The road surface improved and deteriorated again.

'Close your eyes. Do not speak.'

We stopped. The van's engine was switched off, and it was deathly quiet. I climbed out, squinting through half-closed eyes. We were in a garage. I was guided to a far corner, where a trapdoor in the floor had been lifted.

'Step down.'

I looked down. There was a drop of about nine feet to an under-ground room.

'It's too far to step down.'

Someone below, wearing a scarf to conceal his face, pushed a cupboard towards the opening. 'Step on to that and jump.'

I stepped warily on to the cupboard and jumped down to the earthen floor. Both my arms were taken by other masked men.

'Close your eyes.'

They led me across the floor: 12 paces in all. We stopped, someone turned a key, a door opened and I was pushed forward. The door closed behind me, and the key turned again. When I opened my eyes, I was in an empty cell lined with white tiles. I sat down on the floor and looked around. The room was almost seven feet across and about 10 feet long. The height varied between six feet and six feet nine. I could be certain about that because I am six feet seven inches tall and in places it was impossible for me to stand upright. A heavy steel door with several thick iron bars on top secured the entrance. Cautiously, I looked through. There were a number of cells in this underground prison, in which dim lights burnt. I assumed they were occupied. I had heard of the underground prisons of Beirut: 'the Lebanese gulag' as Terry Anderson had described them. There were stories of prisoners being incarcerated for years in such places. I sat down again and began to prepare myself for an ordeal. First, I would strengthen my will by fasting; I would refuse all food for at least a week. Second, I would make three resolutions to support me through whatever was to come: no regrets, no sentimentality, no self-pity. Then I did what generations of prisoners have done before me. I stood up and, bending my head, I began to walk round and round and round and round…

Terry Waite, *Taken on Trust*

Footfalls in Memory

In 1995 Terry Waite reflected further upon his experience of captivity in an anthology, *Footfalls in Memory*, that drew upon the wide variety of books, poems and prayers which had brought him spiritual sustenance throughout his life and which he had been able to recall while in prison. Many of the texts described journeys of various kinds and in the anthology Waite reflects upon the experience of captivity as something which was not altogether negative but also a unique opportunity for reflection.

Recently, when I was speaking at a public function, my audience was anxious to hear about solitary confinement and I attempted to answer questions. One man got to his feet and half apologized for this comment:

'I don't want to belittle what you have been through,' he said, 'but in some ways you have been fortunate. You have been given an opportunity to evaluate your life and go more deeply into inner experience. Most of us are so busy trying to make a living that we never get the chance to reflect.'

I assured him that his apology was unnecessary because there was a great deal of truth in what he said. My captivity was certainly a miserable experience which I would not wish to go through again. And yet, almost despite myself, something had come from it.

When the manuscript of this book was completed in draft, my editor pointed out that I had chosen a number of accounts of journeys. I believe that journeys fascinated me not only because I longed to travel away from my cell but also because I was conscious of the fact that I was in the midst of a unique inner journey. If I have not fully described this here it is perhaps because I am still attempting to interpret the landscape. There are many questions I cannot begin to answer, nor even to frame. I know that I was able to take the experience of captivity and turn it into something creative. There was a cost, a high and painful cost, and at times the pain lingers. There have been benefits. I have learnt to embrace solitude as a friend and I no longer experience the aching loneliness which made me such a compulsive individual. I have long appreciated the beauty of form and order in life, but I no longer feel so insecure that I have to be dogmatic to the point of arrogance. I now understand *in my inner experience* what Eliot was communicating when he wrote:

We shall not cease from exploration
And the end of our exploring
Will be to arrive where we started
And know the place for the first time.
T.S. ELIOT, 'LITTLE GIDDING' FROM 'THE FOUR QUARTETS'

Terry Waite, *Footfalls in Memory*

173

Kathleen Norris

The Rule of St Benedict

In *The Cloister Walk*, the American poet and writer Kathleen Norris (1947–) describes her first encounter with the Rule of St Benedict which led her to set out on a journey of discovery into the meaning of the Benedictine life and the variety of ways in which it is lived.

I met the Rule by happy accident, when I found myself staying in a small Benedictine convent during a North Dakota Council on the Arts residency at a Catholic school. The women were pleasant enough, and I soon learnt that the convent was indeed a heavenly place to return to after a day with lively schoolchildren. I felt it necessary to tell the sisters, however, that I wasn't much of a churchgoer, had a completely Protestant background, and knew next to nothing about them. I said they'd have to tell me if I did anything wrong. In many ways my response was typical of a modern person with little experience of church as an adult; I had the nagging fear that people as religious as these women would find me wanting, and be judgmental.

The sisters listened politely and then one of them said, with a wit I'm just learning to fathom, 'Would you like to read our Rule? Then you'll know if you've done something wrong.' 'Sure,' I said, always a sucker for a good book. She found me a copy, along with a book on Benedictine spirituality that the women were studying. As I went upstairs to begin reading, several of the sisters settled down to watch television, and I appreciated the irony. I began to think that my stay with them would work out fine.

What happened to me then has no doubt happened to many unsuspecting souls in the 1,500-plus years that Benedictines have existed. Quite simply, the Rule spoke to me. Like so many, I am put off by religious language as it's manipulated by television evangelists, used to preach to the converted, the 'saved'. Benedict's language and imagery come from the Bible, but he was someone who read the psalms every day – as Benedictines still do – and something of the psalms' emotional honesty; their grounding in the physical, rubbed off on him. Even when the psalms are at their most ecstatic, they convey holiness not with abstraction but with images from the world we know: rivers clap their hands, hills dance like yearling sheep. The Bible, in Benedict's hands, had a concreteness and vigour that I hadn't experienced since hearing Bible stories read to me as a child.

Kathleen Norris, *The Cloister Walk*

THIRD JOURNEY

Most Third Journeys come at the end of a life of six or seven decades or more; such is the case with Abraham, Pope John XXIII and Cardinal Basil Hume. Other journeys to death can occur in the first years or even months of life, as we read in the letters sent by the parents of Christopher Hope Mitchell.

Some Third Journeys are completed in one's twenties, as with St Thérèse of Lisieux, or in one's thirties, as in the case of Jesus himself, whose Third Journey gave birth to Christianity.

The example of Jesus reminds us that the culmination of a Third Journey may be brought about, not by sickness and other 'natural' causes, but at the hands of those who are inimical to all that we stand for. Such violence led to martyrdom, not only for Jesus and his immediate precursor St John the Baptist, but also for innumerable men and women down the centuries, from St Ignatius of Antioch in the second century, down to Edith Cavell and Dietrich Bonhoeffer during the 20th century.

Some of those whose Third Journeys are included in this section were, like St Ignatius of Antioch, able to interpret the death that was bearing down upon them. In other cases, the interpretation of the final journey is left to others, as happened with St Monica, whose son St Augustine of Hippo left us an unforgettable testimony, and tiny Christopher Hope Mitchell, whose parents wrote about their son's journey to death.

Abraham and Sarah

The Death of Sarah

When Sarah's long life came to an end, Abraham wished to give her an honourable burial. Ephron the Hittite wanted to make Abraham a gift of the cave at Machpelah as a burial place for his wife, but Abraham insisted that payment should be made. He bought the cave for 400 shekels of silver and was eventually buried there himself, next to Sarah, at the age of 175.

The span of Sarah's life was 127 years. She died in Kiriath-arba (that is, Hebron) in the land of Canaan, and Abraham performed the customary mourning rites for her. Then he left the side of his dead one and addressed the Hittites: 'Although I am a resident alien among you, sell me from your holdings a piece of property for a burial ground, that I may bury my dead wife.' The Hittites answered Abraham: 'Please sir, listen to us! You are an elect of God among us. Bury your dead in the choicest of our burial sites. None of us would deny you his burial ground for the burial of your dead.' Abraham, however, began to bow low before the local citizens, the Hittites, while he appealed to them: 'If you will allow me room for burial of my dead, listen to me! Intercede for me with Ephron, son of Zohar, asking him to sell me the cave of Machpelah that he owns; it is at the edge of his field. Let him sell it to me in your presence, at its full price, for a burial place.'

Now Ephron was present with the Hittites. So Ephron the Hittite replied to Abraham in the hearing of the Hittites who sat on his town council: 'Please sir, listen to me! I give you both the field and the cave in it; in the presence of my kinsmen I make this gift. Bury your dead!' But Abraham, after bowing low before the local citizens, addressed Ephron in the hearing of these men: 'Ah, if only you would please listen to me! I will pay you the price of the field. Accept it from me, that I may bury my dead there.' Ephron replied to Abraham,

'Please, sir, listen to me! A piece of land worth 400 shekels of silver – what is that between you and me, as long as you can bury your dead?' Abraham accepted Ephron's terms; he weighed out to him the silver that Ephron had stipulated in the hearing of the Hittites, 400 shekels of silver at the current market value.

Thus Ephron's field in Machpelah, facing Mamre, together with its cave and all the trees anywhere within its limits, was conveyed to Abraham by purchase in the presence of all the Hittites who sat on Ephron's town council. After this transaction, Abraham buried his wife Sarah in the cave of the field of Machpelah, facing Mamre (that is, Hebron) in the land of Canaan. Thus the field with its cave was transferred from the Hittites to Abraham as a burial place.

Genesis 23:1–20

The Death of Abraham

The whole span of Abraham's life was 175 years. Then he breathed his last, dying at a ripe old age, grown old after a full life; and he was taken to his kinsmen. His sons Isaac and Ishmael buried him in the cave of Machpelah, in the field of Ephron, son of Zohar the Hittite, which faces Mamre, the field that Abraham had bought from the Hittites; there he was buried next to his wife Sarah.

Genesis 25:7–10

Ulysses

The Last Voyage

In the poem 'Ulysses' by Alfred, Lord Tennyson (1809–92) we meet the mythical Greek hero who has returned from his wanderings to spend his old age by the fireside. But Ulysses is not content with life at his own hearthstone. The Third Journey beckons and Ulysses wants to make it on his own terms: ''Tis not too late to seek a newer world.'

Ulysses

It little profits that an idle king,
By this still hearth, among these barren crags,
Match'd with an aged wife, I mete and dole
Unequal laws unto a savage race,
That hoard, and sleep, and feed, and know not me,
I cannot rest from travel: I will drink
Life to the lees: all times I have enjoy'd
Greatly, have suffer'd greatly, both with those
That loved me, and alone; on shore, and when
Thro' scudding drifts the rainy Hyades
Vext the dim sea: I am become a name;
For always roaming with a hungry heart
Much have I seen and known; cities of men
And manners, climates, councils, governments,
Myself not least, but honour'd of them all;
And drunk delight of battle with my peers,
Far on the ringing plains of windy Troy.
I am a part of all that I have met;
Yet all experience is an arch wherethro'

Gleams that untravell'd world, whose margin fades
For ever and for ever when I move.
How dull it is to pause, to make an end,
To rust unburnish'd, not to shine in use!
As tho' to breathe were life. Life piled on life
Were all too little, and of one to me
Little remains: but every hour is saved
From that eternal silence, something more,
A bringer of new things; and vile it were
For some three suns to store and hoard myself,
And this grey spirit yearning in desire
To follow knowledge, like a sinking star,
Beyond the utmost bound of human thought.
    This is my son, mine own Telemachus,
To whom I leave the sceptre and the isle —
Well-loved of me, discerning to fulfil
This labour, by slow prudence to make mild
A rugged people, and thro' soft degrees
Subdue them to the useful and the good.
Most blameless is he, centred in the sphere
Of common duties, decent not to fail
In offices of tenderness, and pay
Meet adoration to my household gods,
When I am gone. He works his work, I mine.
    There lies the port: the vessel puffs her sail:
There gloom the dark broad seas. My mariners,
Souls that have toil'd, and wrought, and thought with me —
That ever with a frolic welcome took
The thunder and the sunshine, and opposed
Free hearts, free foreheads — you and I are old;
Old age hath yet his honour and his toil;
Death closes all: but something ere the end,
Some work of noble note, may yet be done,
Not unbecoming men that strove with Gods.
The lights begin to twinkle from the rocks:
The long day wanes: the slow moon climbs: the deep
Moans round with many voices. Come, my friends,
'Tis not too late to seek a newer world.
Push off, and sitting well in order smite
The sounding furrows; for my purpose holds

To sail beyond the sunset, and the baths
Of all the western stars, until I die.
It may be that the gulfs will wash us down:
It may be we shall touch the Happy Isles,
And see the great Achilles, whom we knew.
Tho' much is taken, much abides; and tho'
We are not now that strength which in old days
Moved earth and heaven; that which we are, we are;
One equal temper of heroic hearts,
Made weak by time and fate, but strong in will
To strive, to seek, to find, and not to yield.

'Ulysses', Alfred, Lord Tennyson

St John the Baptist

The Beheading of John the Baptist

Jesus said of John the Baptist, 'there has never been anyone greater'. In the light of the drama that attended John's conception and the fiery uncompromising message he preached, it is perhaps ironical that he dies in order to save Herod from social embarrassment during his birthday banquet. John, who has lived in the desert on a diet of locusts and wild honey, is to lose his life at the whim of a dancing girl because Herod does not want to be seen to refuse her macabre request. We do not know the effect of the sight of John's severed head upon the assembled company, but it is perhaps safe to assume they decided not to prolong the festivities!

Herod… had sent to have John arrested, and had had him chained up in prison because of Herodias, his brother Philip's wife whom he had married. For John had told Herod, 'It is against the law for you to have your brother's wife.' As for Herodias, she was furious with him and wanted to kill him, but she was not able to do so, because Herod was in awe of John, knowing him to be a good and upright man, and gave him his protection. When he had heard him speak he was greatly perplexed, and yet he liked to listen to him.

An opportunity came on Herod's birthday when he gave a banquet for the nobles of his court, for his army officers and for the leading figures in Galilee. When the daughter of this same Herodias came in and danced, she delighted Herod and his guests; so the king said to the girl, 'Ask me anything you like and I will give it you.' And he swore her an oath, 'I will give you anything you ask, even half my kingdom.' She went out and said to her mother, 'What shall I ask for?' She replied, 'The head of John the Baptist.' The girl at once rushed back to the king and made her request. 'I want you to give me John the Baptist's head, immediately, on a dish.' The king was deeply distressed but, thinking of the oaths he had sworn and of his guests, he was reluctant to break his word to her. At once the king sent one of the bodyguard with orders to bring John's head. The man went off and beheaded him in the prison; then he brought the head on a dish and gave it to the girl, and the girl gave it to her mother. When John's disciples heard about this, they came and took his body and laid it in a tomb.

Mark 6:17–29

Artaban

Pearl of Great Price

In *The Story of the Other Wise Man*, the American writer and Presbyterian Minister Henry van Dyke (1852–1933) describes the journeying of Artaban, a fourth wise man who never managed to see the infant Jesus. Artaban had started off for Bethlehem with the other three Magi, whom tradition names as Gaspar, Melchior and Balthazar. He had sold all he possessed in order to purchase three precious jewels to present to the new King. But Artaban is delayed on his journey by a dying man to whom he ministers in a palm grove at Babylon. The other three go ahead and Artaban has to sell his sapphire in order to provide himself with the means to complete the journey. When he eventually arrives in Bethlehem, the holy family have fled and the soldiers of Herod are massacring all the boys in Bethlehem and the vicinity who are two years old and under. Artaban gives up his ruby as a ransom for a baby. But Artaban still possesses a valuable pearl. He dedicates the remainder of his life to seeking the King in order to present him with the jewel. In the final chapter of *The Story of the Other Wise Man*, Henry van Dyke describes the fate of the pearl.

> Three-and-thirty years of the life of Artaban had passed away, and he was still a pilgrim and a seeker after light. His hair, once darker than the cliffs of Zagros, was now white as the wintry snow that covered them. His eyes, that once flashed like flames of fire, were dull as embers smouldering among the ashes.
>
> Worn and weary and ready to die, but still looking for the King, he had come for the last time to Jerusalem. He had often visited the holy city before, and had searched through all its lanes and crowded hovels and black prisons without finding any trace of the family of Nazarenes who had fled from Bethlehem long ago. But

now it seemed as if he must make one more effort, and something whispered in his heart that, at last, he might succeed.

It was the season of the Passover. The city was thronged with strangers. The children of Israel, scattered in far lands all over the world, had returned to the Temple for the great feast, and there had been a confusion of tongues in the narrow streets for many days.

But only this day there was a singular agitation visible in the multitude. The sky was veiled with a portentous gloom, and currents of excitement seemed to flash through the crowd like the thrill which shakes the forest on the eve of a storm. A secret tide was sweeping them all one way. The clatter of sandals, and the soft, thick sound of thousands of bare feet shuffling over the stones, flowed unceasingly along the streets that lead to the Damascus gate.

Artaban joined company with a group of people from his own country, Parthian Jews who had come up to keep the Passover, and inquired of them the cause of the tumult, and where they were going.

'We are going', they answered, 'to the place called Golgotha, outside the city walls, where there is to be an execution. Have you not heard what has happened? Two famous robbers are to be crucified, and with them another, called Jesus of Nazareth, a man who has done many wonderful works among the people, so that they love him greatly. But the priests and elders have said that he must die, because he gave himself out to be the Son of God. And Pilate has sent him to the cross because he said that he was the "King of the Jews".'

How strangely these familiar words fell upon the tired heart of Artaban! They had led him for a lifetime over land and sea. And now they came to him darkly and mysteriously like a message of despair. The King had risen, but he had been denied and cast out. He was about to perish. Perhaps he was already dying. Could it be the same who had been born in Bethlehem, 33 years ago, at whose birth the star had appeared in heaven, and of whose coming the prophets had spoken?

Artaban's heart beat unsteadily with that troubled, doubtful apprehension which is the excitement of old age. But he said within himself, 'The ways of God are stranger than the thoughts of men, and it may be that I shall find the King, at last, in the hands of his enemies, and shall come in time to offer my pearl for his ransom before he dies.'

So the old man followed the multitude with slow and painful steps towards the Damascus gate of the city. Just beyond the entrance of the guard-house a troop of Macedonian soldiers came down the street, dragging a young girl with torn dress and dishevelled hair. As the Magian paused to look at her with compassion, she broke suddenly from the hands of her tormentors, and threw herself at his feet, clasping him around the knees. She had seen his white cap and the winged circle on his breast.

'Have pity on me,' she cried, 'and save me, for the sake of the God of purity! I also am a daughter of the true religion which is taught by the Magi. My father was a merchant of Parthia, but he is dead, and I am seized for his debts to be sold as a slave. Save me from worse than death!'

Artaban trembled.

It was the old conflict in his soul, which had come to him in the palm-grove of Babylon and in the cottage of Bethlehem – the conflict between the expectation of faith and the impulse of love. Twice the gift which he had consecrated to the worship of religion had been drawn from his hand to the service of humanity. This was the third trial, the ultimate probation, the final and irrevocable choice.

Was it his great opportunity, or his last temptation? He could not tell. One thing only was clear in the darkness of his mind – it was inevitable. And does not the inevitable come from God?

One thing only was sure to his divided heart – to rescue this helpless girl would be a true deed of love. And is not love the light of the soul? He took the pearl from his bosom. Never had it seemed so luminous, so radiant, so full of tender, living lustre. He laid it in the hand of the slave. 'This is thy ransom, daughter! It is the last of my treasures which I kept for the King.'

While he spoke the darkness of the sky thickened, and shuddering tremors ran through the earth, heaving convulsively like the breast of one who struggles with mighty grief.

The walls of the houses rocked to and fro. Stones were loosened and crashed into the street. Dust clouds filled the air. The soldiers fled in terror, reeling like drunken men. But Artaban and the girl whom he had ransomed crouched helpless beneath the wall of the Praetorium.

What had he to fear? What had he to live for? He had given away the last remnant of his tribute for the King. He had parted with the last hope of finding him. The quest was over, and it had failed. But, even in that thought, accepted and embraced, there was peace. It was not resignation. It was not submission. It was something more profound and searching. He knew that all was well, because he had done the best that he could, from day to day. He had been true to the light that had been given to him. He had looked for more. And if he had not found it, if a failure was all that came out of his life, doubtless that was the best that was possible. He had not seen the revelation of 'life everlasting, incorruptible and immortal'. But he knew that even if he could live his earthly life over again, it could not be otherwise than it had been.

One more lingering pulsation of the earthquake quivered through the ground. A heavy tile, shaken from the roof, fell and struck the old man on the temple. He lay breathless and pale, with his grey head resting on the young girl's shoulder, and the blood trickling from the wound. As she bent over him, fearing that he was dead, there came a voice through the twilight, very small and still, like music sounding from a distance, in which the notes are clear but the words are lost. The girl turned to see if some one had spoken from the window above them, but she saw no one.

Then the old man's lips began to move, as if in answer, and she heard him say in the Parthian tongue:

'Not so, my Lord! For when saw I thee hungered, and fed thee? Or thirsty, and gave thee drink? When saw I thee a stranger, and took thee in? Or naked, and clothed thee? When saw I thee sick or in prison, and came unto thee? Three-and thirty years have I looked for thee; but I have never seen thy face, nor ministered to thee, my King.'

He ceased, and the sweet voice came again. And again the maid heard it, very faintly and far away. But now it seemed as though she understood the words:

'Verily I say unto thee, inasmuch as thou hast done it unto one of the least of these my brethren, thou hast done it unto me.'

A calm radiance of wonder and joy lighted the pale face of Artaban like the first ray of dawn on a snowy mountain-peak. One long, last breath of relief exhaled gently from his lips.

His journey was ended. His treasures were accepted. The other wise man had found the King.

Henry van Dyke, *The Story of the Other Wise Man*

Jesus

The Way of the Cross

Jesus undertook his final journey to crucifixion and death in shame and ignominy. The great crowd who had greeted his triumphal entry into Jerusalem with glad hosannas were now shouting, 'Take him away! Crucify him!' His chosen followers fled as soon as the Roman soldiers appeared in the Garden of Gethsemane to arrest him. Peter followed Jesus at a distance, only to deny when challenged that he had anything to do with him. At the end only John and the women remained beside the cross. Joseph of Arimathea and Nicodemus took charge of the burial. There is no scriptural evidence that anybody believed that Jesus meant precisely what he said when he told them that he would rise again on the third day.

> Carrying his own cross, he went out to the Place of the Skull (which in Aramaic is called Golgotha). Here they crucified him, and with him two others – one on each side and Jesus in the middle.
> Pilate had a notice prepared and fastened to the cross. It read: JESUS OF NAZARETH, THE KING OF THE JEWS. Many of the Jews read this sign, for the place where Jesus was crucified was near the city, and the sign was written in Aramaic, Latin and Greek. The chief priests of the Jews protested to Pilate, 'Do not write "The King of the Jews", but that this man claimed to be king of the Jews.'
> Pilate answered, 'What I have written, I have written.'
> When the soldiers crucified Jesus, they took his clothes, dividing them into four shares, one for each of them, with the undergarment remaining. This garment was seamless, woven in one piece from top to bottom.
> 'Let's not tear it,' they said to one another. 'Let's decide by lot who will get it.'
> This happened that the scripture might be fulfilled which said,

*'They divided my garments among them
and cast lots for my clothing.'*

So this is what the soldiers did.

Near the cross of Jesus stood his mother, his mother's sister, Mary the wife of Clopas, and Mary Magdalene. When Jesus saw his mother there, and the disciple whom he loved standing nearby, he said to his mother, 'Dear woman, here is your son,' and to the disciple, 'Here is your mother.' From that time on, this disciple took her into his home.

Later, knowing that all was now completed, and so that the scripture would be fulfilled, Jesus said, 'I am thirsty.' A jar of wine vinegar was there, so they soaked a sponge in it, put the sponge on a stalk of the hyssop plant, and lifted it to Jesus' lips. When he had received the drink, Jesus said, 'It is finished.' With that, he bowed his head and gave up his spirit.

Now it was the day of Preparation, and the next day was to be a special Sabbath. Because the Jews did not want the bodies left on the crosses during the Sabbath, they asked Pilate to have the legs broken and the bodies taken down. The soldiers therefore came and broke the legs of the first man who had been crucified with Jesus, and then those of the other. But when they came to Jesus and found that he was already dead, they did not break his legs. Instead, one of the solders pierced Jesus' side with a spear, bringing a sudden flow of blood and water. The man who saw it has given testimony, and his testimony is true. He knows that he tells the truth, and he testifies so that you also may believe. These things happened so that the scripture would be fulfilled: 'Not one of his bones will be broken,' and, as another scripture says, 'They will look on the one they have pierced.'

Later, Joseph of Arimathea asked Pilate for the body of Jesus, but secretly because he feared the Jews. With Pilate's permission, he came and took the body away. He was accompanied by Nicodemus, the man who earlier had visited Jesus at night. Nicodemus brought a mixture of myrrh and aloes, about 75 pounds. Taking Jesus' body, the two of them wrapped it, with the spices, in strips of linen. This was in accordance with Jewish burial customs. At the place where Jesus was crucified, there was a garden, and in the garden a new tomb, in which no one had ever been laid. Because it was the Jewish day of Preparation and since the tomb was nearby, they laid Jesus there.

Early on the first day of the week, while it was still dark, Mary Magdalene went to the tomb and saw that the stone had been removed from the entrance. So she came running to Simon Peter and the other disciple, the one Jesus loved, and said, 'They have taken the Lord out of the tomb, and we don't know where they have put him!'

So Peter and the other disciple started for the tomb. Both were running, but the other disciple outran Peter and reached the tomb first. He bent over and looked in at the strips of linen lying there but did not go in. Then Simon Peter, who was behind him, arrived and went into the tomb. He saw the strips of linen lying there, as well as the burial cloth that had been around Jesus' head. The cloth was folded up by itself, separate from the linen. Finally the other disciple, who had reached the tomb first, also went inside. He saw and believed. (They still did not understand from scripture that Jesus had to rise from the dead.)

Then the disciples went back to their homes, but Mary stood outside the tomb crying. As she wept, she bent over to look into the tomb and saw two angels in white, seated where Jesus' body had been, one at the head and the other at the foot.

They asked her, 'Woman, why are you crying?'

'They have taken my Lord away,' she said, 'and I don't know where they have put him.' At this, she turned round and saw Jesus standing there, but she did not realize that it was Jesus.

'Woman,' he said, 'why are you crying? Who is it you are looking for?'

Thinking he was the gardener, she said, 'Sir, if you have carried him away, tell me where you have put him, and I will get him.'

Jesus said to her, 'Mary.'

She turned towards him and cried out in Aramaic, 'Rabboni!' (which means Teacher).

Jesus said, 'Do not hold on to me, for I have not yet returned to the Father. Go instead to my brothers and tell them, 'I am returning to my Father and your Father, to my God and your God.'

Mary Magdalene went to the disciples with the news: 'I have seen the Lord!' And she told them that he had said these things to her.

John 19:17 – 20:18

St Ignatius of Antioch

Ground by Lion's Teeth

St Ignatius (c. 35–c. 107) was either the second or third bishop of Antioch in succession to St Peter. In his *Letter to the Romans* he describes his desire for martyrdom, and begs his fellow Christians not to deprive him of this privilege by interceding with the Roman authorities, who are having him transferred from Antioch to Rome under a guard of 10 soldiers. The *Letter to the Romans* reveals a man passionately devoted to God and longing only to be with him.

Ignatius Theophorus to the church on which the majesty of the most high Father and of Jesus Christ, his only Son, has had mercy; to the church beloved and enlightened by the faith and charity of Jesus Christ, our God, through the will of him who has willed all things that exist – the church in the place of the country of the Romans which holds the primacy. I salute you in the name of Jesus Christ, the Son of the Father. You are a church worthy of God, worthy of honour, felicitation and praise, worthy of attaining to God, a church without blemish, which holds the primacy of the community of love, obedient to Christ's law, bearing the Father's name. To you who are united, outwardly and inwardly, in the whole of his commandment and filled with grace, in union with God and with every alien stain filtered away, I wish every innocent joy in Jesus Christ, our God.

In answer to my prayer and beyond all I asked for, I have at last seen the faces I have longed to see. In chains as I am for Jesus Christ, I hope to salute you, if only it be his will to grant me grace to reach my goal. I shall know that the beginning is providential if, in the end, without hindrance, I am to obtain the inheritance. But I am afraid of your love; it may do me wrong. It is easy for you to have your way, but if you do not yield to me, it will be hard for me to reach God.

I would have you think of pleasing God – as indeed you do – rather than men. For at no later time shall I have an opportunity like this of reaching God; nor can you ever have any better deed ascribed to you – if only you remain silent. If only you will say nothing in my behalf, I shall be a word of God. But, if your love is for my body, I shall be once more a mere voice. You can do me no greater kindness than to suffer me to be sacrificed to God while the place of sacrifice is still prepared. Thus forming yourselves into a chorus of love, you may sing to the Father in Jesus Christ that God gave the bishop of Syria the grace of being transferred from the rising to the setting sun. It is good to set, leaving the world for God, and so to rise in him.

Never have you envied anyone. You have been others' teachers. I trust that what you have taught and prescribed to others may now be applied to yourselves. Beg only that I may have inward and outward strength, not only in word but in will, that I may be a Christian not merely in name but in fact. For, if I am one in fact, then I may be called one and be faithful long after I have vanished from the world. Nothing merely visible is good, for our God, Jesus Christ, is manifest the more now that he is hidden in God. Christianity is not the work of persuasion, but, whenever it is hated by the world, it is a work of power.

I am writing to all the churches to tell them all that I am, with all my heart, to die for God – if only you do not prevent it. I beseech you not to indulge your benevolence at the wrong time. Please let me be thrown to the wild beasts; through them I can reach God. I am God's wheat; I am ground by the teeth of the wild beasts that I may end as the pure bread of Christ. If anything, coax the beasts on to become my sepulchre and to leave nothing of my body undevoured so that, when I am dead, I may be no bother to anyone. I shall be really a disciple of Jesus Christ if and when the world can no longer see so much as my body. Make petition, then, to the Lord for me, so that by these means I may be made a sacrifice to God. I do not command you, as Peter and Paul did. They were Apostles; I am a condemned man. They were free men; I am still a slave. Still, if I suffer, I shall be emancipated by Jesus Christ and, in my resurrection, shall be free. But now in chains I am learning to have no wishes of my own.

I am already battling with beasts on my journey from Syria to Rome. On land and at sea, by night and by day, I am in chains with 10 leopards around me – or at least with a band of guards who grow more brutal the better they are treated. However, the wrongs they do me make me a better disciple. But that is not where my justification lies. May I find my joy in the beasts that have been made ready for me. My prayer is that they will be prompt in dealing with me. I shall coax them to devour me without delay and not be afraid to touch me, as has happened in some cases. And if, when I am ready, they hold back, I shall provoke them to attack me. Pardon me, but I know what is good for me. I am now beginning to be a disciple; may nothing visible or invisible prevent me from reaching Jesus Christ. Fire and roses and battling with wild beasts, (their clawing and tearing,) the breaking of bones and mangling of members, the grinding of my whole body, the wicked torments of the devil — let them all assail me, so long as I get to Jesus Christ.

Neither the kingdoms of this world nor the bounds of the universe can have any use for me. I would rather die for Jesus Christ than rule the last reaches of the earth. My search is for him who died for us; my love is for him who rose for our salvation. The pangs of new birth are upon me. Forgive me, brethren. Do nothing to prevent this new life. Do not desire that I shall perish. Do not hand over to the world a man whose heart is fixed on God. Do not entice me with material things. Allow me to receive the pure light. When I reach it, I shall be fully a man. Allow me to be a follower of the passion of my God. Let those who hold him in their hearts understand what urges me, realize what I am choosing, and share my feelings.

The prince of this world is eager to tear me to pieces, to weaken my will that is fixed on God. Let none of you who are watching the battle abet him. Come in, rather on my side, for it is the side of God. Do not let your lips be for Jesus Christ and your heart for the world. Let envy have no place among you. And even, when I am come, if I should beseech you, pay no attention to what I say; believe, rather, what I am writing to you now. For alive as I am at this moment of writing, my longing is for death. Desire within me has been nailed to the cross and no flame of material longing is left. Only the living water speaks within me saying: Hasten to the Father. I have no taste for the food that perishes nor the pleasures of this life. I want the Bread of God which is the Flesh of Christ, who was the seed of David; and for drink I desire his blood which is love that cannot be destroyed.

I desire no longer to live a purely human life; and this desire can be fulfilled if you consent. Make this your choice, if you yourselves would be chosen. I make my petition in a few words. Please believe me; Jesus Christ will make it clear to you that I speak the truth, for he was the mouth without deceit through which the Father truly spoke. Beg for me that, through the Holy Spirit, I may not fail. I have not written to you after the manner of men, but according to the mind of God. If I die, it will prove you loved me; if I am rejected, it will be because you hated me.

Remember in your prayers that Church of Syria, which now, in place of me, has God for its pastor. Jesus Christ, along with your love, will be its only bishop. For myself, I am ashamed to be called one of them, for I am not worthy, being the last among them and, as it were, born out of due time. If I reach God, I shall be some one only by his mercy. My spirit salutes you – and with it the love of the churches which welcomed me in the name of Jesus Christ. They treated me as more than a passing pilgrim; for even the communities that did not lie along the route I was taking conducted me from city to city.

I am writing this letter to you from Smyrna by the hands of the Ephesians, who deserve all praise. Among many others who are with me there is my dear friend Crocus. I trust you have come to know those who went ahead of me from Syria to Rome for the glory of God. Please tell them that I am not far away. All of them are worthy of God and of yourselves. You will do well to help them in every way. The date of this writing is the ninth day before the calends of September.

Farewell, and persevere to the end in Jesus Christ.

St Ignatius of Antioch, *Letter to the Romans*

St Monica

The Death of Monica

In his *Confessions*, St Augustine (354–430) writes movingly of the final days of his mother St Monica (c. 331–387) who died in Ostia while accompanying Augustine from Rome back to North Africa. Monica had achieved her heart's desire when Augustine rediscovered his Christian faith and was baptized. In their colloquy Monica and Augustine reflect on the insignificance of earthly pleasures when weighed against the eternal joys to come.

The day was imminent when she was to depart this life (the day which you knew and we did not). It came about, as I believe by your providence through your hidden ways, that she and I were standing leaning out of a window overlooking a garden. It was at the house where we were staying at Ostia on the Tiber, where, far removed from the crowds, after the exhaustion of a long journey, we were recovering our strength for the voyage.

Alone with each other, we talked very intimately. 'Forgetting the past and reaching forward to what lies ahead' (Philippians 3:13), we were searching together in the presence of the truth which is you yourself. We asked what quality of life the eternal life of the saints will have, a life which 'neither eye has seen nor ear heard, nor has it entered into the heart of man' (1 Corinthians 2:9). But with the mouth of the heart wide open, we drank in the waters flowing from your spring on high, 'the spring of life' (Psalm 35:10) which is with you. Sprinkled with this dew to the limit of our capacity, our minds attempted in some degree to reflect on so great a reality.

The conversation led us towards the conclusion that the pleasure of the bodily senses, however delightful in the radiant light of this physical world, is seen by comparison with the life of eternity to be not even worth considering. Our minds were lifted up by an ardent affection towards eternal being itself. Step by step we climbed beyond all corporeal objects and the heaven itself, where sun, moon, and stars shed light on the earth. We ascended even further by internal reflection and dialogue and wonder at your works, and we entered into our own minds. We moved up beyond them so as to attain to the region of inexhaustible abundance where you feed Israel eternally with truth for food. There life is the wisdom by which all creatures come into being, both things which were and which will be. But wisdom itself is not brought into being but is as it was and always will be. Furthermore, in this wisdom there is no past and future, but only being, since it is eternal. For to exist in the past or in the future, is no property of the eternal. And while we talked and panted after it, we touched it in some small degree by a moment of total concentration of the heart. And we sighed and left behind us 'the firstfruits of the Spirit' (Romans 8:23) bound to that higher world, as we returned to the noise of our human speech where a sentence has both a beginning and an ending. But what is to be compared with your word, Lord of our lives? It dwells in you without growing old and gives renewal to all things.

Therefore, we said: If to anyone the tumult of the flesh has fallen silent, if the images of earth, water, and air are quiescent, if the heavens themselves are shut out and the very soul itself is making no sound and is surpassing itself by no longer thinking about itself, if all dreams and visions in the imagination are excluded, if all language and every sign and everything transitory is silent – for if anyone could hear them, this is what all of them would be saying, 'We did not make ourselves, we were made by him who abides for eternity' (Psalm 79:3, 5) – if after this declaration they were to keep silence, having directed our ears to him that made them, then he alone would speak not through them but through himself We would hear his word, not through the tongue of the flesh, nor through the voice of an angel, nor through the sound of thunder, nor through the obscurity of a symbolic utterance. Him who in these things we love we would hear in person without their mediation. That is how it was when at that moment we extended our reach and in a flash of mental energy attained the eternal wisdom which abides beyond all things. If only it could last, and other visions of a vastly inferior kind could be withdrawn! Then this alone could ravish and absorb and enfold in inward joys the person granted the vision. So too eternal life is of the quality of that moment of understanding after which we sighed. Is not this the meaning of 'Enter into the joy of your Lord' (Matthew 25:21)? And when is that to be? Surely it is when 'we all rise again, but are not all changed' (I Corinthians 15:51).

I said something like this, even if not in just this way and with exactly these words. Yet, Lord, you know that on that day when we had this conversation, and this world with all its delights became worthless to us as we talked on, my mother said, 'My son, as for myself, I now find no pleasure in this life. What I have still to do here and why I am here, I do not know. My hope in this world is already fulfilled. The one reason why I wanted to stay longer in this life was my desire to see you a Catholic Christian before I die. My God has granted this in a way more than I had hoped. For I see you despising this world's success to become his servant. What have I to do here?'

The reply I made to that I do not well recall, for within five days or not much more she fell sick of a fever. While she was ill, on one day she suffered loss of consciousness and gradually became unaware of things around her. We ran to be with her, but she quickly recovered consciousness. She looked at me and my brother standing beside her, and said to us in the manner of someone looking for something, 'Where was I?' Then seeing us struck dumb with grief, she said: 'Bury your mother here.' I kept silence and fought back my tears. But my brother, as if to cheer her up, said something to the effect that he hoped she would be buried not in a foreign land but in her home country. When she heard that, her face became worried and her eyes looked at him in reproach that he should think that. She looked in my direction and said, 'See what he says,' and soon said to both of us, 'Bury my body anywhere you like. Let no anxiety about that disturb you. I have only one request to make of you, that you remember me at the altar of the Lord, wherever you may be.' She explained her thought in such words as she could speak, then fell silent as the pain of her sickness became worse.

But as I thought about your gifts, invisible God, which you send into the hearts of your faithful, and which in consequence produce wonderful fruits, I was filled with joy and gave thanks to you as I recalled what I knew of the great concern which had agitated her about the tomb which she had foreseen and prepared for herself next to the body of her husband. Because they had lived together in great concord, she had expressed the wish (so little is the human mind capable of grasping divine things) that a further addition might be made to her happiness and that posterity might remember it: she wished it to be granted to her that after her travels overseas the two partners in the marriage might be joined in the same covering of earth. But when, by your bountiful goodness, this vain thought began to disappear from her mind, I did not know. I was delighted and surprised that my mother had disclosed this to me. Yet even at the time of our conversation at the window, when she said, 'What have I to do here now?' she made it evident that she did not want to die at home. Moreover, I later learnt that before, when we were at Ostia, she conversed one day with some of my friends with all a mother's confidence, and spoke of her contempt for this life and of the beneficence of death. I had not been present on this occasion. But they were surprised at the courage of the woman (for you had given it to her), and asked whether she were not afraid to leave her body so far from her own town. 'Nothing', she said 'is distant from God, and there is no ground for fear that he may not acknowledge me at the end of the world and raise me up.'

On the ninth day of her illness, when she was aged 56, and I was 33, this religious and devout soul was released from her body.

St Augustine of Hippo, *Confessions* **IX:10:23–IX:11:28**

St Thomas More

Together in Heaven

Sir Thomas More (1478–1535) served as King Henry VIII's Lord Chancellor from 1529 to 1534. He chose to accept martyrdom rather than betray his conscience by giving his assent to the King's intention to become Supreme Head of the Church in England in place of the Pope. More was confined to the Tower of London in 1534, tried and sentenced to death. In this letter to his favourite daughter, Margaret, he describes his feelings as he faces execution.

Mistrust him, Meg, will I not, though I feel me faint. Yea, and though I should feel my fear even at point to overthrow me too, yet shall I remember how Saint Peter with a blast of a wind began to sink for his faint faith, and shall do as he did, call upon Christ and pray him to help. And then I trust he shall set his holy hand unto me, and in the stormy seas hold me up from drowning. Yea, and if he suffer me to play Saint Peter further, and to fall full to the ground, and swear and forswear too (which our Lord for his tender passion keep me from, and let me lose if it so fall, and never win thereby): yet after shall I trust that his goodness will cast upon me his tender piteous eye, as he did upon Saint Peter, and make me stand up again, and confess the truth of my conscience afresh, and abide the shame and the harm here of mine own fault. And finally, Marget, this wot I very well, that without my fault he will not let me be lost... And therefore, mine own good daughter, never trouble thy mind, for any thing that ever shall hap me in this world. Nothing can come, but that that God will... And if anything hap me that you would be loth, pray to God for me, but trouble not yourself: as I shall full heartily pray for us all, that we may meet together once in heaven, where we shall make merry for ever, and never have trouble after.

St Thomas More, from a letter to his daughter, Margaret Roper, written in 1534

St Paul Miki

Jesuit Martyr

During the late 16th century fierce persecution broke out against Christians in Japan. The Japanese Jesuit priest St Paul Miki (c. 1564–97) and 25 other Christians were seized, subjected to terrible torture and finally crucified at Nagasaki on 5 February 1597. This contemporary account describes their final hours.

When the crosses had been erected, it was wonderful to see how steadfast all were…

Our brother, Paul Miki, seeing that he was standing in the most honoured pulpit of any he had ever been in, first of all declared to the onlookers that he was both a Japanese and a Jesuit. He told them that he was dying because he had preached the gospel, and that he gave thanks to God for such a singular privilege. Then he added the following words, 'Since I have now come to this moment, I do not think there is anyone among you who would believe that I would willingly tell a lie. I tell you openly, then, that there is no other way of salvation than that of the Christians. Since that way teaches me to forgive my enemies and all who have done me violence, I willingly forgive the king and those who have a hand in my death, and I entreat them to seek the initiation of Christian baptism.'

Then, looking to his companions, he began to encourage them in this last agony. On the face of each of them there appeared a great joy, and this was especially true of Louis. When one of the other Christians cried out that soon he would be in Paradise, he responded with such a joyful movement of his hands and his whole body that he attracted the attention of all the onlookers.

Anthony, who was beside Louis, with his eyes fixed on heaven, called on the most holy names of Jesus and Mary, and then sang the psalm, *Laudate, pueri, Dominum*. He had learnt this at the catechetical school in Nagasaki, for among the tasks given to the children there had been included the learning of some psalms such as these.

The others kept repeating, 'Jesus, Mary,' and their faces showed no sign of distress. Some of them, indeed, were encouraging the bystanders to lead good Christian lives. By these actions and by others like them, they gave ample proof of their willingness to die.

Then the four executioners began to take their spears out of the sheaths that the Japanese use. When they saw those terrible spears, all the faithful cried out, 'Jesus, Mary.' What is more, a sad lamentation assailed heaven itself. The executioners despatched each of them in a very short time with one or two thrusts.

St Paul Miki, from a contemporary account

Sydney Carton

Heroic Self-Sacrifice

In the final chapter of *A Tale of Two Cities* the English novelist Charles Dickens (1812–70) describes the final hours of Sydney Carton, who is taking the place of Charles Darnay on the scaffold during the French Revolution of 1789. Darnay has been sentenced to death because he is a descendant of the family of Evrémonde. Carton's unrequited love for Darnay's wife leads him to exploit the physical resemblance between himself and his successful rival in order to make the act of heroic self-sacrifice with which he redeems an otherwise misspent life. The prison 'Spy' is the only person to know of the substitution because he has been persuaded to assist.

There is a guard of sundry horsemen riding abreast of the tumbrils, and faces are often turned up to some of them and they are asked some question. It would seem to be always the same question, for, it is always followed by a press of people towards the third cart. The horsemen abreast of that cart, frequently point out one man in it with their swords. The leading curiosity is, to know which is he; he stands at the back of the tumbril with his head bent down, to converse with a mere girl who sits on the side of the cart, and holds his hand. He has no curiosity or care for the scene about him, and always speaks to the girl. Here and there in the long Street of St Honoré, cries are raised against him. If they move him at all, it is only to a quiet smile, as he shakes his hair a little more loosely about his face. He cannot easily touch his face, his arms being bound.

On the steps of a church, awaiting the coming-up of the tumbrils, stands the Spy and prison-sheep. He looks into the first of them: not there. He looks into the second: not there. He already asks himself, 'Has he sacrificed me?' when his face clears, as he looks into the third.

'Which is Evrémonde?' says a man behind him.

'That. At the back there.'

'With his hand in the girl's?'

'Yes.'

The man cries 'Down, Evrémonde! To the guillotine all aristocrats! Down, Evrémonde!'

'Hush, hush!' the Spy entreats him, timidly.

'And why not, citizen?'

'He is going to pay the forfeit; it will be paid in five minutes more. Let him be at peace.'

But, the man continuing to exclaim, 'Down, Evrémonde!' the face of Evrémonde is for a moment turned towards him. Evrémonde then sees the Spy, and looks attentively at him, and goes his way.

The clocks are on the stroke of three, and the furrow ploughed among the populace is turning round, to come on into the place of execution, and end. The ridges thrown to this side and to that, now crumble in and close behind the last plough as it passes on, for all are following to the Guillotine. In front of it, seated in chairs as in a garden of public diversion, are a number of women, busily knitting. On one of the foremost chairs, stands The Vengeance, looking about for her friend.

'Thérèse!' she cries, in her shrill tones. 'Who has seen her? Thérèse Defarge!'

'She never missed before,' says a knitting-woman of the sisterhood.

'No; nor will she miss now,' cries The Vengeance, petulantly. 'Thérèse.'

'Louder,' the woman recommends.

Ay! Louder, Vengeance, much louder, and still she will scarcely hear thee. Louder yet, Vengeance, with a little oath or so added, and yet it will hardly bring her. Send other women up and down to seek her, lingering somewhere; and yet, although the messengers have done dread deeds, it is questionable whether of their own wills they will go far enough to find her!

'Bad Fortune!' cries The Vengeance, stamping her foot in the chair, 'and here are the tumbrils! And Evrémonde will be despatched in a wink, and she not here! See her knitting in my hand, and her empty chair ready for her. I cry with vexation and disappointment!'

As The Vengeance descends from her elevation to do it, the tumbrils begin to discharge their loads. The ministers of Sainte Guillotine are robed and ready. Crash! – A head is held up, and the knitting-women who scarcely lifted their eyes to look at it a moment ago when it could think and speak, count One.

The second tumbril empties and moves on; the third comes up. Crash! – And the knitting-women, never faltering or pausing in their work, count Two.

The supposed Evrémonde descends, and the seamstress is lifted out next after him. He has not relinquished her patient hand in getting out, but still holds it as he promised. He gently places her with her back to the crashing engine that constantly whirs up and falls, and she looks into his face and thanks him.

'But for you, dear stranger, I should not be so composed, for I am naturally a poor little thing, faint of heart; nor should I have been able to raise my thoughts to him who was put to death, that we might have hope and comfort here today. I think you were sent to me by heaven.'

'Or you to me,' says Sydney Carton. 'Keep your eyes upon me, dear child, and mind no other object.'

'I mind nothing while I hold your hand. I shall mind nothing when I let it go, if they are rapid.'

'They will be rapid. Fear not!'

The two stand in the fast-thinning throng of victims, but they speak as if they were alone. Eye to eye, voice to voice, hand to hand, heart to heart, these two children of the Universal Mother, else so wide apart and differing, have come together on the dark highway, to repair home together and to rest in her bosom.

'Brave and generous friend, will you let me ask you one last question? I am very ignorant, and it troubles me – just a little.'

'Tell me what it is.'

'I have a cousin, an only relative and an orphan, like myself, whom I love very dearly. She is five years younger than I, and she lives in a farmer's house in the south country. Poverty parted us, and she knows nothing of my fate – for I cannot write – and if I could, how should I tell her! It is better as it is.'

'Yes, yes: better as it is.'

'What I have been thinking as we came along, and what I am still thinking now, as I look into your kind strong face which gives me so much support, is this: – If the Republic really does good to the poor, and they come to be less hungry, and in all ways to suffer less, she may live a long time; she may even live to be old.'

'What then, my gentle sister?'

'Do you think:' the uncomplaining eyes in which there is so much endurance, fill with tears, and the lips part a little more and tremble: 'that it will seem long to me, while I wait for her in the better land where I trust both you and I will be mercifully sheltered?'

'It cannot be, my child; there is no time there, and no trouble there.'

'You comfort me so much! I am so ignorant. Am I to kiss you now? Is the moment come?'

'Yes.'

She kisses his lips; he kisses hers; they solemnly bless each other. The spare hand does not tremble as he releases it; nothing worse than a sweet, bright constancy is in the patient face. She goes next before him – is gone; the knitting-women count 22.

'I am the Resurrection and the Life, saith the Lord: he that believeth in me, though he were dead, yet shall he live: and whosoever liveth and believeth in me, shall never die.'

The murmuring of many voices, the upturning of many faces, the pressing on of many footsteps in the outskirts of the crowd, so that it swells forward in a mass, like one great heave of water, all flashes away. Twenty-three.

They said of him, about the city that night, that it was the peacefullest man's face ever beheld there. Many added that he looked sublime and prophetic.

One of the most remarkable sufferers by the same axe – a woman – had asked at the foot of the same scaffold, not long before, to be allowed to write down the thoughts that were inspiring her. If he had given any utterance to his, and they were prophetic, they would have been these:

'I see Barsad, and Cly, Defarge, The Vengeance, the Juryman, the Judge, long ranks of the new oppressors who have risen on the destruction of the old, perishing by this retributive instrument, before it shall cease out of its present use. I see a beautiful city and a brilliant people rising from this abyss, and, in their struggles to be truly free, in their triumphs and defeats, through long years to come, I see the evil of this time and of the previous time of which this is the natural birth, gradually making expiation for itself and wearing out.

'I see the lives for which I lay down my life, peaceful, useful, prosperous and happy, in that England which I shall see no more. I see her with a child upon her bosom, who bears my name. I see her father, aged and bent, but otherwise restored, and faithful to all men in his healing office, and at peace. I see the good old man, so long their friend, in 10 years' time enriching them with all he has, and passing tranquilly to his reward.

'I see that I hold a sanctuary in their hearts, and in the hearts of their descendants, generations hence. I see her, an old woman, weeping for me on the anniversary of this day. I see her and her husband, their course done, lying side by side in their last earthly bed, and I know that each was not more honoured and held sacred in the other's soul, than I was in the souls of both.

'I see that child who lay upon her bosom and who bore my name, a man, winning his way up in that path of life which once was mine. I see him winning it so well, that my name is made illustrious there by the light of his. I see the blots I threw upon it, faded away. I see him, foremost of just judges and honoured men, bringing a boy of my name, with a forehead that I know and golden hair to this place – then fair to look upon, with not a trace of this day's disfigurement – and I hear him tell the child my story, with a tender and a faltering voice.

'It is a far, far better thing that I do, than I have ever done; it is a far, far better rest that I go to, than I have ever known.'

Charles Dickens, *A Tale of Two Cities*

Fyodor Dostoevsky

Back from the Brink

It is possible to travel to the threshold of the final journey, only to be drawn back from the brink. In 1849 the Russian novelist Fyodor Dostoevsky (1821–81) had been condemned to death by the Russian ruler, Tsar Nicholas I (1825–55) for participating in an anti-Tsarist plot. Dostoevsky and his fellow conspirators stood shivering in Semenovsky Square, St Petersburg, as their crimes and the sentence were read aloud. The first three prisoners were tied to stakes in front of open graves and the soldiers took aim. Dostoevsky was in the next group of three and believed that he had just a few more minutes to live. He uttered the words, 'We shall be with Christ.' And at that point all the condemned men were informed that they had been reprieved. The Tsar had never intended any of them to die but had wanted to stage the mock execution and the reprieve in order to demonstrate his 'benevolence' to the people of Russia. But the joy of the conspirators was short-lived. The sentence had been commuted to hard labour in Siberia until 1854. The experience of the mock execution marked Dostoevsky for life. In *The Idiot* he describes it in the words of the endearing and Christlike Prince Myshkin, the 'idiot' of the title who claims to have heard this account from a man he met on his travels.

> This man had once been taken, together with others, to a place of execution where a sentence of death was read out to him. He was to be shot for a political crime. Twenty minutes later his reprieve was read out to him, another penalty for his crime being substituted. Yet the interval between the two sentences – 20 minutes or, at least, a quarter of an hour – he passed in the absolute certainty that in a few minutes he would be dead. I very much liked to listen to him when he used to recall his impressions of those moments, and I questioned him several times about it. He remembered everything with the most

extraordinary distinctness, and he used to say that he would never forget anything he had been through during those minutes. Three posts were dug into the ground about 20 paces from the scaffold, which was surrounded by a crowd of people and soldiers, for there were several criminals. The first three were led to the posts and tied to them; the death vestments (long, white smocks) were put on them, and white caps were drawn over their eyes so that they should not see the rifles; next a company of several soldiers was drawn up against each post. My friend was the eighth on the list and his would therefore be the third turn to be marched to the posts. The priest went to each of them with the cross. It seemed to him then he had only five more minutes to live. He told me that those five minutes were like an eternity to him, riches beyond the dreams of avarice; he felt that during those five minutes he would live through so many lives that it was quite unnecessary for him to think of the last moment, so that he had plenty of time to make all sorts of arrangements: he calculated the exact time he needed to take leave of his comrades, and decided that he could do that in two minutes, then he would spend another two minutes in thinking of himself for the last time, and, finally, one minute for a last look round. He remembered very well that he had decided to do all this and that he had divided up the time in exactly that way. He was dying at 27, a strong and healthy man; taking leave of his comrades, he remembered asking one of them quite an irrelevant question and being very interested indeed in his answer. Then, after he had bidden farewell to his comrades, came the two minutes he had set aside for thinking of himself; he knew beforehand what he would think about: he just wanted to imagine, as vividly and as quickly as possible, how it could be that now, at this moment, he was there and alive and in three minutes he would merely be *something* – someone or something – but what? And where? All that he thought he would be able to decide in those two minutes! There was a church not far off, its gilt roof shining in the bright sunshine. He remembered staring with awful intensity at that roof and the sunbeams flashing from it; he could not tear his eyes off those rays of light: those rays seemed to him to be his new nature, and he felt that in three minutes he would somehow merge with them... The uncertainty and the feeling of disgust with that new thing which was bound to come any minute were dreadful; but he said that the thing that was most unbearable to him at the time was the constant thought, 'What if I had not had to die! What if I could return to life — oh, what an eternity! And all that would be mine! I should turn every minute into an age, I should lose nothing, I should count every minute separately and waste none!' He said that this reflection finally filled him with such bitterness that he prayed to be shot as quickly as possible.

Fyodor Dostoevsky, *The Idiot*

Abraham Lincoln

Advance Warning

Some people receive advance warning of their death, either through a dream or some other form of premonition. Early in April 1865 Abraham Lincoln (1809–65), the 16th President of the United States, was troubled by such a dream. He confided the details to his wife, Mary, and to his friend and long-time associate, Ward Hill Lamon, who was already concerned about the danger of assassination. Lincoln's presidency (1861–65) had been overshadowed by the bitter Civil War between the Northern States and the Southern Confederacy. With the surrender of Southern General Robert E. Lee on 9 April 1865, the war effectively ended, but Southern feeling against President Lincoln and the North continued to run high. In his biography, *With Malice Towards None*, Stephen B. Oates describes the final days of the President.

In his exhausted condition, Lincoln still wasn't sleeping well, troubled lately by strange and ghostly dreams. One night in the second week of April, with Mary, Lamon, and one or two others in the White House, Lincoln started talking about dreams, and Mary commented on how 'dreadful solemn' he seemed. 'I had one the other night which has haunted me ever since,' Lincoln said. After he woke from the dream, he opened the Bible and everywhere he turned his eye fell on passages about dreams, visions, and supernatural visitations.

'You frighten me!' Mary exclaimed. 'What is the matter?'

Maybe he'd 'done wrong' in even mentioning the dream, Lincoln said, 'but somehow the thing has got possession of me'.

What had possession of him? Mary asked. What had he dreamed?

Lincoln hesitated, then began in a voice sad and serious: 'About 10 days ago I retired very late. I had been up waiting for important dispatches from the front. I could not have been long in bed when

I fell into a slumber, for I was weary. I soon began to dream. There seemed to be a death-like stillness about me. Then I heard subdued sobs, as if a number of people were weeping. I thought I left my bed and wandered downstairs. There the silence was broken by the same pitiful sobbing, but the mourners were invisible. I went from room to room; no living person was in sight, but the same mournful sounds of distress met me as I passed along. It was light in all the rooms; every object was familiar to me; but where were all the people who were grieving as if their hearts would break? I was puzzled and alarmed. What could be the meaning of all this? Determined to find the cause of a state of things so mysterious and so shocking, I kept on until I arrived at the East Room, which I entered. There I met with a sickening surprise. Before me was a catafalque, on which rested a corpse wrapped in funeral vestments. Around it were stationed soldiers who were acting as guards; and there was a throng of people, some gazing mournfully upon the corpse, whose face was covered, others weeping pitifully. 'Who is dead in the White House?' I demanded of one of the soldiers. 'The President,' was his answer; 'he was killed by an assassin!' Then came a loud burst of grief from the crowd. As he recounted the dream, Lamon observed Lincoln was 'grave, gloomy, and at times visibly pale'.

'That is horrid!' Mary said. 'I wish you had not told it.'

'Well,' Lincoln said, 'it is only a dream, Mary. Let us say no more about it, and try to forget it.'

Lamon, of course, was just as frightened as Mary. But Lincoln sported with him as always. 'For a long time you have been trying to keep somebody – the Lord knows who – from killing me,' Lincoln said. 'Don't you see how it will turn out? In this dream it was not me, but some other fellow, that was killed. It seems that this ghostly assassin tried his hand on someone else.' In a moment Lincoln grew solemn again. He sighed, as though talking only to himself: 'Well, let it go. I think the Lord in his own good time and way will work this out all right.'...

A few days later on 14 April, Good Friday, the President and his wife had arranged to go to the theatre with their friend Major Henry Rathbone and his fiancée Clara Harris. During the performance, the actor and Southern fanatic John Wilkes Booth was able to gain access to the Presidential box...

It was a foggy night, so gloomy that the Lincolns could scarcely make out the buildings they passed. At street corners, gaslights glimmered eerily in the drifting mist. By the time they picked up Rathbone and Miss Harris, they were so late that the play had begun without them. At 8.30 the carriage pulled up in front of Ford's, blazing with lights, and the two couples hurried inside – Mary on Lincoln's arm, pretty young Clara on Rathbone's. The major was an ebullient fellow with a walrus moustache and a sloping nose. The two couples made their way up the winding stairway and crossed the dress circle at the back of the first balcony. The theatre was packed tonight with high army brass and assorted Washington socialites; when they spotted the President, the audience gave him a standing ovation and the orchestra promptly struck up 'Hail to the Chief'. The Presidential party swept around the back row of chairs now, passed though a door and down a short hallway to the 'state box', which directly overlooked the stage. Lincoln sank into a rocking chair provided by the management, with Mary seated beside him and Rathbone and Miss Harris to their right. The front of the box was adorned with drapes and brilliant regimental and Union flags. On stage, Harry Hawk, the male lead, ad-libbed a line: 'This reminds me of a story, as Mr Lincoln would say.' The audience roared and clapped, and Lincoln smiled, uttering something to Mary. Behind him, the box door was closed but not locked; in all the excitement of Lincoln's arrival, nobody noticed a small peephole dug out of the door. As the play progressed, guard John Parker left his post in the hallway leading to the state box, and either sat down out in the gallery to watch the play or went outside for a drink.

On stage, the players hammed it up in absurd and melodramatic scenes, and waves of laughter rolled over the audience. As the Lincolns picked up the story, Hawk was a homespun American backwoodsman named Asa Trenchard, and Laura Keene, a stunning woman with high cheekbones and braided auburn curls, was his young English cousin Florence Trenchard. A scheming English matron named Mrs Mountchessington, convinced that Trenchard was a rich Yankee, was out to snare him as a husband for her daughter Augusta. In the state box, Lincoln tried to relax, tried to get his mind off reconstruction, tried to lose himself in the play's preposterous humour. Mary rested her hand on his knee, called his attention to situations on stage, and clapped happily at the funniest scenes. One of the actresses noticed that Lincoln never clapped, but that he did laugh 'heartily' from time to time. At one point he felt a chill, as if a cold wind had blown over him, and he got up long enough to put on his overcoat.

During the third act, Mary slipped her hand into Lincoln's and nestled close to him. 'What will Miss Harris think of my hanging on to you so?' she whispered. 'She won't think anything about it,' Lincoln replied.

On stage, Mrs Mountchessington finally discovered the shocking truth about Trenchard: he was 'church mouse poor' and no catch at all for her daughter. In stiff British rage, she sent Augusta to her room, reproached the American for his ill-mannered impertinence, and flounced haughtily into the wings, leaving Trenchard alone on stage. Behind Lincoln, the door opened and a figure, a man, stepped into the box and aimed a derringer at the back of Lincoln's head, not six inches away. Mary was still sitting close to Lincoln and Rathbone and Miss Harris were looking rapturously at Trenchard. 'Don't know the manner of good society, eh?' Trenchard called after Mrs Mountchessington, 'Wal, I guess I know enough to turn you inside out, old gal – you sockdologizing old mantrap.' A gunshot rang out in the state box, and Lincoln's arm jerked up convulsively. For a frozen instant nobody moved – Mary and Miss Harris sat rigid in their seats, and the man stood there enveloped in smoke. As Lincoln slumped forward, Mary reached out instinctively and struggled to keep him from falling. She screamed in deranged, incomprehensible terror. The man jumped out of the smoke brandishing a dagger, a wild-looking man in a black felt hat and high boots with spurs. He yelled something and stabbed at Rathbone, gashing his arm open to the bone. Then he leaped from the box, only to catch his spur in a regimental flag and crash to the stage, breaking his left shinbone in the fall.

The audience was stunned, incredulous. Why, it was the actor John Wilkes Booth. Was this part of the play? An improvised scene? Witnesses heard him shout something in defiance – either *Sic semper tyrannis!* (Thus be it ever to tyrants) or 'The South shall be free!' Then he dragged himself out the back stage door, while Rathbone and Miss Harris both screamed, 'Stop that man! Stop that man!' 'Won't somebody stop that man?' Miss Harris pleaded. 'The President is shot!'

By now the theatre was pandemonium: screams, a medley of voices. 'Is there a doctor in the house!' someone cried. People were shoving into the aisles and rushing for the exits, with Laura Keene yelling at them from the stage, 'For God's sake, have presence of mind and keep your places, and all will be well.' In all the commotion, a young army

213

doctor named Charles A. Leale fought his way to the President's box, where a tearful Clara Harris tried to console Mary, who was holding Lincoln in the rocker and weeping hysterically. Leale lay the President on the floor and removed the blood clot from the wound to relieve the pressure on the brain. The bullet had struck him just behind the left ear, tunnelled through his brain, and lodged behind his right eye. The President was almost dead, Leale thought. He was paralysed, his breath shallow, his wrists without a pulse. Quickly Leale reached into his mouth, opened his throat, and applied artificial respiration in a desperate attempt to revive him. By now another doctor had reached the box, and Leale had him raise and lower the President's arms while Leale himself massaged the left breast with both hands. Then he placed his face against Lincoln's and gave him mouth-to-mouth resuscitation, drawing in his own breath and forcing it again and again into the President's lungs. At last he was breathing on his own, his heart beating with an irregular flutter. But he was still unconscious. Leale shook his head, unable to believe what was happening. 'His wound is mortal,' he said softly; 'it is impossible for him to recover.'

Stephen B. Oates, *With Malice Towards None: The Life of Abraham Lincoln*

St Thérèse of Lisieux

The Night of Faith

The French Carmelite nun St Thérèse of Lisieux (1873–97) died of
tuberculosis at the age of 24. Thérèse's Third Journey was completed in
physical agony and unrelieved spiritual darkness. Her final hours are
described in the Epilogue to her *Collected Letters*.

Suffering almost without respite in mind and body, but serene beneath
the suffering and wholly yielded up to God's will, Thérèse came to the
last day of her exile, 30 September 1897.

Then, more than ever, it was 'sheer suffering, with no single
element of consolation'.

And she cried, in the terrible death-agony, which lasted 12 hours:
'O my God! O sweet Virgin Mary! Come to my aid.'

'The cup is full to the brim! I could never have believed it was
possible to suffer so much... I cannot account for it save by the
extremity of my desire to save souls...'

'O my God! Whatever you will! But have pity on me!'

When she seemed driven to the very depths by the storm, she
mastered herself to assure those around her that the centre of her
soul remained the same:

'All I have written on my desire to suffer terribly for the good
God, oh! It is true.'

On the evening before, she had answered her sister Céline, who
wanted a word of farewell: 'I have said all... all is consummated...
only love counts.'

At 7.15 in the evening of the 30th, after the Angelus, the Prioress
warned her that her agony might go on longer. Thérèse answered
courageously, in a voice barely audible: 'Very well then!... let it
come... oh! I would not want to suffer less!...'

Then, looking at the crucifix she held so tightly in her clasped hands:

'Oh! I love him!… My God… I love you!' She had barely uttered these words in 'the night of faith', when she collapsed; then suddenly, as though hearing a voice from heaven, she sat up in ecstasy, her look radiant, gazing above her.

It was the rending of the cloud, the skies opening, illumination; and in that illumination she died.

St Thérèse of Lisieux, *Collected Letters*

The Aftermath

Thérèse's older sister Céline (1869–1959), now Sister Geneviève, had been at her sister's deathbed and describes the aftermath.

Thérèse had hardly expired when I felt my heart ready to break with grief and I hurriedly left the infirmary. It seemed to me, in my naivety, that I would see her in the sky, but the firmament was covered with clouds, and it was raining. Then, leaning against one of the pillars of the cloister arches, I said, sobbing: 'If only there were some stars in the heavens!' I had hardly pronounced these words when the sky became serene, the stars shone brilliantly in the firmament, and there were no more clouds! My uncle and aunt Guérin, who were on their way back home with their umbrellas, after having spent the whole time of our dear little sister's agony in our chapel, were very much surprised at this sudden change and asked each other what it could mean.

Stéphane-Joseph Piat, OFM, *Céline: Sister Geneviève of the Holy Face*

Edith Cavell

Patriotism is Not Enough

The British nurse Edith Cavell (1865–1915) was matron of the Berkendael Medical Institute in Brussels when it became a Red Cross hospital in 1914 at the outbreak of the First World War. On 5 August 1915 Edith was arrested by the occupying German forces on a charge of assisting Allied soldiers to escape from Belgium. During her trial she admitted that she had helped more than 200 men in this way. The American Legation in Brussels, which was responsible for protecting British interests in occupied Belgium, did everything in its power to intercede for clemency. Edith Cavell was nevertheless sentenced to death and executed by firing squad on the morning of 12 October 1915. Her last visitor was Stirling Gahan, the English chaplain in Brussels. Recruitment to the Allied cause is said to have doubled during the eight weeks following the announcement of Edith Cavell's execution, and her death was believed to have been influential in bringing the United States into the war 18 months later. The following extract is taken from the journal of Hugh Gibson (1883–1954), who was Secretary of the American Legation in Brussels.

It seems the sentence on Miss Cavell was not pronounced in open court. Her executioners, apparently in the hope of concealing their intentions from us, went into her cell and there, behind locked doors, pronounced sentence upon her. It is all of a piece with the other things they have done.

Last night Mr Gahan got a pass and was admitted to see Miss Cavell shortly before she was taken out and shot. He said she was calm and prepared and faced the ordeal without a tremor. She was a tiny thing that looked as though she could be blown away with a breath, but she had a great spirit. She told Mr Gahan that soldiers had come to her and asked to be helped to the frontier; that knowing the risks they ran and the risks she took, she had helped them. She said she had nothing to regret, no complaint to make, and that if she had it all to do over again, she would change nothing. And most pathetic of all was her statement that she thanked God for the six weeks she had passed in prison – the nearest approach to rest she had known for years.

They partook together of the holy communion, and she who had so little need of preparation was prepared for death. She was free from resentment and said: 'I realize that patriotism is not enough. I must have no hatred or bitterness toward anyone.'

She was taken out and shot before daybreak.

She was denied the support of her own clergyman at the end, but a German military chaplain stayed with her and gave her burial within the precincts of the prison. He did not conceal his admiration and said: 'She was courageous to the end. She professed her Christian faith and said that she was glad to die for her country. She died like a heroine.'

Hugh Gibson, *A Journal from Our Legation in Belgium*

The Hindenburg

The Loss of the Hindenburg

On 6 May 1937 the airship *Hindenburg* burst into flames on approaching its mooring point at Lakehurst, New Jersey, at the end of a transatlantic flight from Germany. The airship was the largest ever constructed, the first commercial transatlantic airliner and a source of considerable pride to Hitler and Germany's Nazi leaders. The passengers in the luxurious *Hindenburg* had no inkling that many of them were minutes away from death when the landing ropes were dropped. This extract is taken from the account written by Commander Charles Rosendahl (1892–1977), who was in command of the Lakehurst Naval Air Station and a good friend of the captain of the *Hindenburg*, Ernst Lehmann, who died the following day as a result of burns sustained in the explosion.

At 7.25, or just four minutes after the landing ropes had been dropped, I saw a burst of flame on top of the ship just forward of where the upper vertical fin attaches to the hull. It was a brilliant burst of flame resembling a flower opening rapidly into bloom. I knew at once that the ship was doomed, for nothing could prevent that flame from spreading to the entire volume of hydrogen with which she was inflated. There was a muffled report and the flames spread rapidly through the after quarter of the ship. In the control room, the officers were not aware that anything was wrong until they felt a shudder through the ship that reminded them of the snapping of a landing rope, but a quick glance assured them that it was something else. As the stern section of the ship lost its buoyancy in the fire, it began to settle to the ground on almost an even keel, ablaze throughout and sending huge pillars of flame and smoke to great heights, particularly as the fuel oil began to burn.

As the stern settled, the forward three-quarters of the ship, still having its buoyancy, pointed skywards at an angle of about 45 degrees.

Through the axial corridor of the ship, in reality a huge vent extending along the very central axis, the flame shot upward and forward as though it were going up a stack. Although the travel of the flame was actually progressive, it spread forward so rapidly and so quickly encompassed the entire length of the ship that to some it may have seemed almost instantaneous. The forward section was not long in following the stern to the ground, and within less than a minute from the first appearance of the fire, the ship had settled, not crashed, on to the ground and lay there writhing and crackling from the hottest flame that man knows.

The feelings of those on the ground are difficult to describe. Visitors who stood in the assigned visiting space several hundred yards away were stricken dumb or fled in horror at this amazing spectacle. In order not to be caught under the burning ship, the ground crew were ordered to run from the immediate vicinity. But even before the ship had touched the ground, they had dashed back to effect such rescues as might be possible. In the ground crew were many men who were not only acquainted with many of those on board the ship, but were also familiar with the parts of the ship where passengers and crew were located. To such places they went immediately. On board the ship there was little time for warning or help. Some were surprised in their cabins or at their posts of duty and never knew what overtook them. Others heard shouts from within and from without the ship to jump through the windows and many of the survivors got out by this method. At first glance, it seemed impossible that human beings could come out alive from such an inferno. As I stood off to one side, spellbound by this most unexpected tragedy, I saw the flames eat rapidly along the fabric sides of the hull greedily devouring the illustrious name *Hindenburg* letter by letter.

It is unfortunate that most of the passengers were gathered on the starboard side and that they and perhaps others on board did not realize that the wind on the surface was blowing directly onto the port beam and hence was driving the flames to starboard. Realization of this fact might have saved a few more lives. I do not recall when I have been so startled as when I saw Chief Steward Kubis, Watch Officers Ziegler and Zable, and several others, suddenly emerge from the burning mass of wreckage totally unharmed. There were of course some miraculous escapes, not all of which will ever be recorded. One of the elderly women passengers, as though led by a guardian angel, left the ship by the regular hatchway with the calmness of a somnambulist, receiving only minor burns. Others hearing the call to them to jump, went through the open windows and were then led to safety. Mr George Grant, a British shipping man, escaped without a single scratch or burn by jumping through a window, and then as he was picking himself up to run away from the fire, suffered the great misfortune of having another person leap from the same window and land squarely in the middle of his back injuring him severely. Probably the most miraculous escape was that of Werner Franz, a 14-year-old cabin boy. As he jumped through a hatch in the bottom of the ship and reached the ground, the searing flames began to choke him. Just at that moment, a water tank opened up immediately above him discharging its entire contents upon him and bringing him to his senses. Just then he spied an opening in the wreckage free from flames, worked his way through it and emerged into the open air from this fiery furnace totally unharmed and thoroughly drenched. Another who escaped without injury was Captain Anton Wittemann. Nelson Morris, an American passenger and an experienced airship traveller, jumped through a window on the starboard side and then with his bare hands snapped the red hot structural members about him as though they were twigs, and fought his way clear of the burning wreck with only minor burns.

Those in the control car, as had every member of the crew, stuck to their posts in accordance with the highest traditions. As the forward section of the ship settled to the ground, it rebounded slightly from the resiliency of the forward landing wheel. Then and only then came the word: 'Now everybody out.' There had been plenty of quick thinking in the control car during those seconds of descent. The normal impulse would have been to drop water ballasts to ease the impact of the ship with the ground, but those in the control car in an instant decided not to drop it but to let the weight of that water remain in the ship as long as possible to bring the burning hull to the ground in the shortest space of time. In my opinion, this was one of the outstanding events in the whole disaster.

Captain Pruss was badly burnt, but not so badly as Captain Lehmann who nevertheless was able to stagger away from the ship. Largely because there were many tons of fuel oil still remaining on board, the fire raged for more than three hours despite the efforts of all available fire fighting apparatus. Thirteen out of 36 passengers perished or died subsequently from injuries; of the 61 crew members,

22 fell victim to this awful fire and one civilian member of the ground crew died of burns. To anyone having seen the tragedy, it seems remarkable indeed that out of 97 persons on board, 62 of them or nearly two-thirds have survived. Sad as was the loss of every one of them, no loss will be more keenly felt in the airship world than that of the outstanding pioneer Ernst Lehmann who succumbed to burns.

Commander Charles Rosendahl: this account forms the last chapter of Ernst Lehmann's posthumously published autobiography *Zeppelin*

Dietrich Bonhoeffer

The Cost of Discipleship

The Lutheran pastor and theologian Dietrich Bonhoeffer (1906–45) was a member of the Confessing Church, the group of German evangelical Christians most actively opposed to the German Christian Church Movement sponsored by the Nazis between 1933 and 1945. At the outbreak of war Bonhoeffer was in America on a lecture tour, but felt that it was his duty to return to Germany, where he became deeply involved in the German resistance movement. In 1943 he was arrested, imprisoned and taken to the concentration camp of Buchenwald. On 9 April 1945 he was hanged by the Gestapo in Flossenburg concentration camp. Bonhoeffer's indomitable courage, his unselfishness and his goodness, inspired all who came into contact with him in prison. He even inspired respect in the guards, who smuggled his papers and poems out of prison and apologized for having to lock his door. Bonhoeffer clearly saw death bearing down upon him, and in this poem he acknowledges the difference between the way others see him and the way he perceives himself.

Who Am I?

Who am I? They often tell me
I would step from my cell's confinement
calmly, cheerfully, firmly,
like a squire from his country-house.

Who am I? They often tell me
I would talk to my warders
freely and friendly and clearly,
as though it were mine to command.

Who am I? They also tell me
I would bear the days of misfortune
equably, smilingly, proudly,
like one accustomed to win.

Am I then really all that which other men tell of?
Or am I only what I myself know of myself,
restless and longing and sick, like a bird in a cage,
struggling for breath, as though hands were compressing my throat,
yearning for colours, for flowers, for the voices of birds,
thirsting for words of kindness, for neighbourliness,
tossing in expectation of great events,
powerlessly trembling for friends at an infinite distance,
weary and empty at praying, at thinking, at making,
faint, and ready to say farewell to it all?

Who am I? This or the other?
Am I one person today, and tomorrow another?
Am I both at once? A hypocrite before others,
and before myself a contemptibly woebegone weakling?
Or is something within me still like a beaten army,
fleeing in disorder from victory already achieved?

Who am I? They mock me, these lonely questions of mine.
Whoever I am, thou knowest, O God, I am thine.

Dietrich Bonhoeffer, *Letters and Papers from Prison*

Anna

The Death of Anna

In *Mister God, This is Anna*, Anna's biographer Fynn describes the
extraordinary years he spent with the child who erupted into his life as a
homeless six-year-old wandering the streets of London during the 1930s.
Anna had no family, or none that she cared to acknowledge, so Fynn took
her home to his mother. His account of Anna's philosophical and original
views of 'Mister God', life and the universe has remained a bestseller since
its first appearance in 1974. The last chapter describes Anna's final hours –
the Third Journey which took her into the arms of 'Mister God'.

It was a beautiful sunny day. The street was full of kid noises. Laughter
drowned the sounds of marching feet, when suddenly the world fell to
pieces.

One scream killed the laughter. It was Jackie's. I turned round in
time to catch her in my arms as she hurled herself at me. Her face
was a white mask of horror.

'Fynn! Oh Christ! It's Anna. She's dead! She's dead!'

Her scarlet fingernails dug into my chest and the ice-cold water
of fear flooded over me. I ran down the street. Anna was lying
across the railings, her fingers clinging to the top of a wall. I
lifted her off and cradled her in my arms. A flicker of pain
narrowed her eyes.

'I slipped outa the tree,' she murmured.

'All right, Tich, hold on. I've got you.'

Suddenly I felt terribly sick. Out of the corner of my eyes I had
seen something, something that in a curiously distorted way was
even more terrifying than this injured child in my arms. Her fall had
broken off the top part of one of the railings. A broken iron stump.
A few years ago nobody could see that, now it was clear for all to see.

This iron stump, these crystal mountains, were now red with shame and horror at its part in this dreadful thing.

I carried Anna home and put her to bed. The doctor came and dressed her wounds and left me with her. I held her hands and searched her face. The pain flickered across her eyes but was chased away by a grin that slowly blossomed over her face. The grin won; the pain was hidden somewhere inside her. Thank God, she was going to be all right. Thank God.

'Fynn, is the Princess all right?' Anna whispered.

'She's fine,' I answered. I didn't know if she was all right or not.

'She was stuck up the tree and couldn't get down – I slipped,' said Anna.

'She's all right.'

'She was very frightened. She's only a baby kitten.'

'She's fine, she's all right. You rest. I'll stay with you. Don't be frightened,' I said to Anna.

'Ain't frightened, Fynn, I ain't frightened.'

'Go to sleep, Tich. Have a little sleep, I've got you.'

Her eyes closed and she slept. It was going to be all right. I knew it deep down inside. For two days this feeling that it was going to be all right grew and took over my fears. Her grin and her excited conversations about Mister God made me doubly sure. The knots inside me were coming undone. I was looking out of the window when she called me.

'Fynn!'

'Here, Tich. What d'you want?' I crossed to her.

'Fynn, it is like turning inside out!' There was a look of amazement on her face.

An ice-cold hand gripped my heart and squeezed hard. I remembered Granny Harding.

'Tich,' my voice was too loud, 'Tich, look at me!'

Her eyes flickered and her smile spread. I hurried to the window and flung it up. Cory was there.

'Get the doctor quickly,' I said.

She nodded, turned on her heels and ran. Suddenly I knew what was going to happen. I went back to Anna. It wasn't time for crying, it was never time for crying. The cold dread in my heart had frozen the tears within me. I held Anna's hand. My head pounded with the idea that 'whatever you shall ask in my name...' I asked. I pleaded.

'Fynn,' she whispered, and the smile lit up her face, 'Fynn, I love you.'

226

'I love you too, Tich.'

'Fynn, I bet Mister God lets me get into heaven for this.'

'You betcha. I bet he's waiting for you.'

I wanted to say more, a whole lot more, but she wasn't listening any more, just smiling.

The days burnt up like giant candles, and time melted, ran, and congealed into useless and hideous lumps.

Two days after the funeral I found Anna's seed pouch. It gave me something to do. I went to the cemetery and stayed for a little while. It just made things worse, that much more empty. If only I had been nearer at the time – if only I had known what she was doing, if only – if only – I tipped the seeds on the fresh-turned earth and hurled the pouch from me in misery.

I wanted to hate God, wanted him out of my system, but he wouldn't go. I found God more real, more strangely real than ever before. Hate wouldn't come, but I despised him. God was an idiot, a cretin, a moron. He could have saved Anna, but he didn't; he just let this most stupid of all things happen. This child, this beautiful child, had been cut off – cut off and not yet eight. Just when she was – Hell!

The war years took me out of the East End. The war dragged its bloody boots over the face of the world until the madness was over. Thousands of other children had died, thousands more were maimed and homeless. The madness of war became the madness of victory. Victory? I got good and drunk on VJ night. It was a good way out.

I had been given a bundle of books some time previously, but I hadn't bothered to undo them. There didn't seem much point. It was one of those idle moments; I didn't know what to do with myself. Those years had made my eyes tired with looking and my ears ache with listening. Some sign, some vision, just for a moment. I picked up the books. They didn't seem all that interesting. Nothing seemed very interesting. I flipped through the pages. It wasn't until my eyes fell upon the name of Coleridge that I stopped the pages of the book slipping through my fingers. For me Coleridge is at the top of the heap. I began to read:

'I adopt with full faith the theory of Aristotle that poetry as poetry is essentially ideal, that it avoids and excludes all accident, that is...'

I turned back a few pages and began to read again. Out of the pages of that book Old Woody appeared.

'The process by which the poetic imagination works is illustrated by Coleridge from the following lines of Sir John Davies:

Thus doth she, when from individual states
She doth abstract the universal kinds,
Which then reclothed in divers names and fates,
Steal access thro' our senses to our minds.'

The smoky fires of the 'night-time people' came drifting through my imagination: Old Woody, Convict Bill, Old Lil, Anna and me. A few lines further on my eye caught one word, 'violence'.

'The young poet,' says Goethe, 'must do some sort of violence to himself to get out of the mere general idea. No doubt this is difficult, but it is the very art of living.'

It slowly began to make sense, the bits began to fall into place. Something was happening and it made me cry; for the first time in a long, long time I cried. I went out into the night and stayed out. The clouds seemed to be rolling back. It kept nagging at the back of my mind. Anna's life hadn't been cut short; far from it, it had been full, completely fulfilled.

The next day I headed back to the cemetery. It took me a long time to find Anna's grave. It was tucked away at the back of the cemetery. I knew that it had no headstone, just a simple wooden cross with the name on it, 'Anna'. I found it after about an hour.

I had gone there with this feeling of peace inside me, as if the book had been closed, as if the story had been one of triumph, but I hadn't expected this. I stopped and gasped. This was it. The little cross leant drunkenly, its paint peeling off, and there was the name, ANNA.

I wanted to laugh, but you don't laugh in a cemetery, do you? Not only did I want to laugh, I had to laugh. It wouldn't stay bottled up. I laughed till the tears ran down my face. I pulled up the little cross and threw it into a thicket.

'OK, Mister God,' I laughed, 'I'm convinced. Good old Mister God. You might be a bit slow at times, but you certainly make it all right in the end.'

Anna's grave was a brilliant red carpet of poppies. Lupins stood guard in the background. A couple of trees whispered to each other while a family of little mice scurried backwards and forwards through the uncut grass. Anna was truly home. She didn't need a marker. You couldn't better this with a squillion tons of marble. I stayed for a little while and said goodbye to her for the first time in five years.

As I made my way back to the main gates I passed by hordes of little marble cherubs, angels and pearly gates. I stopped in front of the 12-foot angel, still trying to lay down its bunch of marble flowers, after God knows how many years.

'Hi chum,' I said, saluting the angel, 'you'll never make it, you know.'

I swung on the iron gates as I yelled back into the cemetery. 'The answer is "In my middle."'

A finger of thrill went down my spine and I thought I heard her voice saying, 'What's that the answer to, Fynn?'

'That's easy. The question is "Where's Anna?"'

I had found her again – found her in my middle.

I felt sure that somewhere Anna and Mister God were laughing.

Fynn, *Mister God, This is Anna*

Dylan Thomas

Into the Darkness

The Welsh poet Dylan Thomas (1914–53) wrote this poem in 1951 for his agnostic father who was dying from cancer of the throat.

Do Not Go Gentle into That Good Night

Do not go gentle into that good night,
Old age should burn and rave at close of day:
Rage, rage against the dying of the light.

Though wise men at their end know dark is right,
Because their words had forked no lightning they
Do not go gentle into that good night.

Good men, the last wave by, crying how bright
Their frail deeds might have danced in a green bay,
Rage, rage against the dying of the light.

Wild men who caught and sang the sun in flight,
And learn, too late, they grieved it on its way,
Do not go gentle into that good night.

Grave men, near death, who see with blinding sight
Blind eyes could blaze like meteors and be gay,
Rage, rage against the dying of the light.

And you, my father, there on the sad height,
Curse, bless, me now with your fierce tears, I pray.
Do not go gentle into that good night.
Rage, rage against the dying of the light.

Dylan Thomas

Malcolm Muggeridge

A Turning Point

If life becomes unbearable it is possible to anticipate the Third Journey by taking one's own life or attempting to do so. In a mood of deep depression the British writer and broadcaster Malcolm Muggeridge (1903–90) decided that he would swim out to sea until he could swim no further. In *Jesus Rediscovered* he describes the experience and its aftermath.

There was one point in my life when I decided to kill myself, and I swam out to sea, resolved for a variety of reasons that I didn't want to live any more. Partly it was a mood of deep depression, and partly actual difficulties. I swam out to sea until I felt myself sinking; you get a strange kind of sleepiness that afflicts you, as if you were just about to fall into a deep sleep. I thought that I would take one last look at the coast, and that would be the end. I saw the lights along the coast; and I suddenly realized that that was my home, the earth – the earth my home, and that I must stay on the earth because I belonged there until my life had run its course. Then somehow, I don't know how, I swam back. Now that was a time of great trouble for me... At the same time, it was a terrific turning point. I have never doubted since then that in all circumstances, whatever one's condition may be, or the condition of the society one lives in, or the condition of the world, life is good, and that to gain from this experience of living what has to be gained, and to learn what has to be learnt, it is necessary to live out one's life to the end until the moment comes for one's release. Then, and only then, can one truly rejoice in that moment. There is no catastrophe, as it seems to me, that can befall human beings which is not an illumination, and no illumination which is not in some sense a catastrophe. It's in an age like ours, an age of great superficiality of thought, that people ask how, if God makes a child with Down syndrome he can be a loving God. It's a very superficial thought, because a child with Down syndrome is part of the process whereby man exists, and we can't judge how that comes about, or what are its full consequences. All we can say is that it's part of the experience of living, and, like all other parts, it can shed light or it can shed darkness. Suffering is an essential element in the Christian religion, as it is in life. After all, the cross itself is the supreme example. If Christ hadn't suffered, do you imagine that anyone would have paid the slightest attention to the religion he founded? Not at all.

Malcolm Muggeridge, *Jesus Rediscovered*

Pope John XXIII

Spiritual Testament of
Patriarch Angelo Roncalli

In 1954 Angelo Roncalli (1881–1963), the future Pope John XXIII (1881–1963), had been Cardinal Patriarch of Venice for a year. He was over 70 and this spiritual testament included in his writings, *Journal of a Soul* published in 1964, indicates that he considered his life to be drawing to a close. There is no indication that he had the faintest inkling that his greatest achievements still lay several years ahead: he was elevated to the papacy in 1958 and convened the first session of the Second Vatican Council in 1962.

Venice, 29 June 1954

On the point of presenting myself before the Lord, One and Three, who created me, redeemed me, chose me to be priest and bishop and bestowed infinite graces upon me, I entrust my poor soul to his mercy. Humbly I beg his pardon for my sins and failings; I offer him what little good, even if imperfect and unworthy, I was able with his help to do for his glory and in the service of holy church and for the edification of my fellows, and I implore him finally to welcome me, like a kind and tender father, among his saints in the bliss of eternity.

I wish to profess once more my complete Christian and Catholic faith, belonging and submitting as I do to the holy, apostolic and Roman Church, and my perfect devotion and obedience to its august head, the supreme Pontiff, whom it was my great honour to represent for many years in the various regions of East and West, and who finally sent me here as cardinal and patriarch, and for whom I have always felt a sincere affection, apart from and above any dignity conferred upon me. The sense of my littleness and worthlessness has always kept me good company, making me humble and tranquil, and permitting me the joy of putting my best efforts into a continual exercise of obedience and love for souls and for the interests of the kingdom of Jesus, my Lord and my all. To him be all the glory: for me and for my own merits, only his mercy. 'God's mercy is my only merit. Lord, you know all things: you know that I love you!' This is enough for me.

I ask forgiveness from those whom I have unknowingly offended, and those whom I have not influenced for good. I feel that for my own part I have nothing to forgive anyone, because in all those who knew me and had dealings with me – even if they have offended or despised me or, no doubt justly, had little regard for me, or given me cause to suffer – I recognize only brothers and benefactors, to whom I am grateful and for whom I pray and will pray always.

Born poor, but of humble and respected folk, I am particularly happy to die poor, having distributed, according to the various needs and circumstances of my simple and modest life in the service of the poor and of the holy church which has nurtured me, whatever came into my hands – and it was very little – during the years of my priesthood and episcopate. Appearances of wealth have frequently disguised thorns of frustrating poverty which prevented me from giving to others as generously as I would have wished. I thank God for this grace of poverty to which I vowed fidelity in my youth, poverty of spirit, as a priest of the Sacred Heart, and material poverty, which has strengthened me in my resolve never to ask for anything – positions, money or favours – never, either for myself or for my relations and friends.

To my beloved family according to the flesh, from whom moreover I have never received any material wealth, I can leave only a great and special blessing, begging them to preserve that fear of God which made them always so dear and beloved to me, and to be simple and modest without ever being ashamed of it: it is their true title of nobility. I have sometimes come to their aid, as a poor man to the poor, but without lifting them out of their respected and contented poverty. I pray and I will ever pray for their welfare, glad as I am to see in their new and vigorous shoots the constancy and faithfulness to the religious tradition of the parent stock which will always be their happiness. My most heartfelt wish is that not one of my relations and connections may be missing at the final joyful reunion.

About to leave, as I hope, on the heavenward path, I greet, thank and bless the infinite number of souls who made up, successively, my spiritual family in Bergamo, in Rome, in the East, in France, and in Venice, my fellow citizens, benefactors, colleagues, students, collaborators, friends and acquaintances, priests and lay folk, men and women of the Religious Orders, to all of whom, by the decree of Providence, I was the unworthy brother, father or shepherd.

The kindness shown my humble person by all those I met with along my way has made my life a peaceful one. Now, in the face of death, I remember all and everyone of those who have gone before me on the last stretch of the road, and those who will survive me and follow me. May they pray for me. I will do the same for them from purgatory or paradise where I hope to be received, not, I repeat, through my own merits but through the mercy of my Lord.

I remember them all and will pray for them all. But my Venetian children, the last the Lord has given me, for the final joy and consolation of my priestly life, shall here receive special mention as a sign of my admiration, gratitude and very special love. I embrace them all in the spirit, all, everyone, clergy and lay folk, without distinction, as without distinction I loved them all as belonging to the same family, the object of the same priestly love and care. 'Holy Father, keep them in thy name, whom thou hast given me, and that they may be one, even as we are one' (John 17:11).

In the hour of farewell or, better, of leave-taking. I repeat once more that what matters most in this life is: our blessed Jesus Christ, his holy church, his Gospel, and in the Gospel above all else the Our Father according to the mind and heart of Jesus, and the truth and goodness of his Gospel, goodness which must be meek and kind, hardworking and patient, unconquerable and victorious.

My children, my brothers, I take leave of you. In the name of the Father, the Son and the Holy Ghost. In the name of Jesus our love; of Mary, his sweet Mother and ours; of St Joseph, my first and most beloved protector. In the name of St Peter, of St John the Baptist, and of St Mark; of St Lawrence Giustiniani and St Pius X. Amen.

Pope John XXIII, *Journal of a Soul*

Maura Clarke

No Turning Back

During the 20th century tens of thousands of Christian men and women gave their lives for their faith and for justice and peace. On 2 December 1980 four American churchwomen were brutally slain in El Salvador, Central America, by right-wing military forces who saw their service of the poor as a threat to the powerful ruling class. Maura Clarke and Ita Ford were Maryknoll Sisters, Dorothy Kazel was an Ursuline Sister and 27-year-old Jean Donovan had been working with them. In this article from the American newspaper *National Catholic Reporter*, Moises Sandoval describes the final days of Maura Clarke (1931–80).

In one of her last letters home from El Salvador, Maryknoll Sister Maura Clarke asked her mother for a pair of shoes. She had given her only pair away to a woman who had none. Sister Peggy Healy, who took the new shoes to El Salvador early in November, said: 'I don't think Maura knew how to say no. She just didn't know how to keep people waiting.'

'She was outstanding in her generosity,' said Sister Margarita Jamias, who served with her in Nicaragua and travelled with her in the US giving 'world awareness workshops,' when Clarke came home in 1976 after 17 years in Nicaragua.

'She would give whatever she had to the poor. She was accustomed to living in poverty. We were laughing the other day remembering how in Nicaragua she was always drawing advances on her monthly allowance (about 15 dollars), because as soon as she got it, she gave it away.'

Clarke, the daughter of Irish-born parents from Queens, New York, loved life and always seemed to have a sparkle in her eye. 'Almost every time we got together', Healy remembered from their days in Nicaragua, 'she did a wonderful Irish jig. She had some wonderful songs and dances and loved to celebrate. She never missed a party. We had such wonderful times together.'

But at the same time, in keeping with her giving nature, she was ready, if the Lord asked, to give her life away. In her last days in El Salvador, she began to think this would be asked of her. Speaking of 'unknown, uncelebrated martyrs' in a letter written on 20 November, she said, 'One cries out, "Lord, how long?" And then too, what creeps into my mind is a little fear or big, that when it touches me very personally, will I be faithful?... I keep saying to him, "I want to trust, I want to believe, help me!"'...

Clarke went to El Salvador on a trial basis, reserving the final decision for the Maryknoll regional assembly that concluded in Managua on the day she died. But after arriving in El Salvador, she saw overwhelming need that could not be ignored.

One day, she wrote to Sister Margarita, a 12-year-old boy appeared at the door with six younger brothers and sisters. His parents had been killed and the children were 'nothing but skin and bone'.

So there was no turning back. By early November she made her decision to stay. On 22 November she wrote, 'What is happening here is impossible, but happening. The endurance of the poor and their faith through this terrible pain is constantly pulling me to a deeper faith response. My fear of death is being challenged constantly as children, lovely young girls, and old people, are being shot and some cut up with machetes and bodies thrown by the road, and people prohibited from burying them... I want to stay on now. I believe right now that this is right... God is present in his seeming absence.'

Moises Sandoval, from an article in *National Catholic Reporter*, 19 December 1980

Christopher Hope Mitchell

A Special Child

Christopher Hope Mitchell was born with a condition called Edwards syndrome (Trisomy 18) which his parents were told was 'incompatible with life'. Verity and Alan Mitchell learnt that all was not well when Verity went for a routine prenatal scan at 20 weeks. Most parents opt for an abortion when a child is diagnosed with such a severe foetal abnormality. But the Mitchells were determined to give their baby the chance to live and Christopher was born near London on 5 November 1996 by caesarean section. Alan and Verity decided that the best way to introduce Christopher to their family and friends was to allow him to speak for himself! In Christopher's 'Letters' we meet someone whose existence clearly had a purpose and who touched the hearts and minds of many during his short life.

The diary of Christopher Hope Mitchell, aged one week: 12 November 1996

I have had so many letters, phone calls and flowers from my friends, even though I have met hardly any of them, that I thought it would be good to send you all a copy of my diary to let you know how I am getting on.

My Mummy was wonderfully well throughout the whole pregnancy and was able to carry on working right up till 22 October, three weeks before my due date. I was quite comfortable inside and wasn't very keen to come out into the world so eventually the doctors decided that her labour should be induced. Now I didn't like this at all. Every time she had a contraction my heart rate dropped and didn't recover and it was decided to deliver me quickly as the doctors thought I might not survive a long labour. Daddy arrived just in time to get dressed up and go into the operating theatre where Mummy had a caesarean section. I was born at Farnborough Hospital at 8 a.m. on Tuesday 5 November and weighed five pounds four and a half ounces.

I was shown to Mummy and given a kiss and then I was whisked off to the Special Care Baby Unit (SCBU) where I was popped in a nice warm incubator. My heart rate soon stabilized and I didn't need any help with my breathing. This was very comfy for me, but of course Mummy wanted to see me and so after a few hours they wheeled her bed through the hospital corridors and into the SCBU right up to my incubator. They lifted me out with all my monitor leads and drips attached and let her cuddle me on the side of her bed for half an hour. They don't normally do this but it was a very special moment for us.

I am 'special' because I've got Edwards syndrome (Trisomy 18) which means that all my cells have an extra chromosome 18. Because of this I have lots of different things wrong with me: a hole in the heart, rather a funny upper lip, ears that are a bit lower than normal and feet that seem to come out from my ankles at the wrong angle. Most of these things really don't worry me or Mummy and Daddy, who think I'm wonderful. Some people thought I might look rather strange, but in fact everyone says that I've got a lovely face – I mainly look like my Dad but I've definitely got Mummy's nose.

My most serious problem was a hernia coming from my umbilical cord containing some of my small intestine. Unless the contents were put back inside my abdomen, I wouldn't be able to digest any food so it was decided that I should be sent to Lewisham Hospital where there is a specialist paediatric surgeon. She was amazing because when she came to see me the following morning she said that I didn't need an operation at all. With her nimble fingers she managed to push my insides back where they belonged. This was great because now they could start giving me Mummy's milk down a tube into my stomach.

An ambulance brought Mummy over to the new hospital and she was given a private room because I was in intensive care. The nurses soon saw how much time my Daddy was spending with me and so they brought an extra bed in for him so that we could all stay together as a family in the hospital.

After a few days I was feeling much more stable and so I was able to go back to the SCBU at Farnborough. Mummy and Daddy are now back home but they come to visit me every day for hours and hours. They feed me, change me and sometimes Daddy sits me on his lap, holds my hand and just looks at me. The doctors have taken away almost all of my monitoring machines now, and if I carry on making progress I may be able to go home at the weekend. Daddy has been given extra time off work because he has not only to look after me, but also Mummy since she won't be able to drive or carry anything heavy for six to eight weeks after her operation.

The consultant who is looking after me is called Andy Long. He has a daughter called Verity and when he was little he went to the same church as my Mummy. He says he really doesn't know how long I will live. I might die quietly in my sleep tomorrow or I might live for a few weeks or months. It is not likely to be much more than that. Most babies like me only survive for a few days. I get very tired and have to sleep a lot and I don't have enough strength to feed myself. I am not in any pain and with all the tender loving care I get from my family and the doctors and nurses, my quality of life really couldn't be better. There is no doubt my Mummy and Daddy love me and think of me as a very special gift from God, all the more precious because we may not have very long together. There is no reason why any of their future children should be like me but I know they will always remember me as their first little boy.

I hope I may be able meet you one day but if not I am sure you will see some photographs of me.

Lots of love
Christopher

The Easter diary of Christopher Hope Mitchell, aged four and a half months: 23 March 1997

It seems an awfully long time since I sent you my first letter and, although I have seen some of my friends regularly, there are some people I haven't even met yet, so I thought you might like to know how I have been getting on.

I still only weigh four pounds fourteen ounces, which is half a pound less than my birth weight, but curiously enough I have managed to grow one inch longer. I have a very slow heart rate and rather irregular breathing and I use up all my strength to stay as I am, so I don't have any spare energy for growing.

When I was four months old I had a check up at the hospital and all the doctors seemed very pleased with me. They said I was extra special because no one thought that I would survive as long as this. The consultant asked if my Mummy would bring me in again another day so that the hospital photographer could take some pictures of me to put in the big fat file which has my name on the outside. (I must say I thought this seemed very odd since Mummy and Daddy already have hundreds of photos of me.) Two people have even taken videos of me – I like these because if you listen carefully you can hear me squeaking in the background.

No one seems to know how much longer I will live, but I've successfully passed various landmarks over the last few months. The first was just to be born alive and I am so grateful Mummy was prepared to have a caesarean operation, because otherwise I might well have died during labour. The next stage was the two weeks I spent in the Special Care Baby Unit in hospital before I was allowed to come home. That was a really exciting day, especially as it was snowing.

When the Rector at All Souls' heard that I might not live for very long he said I could have a special baptism as part of an evening service. The church was absolutely packed and when Mummy and Daddy explained why I was so special, lots of people had to reach for their hankies. I am now the smallest member of the church family. There was someone in the congregation from Premier, the new radio station in London, and he asked if they could do a feature about me during the following week. Lots more people were able to hear my story.

Christmas was the next landmark, then Mother's Day (I picked some daffodils from the garden with Daddy's help and brought Mummy breakfast in bed), and now here we are almost at Easter. I am about to go on holiday to Cornwall to visit my Great Aunt and just the other day I overheard Mummy saying that she might have to get me a passport for my summer holiday.

I have made lots and lots of friends, although it is a bit odd when I meet other babies that are the same age as me since they usually seem to be twice as big as I am. One of the interesting things I have done is to visit our local hospice, St Christopher's (nice name), where they have a special service when someone puts their hands on my head and says a prayer for me. Mummy and I then go to visit some of the patients who are dying. Often they like to hold me and it seems to help them to know that it is not just elderly people that need terminal care.

Mum and Dad say that having me around has helped deepen a lot of their friendships. People seem to open up much more about their own pains and sorrows, and we have heard some very sad stories about multiple miscarriages or children who have died young. Some people use big words to talk about the theology of suffering but I think perhaps they have missed the point. I'm not really suffering pain at all – I get sticky eyes and a sore bottom occasionally, but that is really no different from other babies. It's just that because of my extra chromosome I am not going to live for very long.

Nowadays many foetal abnormalities can be spotted early in the pregnancy and the result is that most babies like me, or even those who just have a small physical handicap, are terminated before birth. I often hear Mummy and Daddy say that they are so glad they didn't deny me the chance to live. I don't ask for very much, just Mummy's milk, warmth and lots of cuddles. Some doctors say that my condition is 'incompatible with life' or that I cannot have a 'meaningful' life. Well, it may not be compatible with long-term survival, but perhaps I am only supposed to have a lifespan of a certain length. And who is to say what is 'meaningful'? I don't suppose I am going to achieve very much in one sense but that doesn't mean I have nothing to offer. I'm the person that I am and I'm sure my life does have a purpose. I must have been cuddled by well over a hundred people now and I suspect many of them will remember me long after I have gone.

If it is true that we are all made in the image of God, then perhaps I reflect a Good Friday portrait of God, the broken body of Christ on the cross. Of course the wonderful news of Easter day for me is that Jesus came back from the grave in a new resurrection body. In eternal life I will not be deformed, weak or helpless any more. I will be a new creation.

Lots of love
Christopher

Christopher Hope Mitchell, 5 November 1996–29 May 1997

'Christopher died in the early hours of Thursday 29 May in his parents' arms aged six and a half months. In his short life we and many others had grown to know and love him as a very special and precious individual. In the last few weeks as his heart began to fail, life took on a new intensity. He himself sensed the change through his discomfort and demanded to be held constantly. This we were privileged to do and were able to accompany him on his final journey. When he was not in pain he was as responsive as ever, staring up at us with his big blue eyes.

Christopher himself was unable to grow physically, yet he enabled others to grow both emotionally and spiritually. He touched the lives of those who were in contact with him and many more who were never able to meet him. It seems that his gift was to draw love out of people and it was beautiful to watch as he softened hearts and the tears fell.

His name Christopher means 'the bearer of Christ' and, remarkably, it was through his very frailty and weakness that he shone the light and love of God into our lives. His light has now been extinguished but we are left with many joyous memories that we will treasure for ever.

He was a special child and it was an honour and blessing to be given the charge of his care if only for a very short time. We have received so much support from our family and friends over the recent months and this has played an enormous part in helping us cope with the responsibility of parenthood.

With much love

Alan and Verity

Christopher's 'Letters' by Alan and Verity Mitchell

Cardinal Basil Hume

Into the Presence of God

George Basil Hume (1923–99), Cardinal Archbishop of Westminster, learnt of his approaching death in April 1999. George Hume was born in Newcastle in the North of England. He joined the Benedictine community of Ampleforth as Brother Basil at the age of 18 and served as Abbot from 1963 until he was appointed to the archdiocese of Westminster and made Cardinal in 1976. When Cardinal Hume received the diagnosis of an advanced cancer he described himself as 'uncharacteristically calm and at peace'. His private secretary Father James Curry described Cardinal Hume's final journey towards death in the journal *Priests and People*.

The disease progressed rapidly and it soon became apparent to the Cardinal that Archbishop's House was not the place to be at this time. We explored the possibility of home nursing but he decided for the sake of the Sisters and the household that he would return to hospital. He wasn't anxious either to emulate one of his predecessors, Cardinal Wiseman, who, on his deathbed, delivered an oration to the Chapter of Canons of Westminster. Much as he admired the present Chapter he felt it would be too much for all concerned! His sense of humour was still intact.

The day before he left for hospital he watched the Cup Final with some fellow football fanatics. His spirits were low – not just because Newcastle lost 2–0 to Manchester United. Then on 23 May he returned to the hospital. The Cardinal had total trust in those who nursed him. He would often remark that you could hide nothing from someone who had to assist you in the most necessary functions in life. For one who was so private and independent, it must have been difficult to give himself completely into the care of those who were looking after him. He was immensely appreciative of all that was done for him and felt that nurses were among the unsung heroes of our society. When the Cardinal left Archbishop's House we felt that he would never return. We were wrong. We started to plan his funeral with others. I told him that we were entering this stage. 'Good,' he said. That was the last time we mentioned it…

The Cardinal's serenity had never been more obvious than when he sat us down to discuss his funeral arrangements. He was quite clear about the readings and the lack of fuss. He hated the notion of a lying in state. We all joked that at that stage he wouldn't have much of a say in the proceedings. Two things he was adamant about though were the singing of the *Suscipe* before he was buried, and that the whole occasion should end on a note of praise to God. Accordingly at the funeral Mass the monks of Ampleforth sang the *Suscipe*. This is sung three times before a monk makes his final profession: *Suscipe me Domine, secundum eloquium tuum et vivam, et non confundas me ab expectatione mea.* 'Receive me, Lord, according to thy word, and I shall live, and let me not be disappointed in my expectation.'

After discussing other arrangements, the final hymn which we chose was Charles Wesley's 'Love Divine', which of course ends with the line 'Lost in wonder, love and praise'.

After that he was happy to leave the rest to us. He continued to carry out some duties but he was increasingly tired. I remember waking him the night the Soho bomb exploded in central London. The next morning he was on the BBC's *Today* programme. After all, he had said 'business as usual'.

On the morning of 5 May I walked into his study. I could see an envelope from Buckingham Palace. I joked about an invitation to tea. It was in fact the invitation from the Queen to be appointed to the Order of Merit. He was in many ways embarrassed to have been singled out in this way. He mused that if he was to accept it he would regard it as an honour for the whole Catholic community. However, I understand that when he met the Queen she insisted that the Order of Merit was an honour for him from her. He was embarrassed, too, when the Dalai Lama who was in London asked if he might call. The sight of these two spiritual leaders dressed in their respective monastic robes was very moving. The Dalai Lama placed a scarf around the Cardinal's shoulders and whispered into his ear, and, as always, left with his infectious laugh hanging in the air. He called out to the Cardinal as he left, 'I hope to see you again.' The Cardinal replied, 'I hope we meet again in whatever awaits us.'

246

The day was fast approaching when the Cardinal was due to go to the palace. This was a few days before he moved from one hospital to another: that of St John and St Elizabeth. The palace were most anxious to be as helpful as possible. We were informed that the Queen would like to make the presentation but if the Cardinal was not well enough to travel to the palace a senior member of the Royal Family would come to him. The Cardinal was determined to go to the palace. A date was set which would fall at the end of the second cycle of chemotherapy. It was thought that at that stage the Cardinal would have recovered sufficiently from the initial bad reaction to be able to travel to the palace. The doctors ensured that he would be strong enough for the day.

We collected him from the hospital and brought him back to Archbishop's House. Having bathed, he dressed as a cardinal of the Catholic Church, and we set off. As we drove up to the gates there was a group of his family waving and cheering. His face lit up with delight. We drove into the courtyard and up to the carriage entrance. There we were greeted by officials and the Queen's Piper, though without his bagpipes. The palace had provided a wheelchair to take the Cardinal to the room where the audience would take place. The Queen had moved the audience from her private apartments to a reception room on the ground floor of the palace. The audience was to be private and one-to-one. Those with him were to wait in an ante-room. We asked him if he wanted to be wheeled in. He declined, preferring to walk in to greet his monarch, and so he did. At the end of the audience the plan was that one of us would go to the doors of the room and, as they opened, go forward to give the Cardinal assistance. There was no need. No sooner had the doors opened than the Cardinal drew himself up from the chair where he was seated. He bowed and walked out. I cannot adequately describe the atmosphere at that moment save to say that it was electric. His only comment was, 'What a marvellous woman.'

There were tears in more eyes than mine. As I reflect on that encounter I cannot help thinking that here were two people who, though they rarely met, understood each other and the nature of duty and the demands of office. It was as if few words were needed. We returned to Archbishop's House having stopped to show the Badge of the Order of Merit to his family outside. After changing into easy clothes at the house he took the opportunity to say goodbye individually to those who worked there. They all gathered to cheer him as he left. The front door closed behind him as he went down the steps of what had been his home for the last 22 years and then into the car waiting in Ambrosden Avenue. Now he had left us for the last time.

In the last days of his life the Cardinal increasingly prayed through the sense of touch. He held a small crucifix in his hand and touched the wounds on the Christ-figure. A devotion that had sustained him throughout his life was the meditation on the Seven Last Words of Christ from the Cross…

Recently, he had sometimes been expressing impatience, asking, 'Why doesn't God take me? Why is he keeping me waiting?' Now the calm that had been such a feature of the early days of his illness became more apparent again. The chemotherapy had upset his equilibrium for a while and had brought with it a kind of darkness. It was not despair; but rather the kind of frustration that overtakes a man who was once so strong, but has become enfeebled and bound to his bed. He disliked the thought that any of us were staying around in the hospital. He never wanted to burden others. The night before he died it was suggested that one of us might stay the night…

The next morning I was relieved by a colleague. I returned to the house, brought everyone up to date with the situation and then returned to the hospital at midday. Members of the family visited and prayed with the Cardinal. One great-niece arrived with a Cardinal's hat she had made for him, reminding him he had promised not to die before it was finished. He looked at it and smiled. A nephew of his decided he would like to stay for a while. For the first time the Cardinal was given some medication as he had become restless and was drifting in and out of consciousness. We took turns in sitting with him. At about 5.15 p.m. the nurse came in to make him comfortable and we left the room for a moment. Shortly afterwards we were called in. There had been a decline in his condition. I anointed him and prayed:

Go forth, Christian soul, from this world, in the name of God the almighty Father who created you, in the name of Jesus Christ, Son of the living God, who suffered for you, in the name of the Holy Spirit who was poured out upon you. Go forth, faithful Christian.

May you live in peace this day; may your home be with God in Zion, with Mary, the virgin Mother of God, with Joseph and all the angels and saints.

As we prayed, he died.

He was a man ready to die; impatient to see God. It was as if he lay in a boat and we gently gave that boat a nudge and it sailed into the presence of God.

Father James Curry, from an article in *Priests and People*, November 2000

Bibliography

First Journey

pp. 13–14, 15, 16–17, 17–18, 19, 20–21, 77–78, 81–82, 83–84, 188–90: scripture quotations taken from the *Holy Bible, New International Version* are copyright © 1973, 1978, 1984 by the International Bible Society. Used by permission of Hodder & Stoughton Ltd. All rights reserved. 'NIV' is a registered trademark of the International Bible Society. UK trademark number 1448790.

pp. 22–23, 92–94, 195–98: from St Augustine of Hippo, *Confessions*, translated by Henry Chadwick, copyright © Henry Chadwick 1991. Reprinted by permission of Oxford University Press.

pp. 24–25: Régine Pernoud, *Joan of Arc: By Herself and Her Witnesses*, translated from the French by Edward Hyams, London: Macdonald, 1964.

pp. 26–27: William Shakespeare, *As You Like It*, c. 1599.

pp. 28–30, 101–104: John Wesley, *John Wesley's Journal*, abridged by Nehemiah Curtin, Epworth Press, 1949.

pp. 31–32: Cecil Woodham-Smith, *Florence Nightingale*, London: Constable, 1950.

pp. 33–37: Louisa M. Alcott, *Good Wives*, 1869.

pp. 38–39: Katherine Burton, *The Life of Katharine Drexel*, Dublin: Clonmore and Reynolds, 1961. Published in the USA by P.J. Kennedy and Sons as *The Golden Door*.

pp. 40–41: St Thérèse of Lisieux, *The Autobiography of a Saint* (1898), translated by Ronald Knox, Collins, 1958.

pp. 42–44: Miles Franklin, *My Brilliant Career*, Melbourne: Angus & Robertson, 1901.

pp. 45–46: Ronald Knox, *A Spiritual Aeneid*, 1918.

pp. 47–48: Edith Piaf, *The Wheel of Fortune*, translated from the French, London: Peter Owen, 1965.

pp. 49–52: Billy Graham, *Just as I Am*, copyright © 1997 by Billy Graham Evangelistic Association, published in the UK by HarperCollins Publishers Ltd, London, 1997; published in the USA by HarperCollins Publishers, Inc., New York. Reproduced by permission of the publishers.

pp. 53–57: Maya Angelou, *I Know Why the Caged Bird Sings*, copyright © 1969 and renewed 1997 by Maya Angelou. Published in the UK by Little, Brown and Company, London, 1984; published in the USA by Random House, Inc., New York. Used by permission of the publishers.

p. 58: Jean Vanier, *A Door of Hope*, London: Hodder and Stoughton, 1996.

pp. 59–60: Anne Frank, *The Diary of a Young Girl*, Harmondsworth: Viking, 1997; New York: Doubleday, 1995.

pp. 61–64: Nicholas Alkemade, *Readers Digest*, August 1953.

pp. 65–67: Barbara Kingsolver, *The Poisonwood Bible*, copyright © 1998 Barbara Kingsolver, published in the UK by Faber & Faber Ltd; published in the USA by HarperCollins Publishers, Inc., New York. Reprinted by permission of the publishers.

pp. 68–70: Sally Trench, *Bury Me in My Boots*, London: Hodder & Stoughton, 1968. Reproduced by permission of Hodder & Stoughton Ltd.

pp. 71–75: Mary McAleese, *Reconciled Being: Love in Chaos*, London: Medio Media, 1997. (The original event was the John Main Seminar, 1997.)

Second Journey

pp. 79–80, 85–86, 87–88, 182–83: excerpts from *The Jerusalem Bible*, published and copyright © 1966, 1967 and 1968 by Darton, Longman & Todd Ltd and Doubleday, a division of Random House,

Third Journey

pp. 177–78, 178: scripture excerpts are taken from the *New American Bible*, copyright © 1970 Confraternity of Christian Doctrine, Inc., Washington, DC. Used with permission. All rights reserved. No part of the *New American Bible* may be reproduced by any means without permission in writing from the copyright owner.

pp. 179–81: Alfred Lord Tennyson, 'Ulysses', 1842.

pp. 184–87: Henry van Dyke, *The Story of the Other Wise Man*, 1893. Published by *Harpers* magazine.

pp. 191–94: St Ignatius of Antioch, *Letter to the Romans*, in *Fathers of the Church*, Vol. 1: *The Apostolic Fathers*, Francis X. Glimm, Joseph M.F. Marique, SJ, and Gerald G. Walsh, SJ, Washington, DC: the Catholic University of America Press, 1947. Reprinted by permission.

p. 199: St Thomas More, from a letter written to his daughter, Margaret Roper, in 1534.

pp. 200–201: St Paul Miki, from a contemporary account of the events of 5 February 1597.

pp. 202–206: Charles Dickens, *A Tale of Two Cities*, 1859.

pp. 207–209: extract from Fyodor Dostoevsky, *The Idiot* (1869), translated by David Magarshack, London: Penguin Classics, 1955. Copyright © 1955 David Magarshack. Reproduced by permission of Penguin Books Ltd.

pp. 210–14: excerpt from pp. 425–26 of *With Malice Towards None: The Life of Abraham Lincoln* by Stephen B. Oates, copyright © 1977, 1994 Stephen B. Oates. Reprinted by permission of HarperCollins Publishers, Inc., New York.

pp. 215–16: St Thérèse of Lisieux, *Collected Letters of St Thérèse of Lisieux*, translated by F.J. Sheed, London: Sheed & Ward, 1949. Published in the USA by Sheed & Ward, Franklin, Wisconsin. Reprinted by permission of the publishers.

p. 216: Sister Geneviève of the Holy Face, 'Conseils et Souvenirs', in *Céline: Sister Geneviève of the Holy Face* by Stéphane-Joseph, Piat, OFM, translated by the Carmelite Sisters of the Eucharist, Colchester, Connecticut; San Francisco: Ignatius Press, 1997.

pp. 217–18: Hugh Gibson, *A Journal from Our Legation in Belgium*, Garden City, New York: Doubleday, Page and Company, 1917.

pp. 219–22: this account by Charles Rosendahl appears as the final chapter of *Zeppelin: The Story of the Lighter-Than-Air Craft* by Ernst Lehmann, published by Addison, Wesley and Longman, 1937.

pp. 223–24: Dietrich Bonhoeffer, 'Who Am I?' from *Letters and Papers from Prison*, the Enlarged Edition, copyright © 1953, 1967, 1971 by SCM Press Ltd, London. Reprinted with the permission of SCM Press and Scribner, a division of Simon & Schuster, Inc.

pp. 225–29: Fynn, *Mister God, This is Anna*, London: HarperCollins Publishers Ltd, 1974. Reprinted by permission.

pp. 230–31: Dylan Thomas, 'Do Not Go Gentle into That Good Night' (1951), from *The Poems of Dylan Thomas*, copyright © 1952 Dylan Thomas. Published in the UK by J.M. Dent and in the USA by New Directions. Reprinted by permission of David Higham Associates Ltd and New Directions Publishing Corp.

pp. 232–33: Malcolm Muggeridge, *Jesus Rediscovered*, London: Collins Fontana, 1969.

pp. 234–36: Pope John XXIII, *Journal of a Soul*, translated from the Italian by Dorothy White, Geoffrey Chapman, 1964.

pp. 237–38: Moises Sandoval, from an article on Maura Clarke in *National Catholic Reporter* (www.natcath.org), 19 December 1980. Reprinted by permission.

pp. 239–44: Christopher's 'Letters', copyright © Alan and Verity Mitchell.

pp. 245–49: Father James Curry, from an article on Cardinal Basil Hume in *Priests and People*, November 2000. Reprinted by permission.

Index